The MADE IN AUSTRALIA Food Book

·······························

WITH OVER 200 RECIPES

·······························

Tess Mallos

A Lothian Book

To my grandchildren, Stephanie and John, and your grandchildren — may we grown-ups keep paving the way to a better, more caring and more prosperous Australia for their sakes.

Cover photograph: Tomato and Basil Salad with Bocconcini (page 139), Green Salad with Macadamia Dressing (page 140), shown with Australian oils.

A Lothian Book
First published 1994
Thomas C. Lothian Pty Ltd
11 Munro Street, Port Melbourne, Victoria 3207

Copyright © Tess Mallos 1994

This book is copyright. Apart from any fair dealing for the purposes of private study, research, criticism or review as permitted under the Copyright Act, no part may be reproduced by any process without written permission. Enquiries should be made to the publisher.

National Library of Australia
Cataloguing-in-Publication data:

Mallos, Tess
Made in Australia

Bibliography.
Includes index.
ISBN 0 85091 655 0.

1. Cookery, Australian. I. Title.

641.5994

Designed and illustrated by Lynn Twelftree
Photography: Reg Morrison
Food styling and preparation: Margaret Alcock
Assistant for food preparation: Fiona Grieve
Photograph of author: Scott Cameron
Typeset in Australia by Image Makers
Colour separations by Type Scan, South Australia
Printed in Australia on Australian paper
by Pirie Printers Pty Limited, ACT

Foreword

Buying Australian has been the subject of much public debate in recent times. It is an issue of importance to us all as we seek to do the right thing by ourselves as consumers, and by an Australian industry responsible for the creation and maintenance of jobs for Australians.

Local manufacturers and producers will always battle competition in the form of imports. This competition is a valuable characteristic of the Australian marketplace. It is one of the reasons why Australian producers and manufacturers continue to strive for high standards for their products across all industries, the dynamic Australian food industry notwithstanding.

Since its establishment in 1986 as a vehicle through which to educate Australians about the benefits of buying Australian, the Australian Made Campaign has sought to change consumer perceptions about the quality, value and innovation of Australian Made products. Importantly, our licensees believe the campaign helps them compete more successfully against comparable imported products, and that it has increased their sales by $185–350 million in recent years. The benefits of this extra production include additional jobs and investments in Australian manufacturing. Food companies comprise a significant percentage of our licensees.

The Australian Made symbol of the gold kangaroo on the green triangle, as the only product symbol officially endorsed by the Commonwealth Government, has served to highlight the Australian choice to consumers for almost a decade. The alternative wording, Produce of Australia, is also available to industries that process and package Australian-grown produce.

According to ongoing research, three in four Australians believe an increasingly wide range of locally made products are of good quality and at least as good as imported products. It is also very pleasing to know that consumers continue to be motivated by such factors as helping the economy and creating jobs.

Some people argue that we should only support Australian-owned companies. However, Australian Made products are manufactured in Australia by workers employed by both Australian and overseas-owned companies. It is not company ownership that is important, but the single aim all manufacturers share — providing jobs and a future for all Australians.

In fact, for every $1 million worth of imports replaced by locally made goods, approximately thirty jobs are created. The author suggests that Australia's 5.4 million households should spend $10 more per month on locally produced food rather than the imported equivalents; this translates into over 19 000 jobs.

Australian-manufactured goods continue to be preferred in major categories such as processed food. Here there is a strong belief in the local product, particularly when compared with those manufactured in third-world countries.

With the decision on how we are to identify Australian Made goods in the future soon to be made law, now is the ideal time to familiarise ourselves with our choices across all product categories.

Food, as the consumable none of us can live without, is an ideal starting point for this valuable learning process, and this book is the ideal tool. In addition to building our pride in the vast array of quality food already produced and manufactured in our great country, the book also acknowledges our limitations and offers 'next best' choices.

Essential in every Australian kitchen, whether used by the home cook, the restaurateur, the hotel chef or the caterer, The *Made in Australia Food Book* is an invaluable guide to our country's increasing array of home-grown culinary ingredients and delights, and a practical guide on how to prepare them.

Norm Spencer
Executive Director, Advance Australia Foundation

Contents

Foreword   iii
Introduction   vii

EATING WITHIN OUR MEANS   1
   Food Labelling — Is It Australian?   2
   The Australian Vegetarian   7
   Indigenous Foods   7
   Spreading the Word   7
   The Food Statistics   8
   Using the Recipes   8

Buyer's Guides and Recipes

CEREALS AND GRAINS   10

PULSES, NUTS AND SEEDS   39

DAIRY FOODS   58

OILS, FATS AND SPREADS   76

SEAFOODS   84

MEAT AND POULTRY   100

VEGETABLES   126

FRUIT   144

HERBS AND SPICES   161

PICKLES, SAUCES AND CONDIMENTS   171

JAMS, SYRUPS AND HONEY   182

CONFECTIONERY AND SNACK FOODS   192

BEVERAGES   198

Weights and Measures   206
Glossary   208
Further Reading   209
Acknowledgements   210
Index — Recipes   212
Index — General   214

INTRODUCTION

*H*ow fortunate we are to live in a country capable of producing an immense range of foods of excellent quality. Visitors of all kinds, including chefs and food writers, wax lyrical over the quality and variety of foods and wines we seem to take for granted. But we are not content with our lot. We must have more. We also demand cheaper foods, even though we spend less of our income on keeping ourselves fed than many other developed nations.

This book is about knowing what we produce or manufacture, and choosing those foods and beverages, rather than using similar imported foods. We reap the benefits in the long term by keeping present industries going, and encouraging new endeavours with our support. If we don't produce a specific food (chocolate, for example) or don't produce enough of it to meet demand (as with tea and coffee), it costs Australia less if we buy food products that are value-added in Australia rather than in countries that are not producers of the base product. I have endeavoured to show you how to make the right choices for such products.

Every now and then there is a media story about food imports, and the need to buy Australian, which is commendable, but how does one put it into practice? Package labelling, while giving a fair indication as to the source of products, is not always a reliable guide if you are not totally familiar with the kinds of foods we produce. This book has been written to help you make the right choices when buying food, whether for home preparation, take-aways or eating at a restaurant.

The recipes put into practice what is preached. They are all devised to use Australian-produced products with a minimum of imported ingredients. To extend the 'buy Australian' message, Australian ceramics, pottery, glassware and other handicrafts have been used in most of the photographs (these are identified in the Acknowledgements). Even this book is a wholly Australian product, including the paper used.

vii

Our food and beverage imports cost some $2.7 billion. Now that may not seem a great deal when we spend $38 billion annually on all foods and beverages, at home and away from home. As the $38 billion is based on retail sales, the $2.7 billion could realistically be increased by 75 per cent to $4.7 billion — 12 per cent of our total food and beverage expenditure. Import statistics give the Free On Board (FOB) value — the importer pays transport costs from the country of export. Add to that all other costs, from tariffs and local transport to manufacturer or middleman, through to the retailer.

If each Australian household made a conscientious effort to spend a mere $10 per month more on wholly Australian-produced foods rather than on imported equivalents, we can reduce the FOB expenditure of $2.7 billion by $648 million. Assuming that half of the 5.4 million Australian households care enough to make that expenditure, those of us who are genuinely concerned should endeavour to increase expenditure to $20 per month.

That $20 a month could save jobs, even create jobs, not only in the food industry but also in associated industries such as packaging and packaging materials: steel turned into cans, glass turned into bottles, paper and cardboard turned into packs and cartons, plastics turned into bags and containers, and all those other businesses and utilities involved in getting the food from the producer to the manufacturer, to the warehouse, to the retail outlet and into your shopping basket.

We consumers are *the* force in the marketplace. This book is a means of changing our buying habits now. And wouldn't it be wonderful to be able to boast, during the 2000 Olympic Games, that the majority of foods and beverages served to the visiting athletes is Australian produced or made!

Tess Mallos

Eating within our means

If Australia was suddenly isolated from the rest of the world, we could survive very well indeed. There would be a few items we would have to do without, such as some spices and chocolate, but our small band of tea, coffee and pepper producers would have the incentive to increase production, the vanilla orchid could blossom in our tropical north along with the cacao tree; in fact there would be very little we could not produce if the need arose.

Those of us who remember the years of World War II would remember how we survived very well with our victory gardens for vegetables and fruit, our chook runs for poultry and eggs, and took the rationing of meat, butter, tea and sugar in our stride. Even those of us who had a non-Australian kitchen could still produce traditional foods with the available local and home-grown ingredients.

These days, with our smallgoods industries producing all types of preserved meats and poultry, our cheese makers producing the pick of the cheeses of the world plus our very own cheeses, our bakers baking breads of infinite variety, our bean curd and soy sauce manufacturers, our pasta and noodle manufacturers … we would hardly be aware of any changes on our table.

We are capable of living on what we produce, and the need to do so has now arisen, not because of isolation, but because we are living beyond our means. We are spending too much on imports, and while exports and imports of all commodities in total amount to much the same in dollar terms, we cannot afford to continue in this way. Our imports have to be reduced and exports increased if Australia's economy is to improve, and an improved economy means more jobs!

So let us start in the kitchen and learn to eat within our means, to make a concerted effort to use the foods we produce well and in abundance. Once we begin in earnest to support our own food industries there will be a ripple effect, making us more conscious of many other Australian-produced goods we could use in place of imports. Even when testing recipes for this book, I began to look at the equipment and cooking aids I was using. One change I made was to use greaseproof paper rather than the non-stick baking paper I rather liked, because the latter, though packaged here, is imported.

Go to your refrigerator, your freezer and your pantry and look at the country of origin of your goods. With the aid of the Buyer's Guides, you will be able to see where you can make changes on your next shopping trip. And if you wear reading glasses, take them along — you'll need them!

Food Labelling — Is It Australian?

The Australian Food Standards Code, which is developed and maintained by the National Food Authority (NFA), requires the label on every food package to include a statement of the country in which the food was made or produced. The Code is incorporated by reference into State and Territory law. This means that the food standards set out in the Code are in effect State/Territory laws and are enforced by the relevant State/Territory Department of Health.

In 1993 the NFA prepared a proposal to vary the country-of-origin labelling requirements in the Code, to provide consumers with better information so that they could make informed choices about foods, and to prevent fraud and deception. The NFA sought public submissions on that proposal, and prepared and released a Discussion Paper in May, 1994. After the receipt of public comment, recommendations will be made to the National Food Standards Council on changes to the Code.

Another piece of legislation which affects the labelling of food, and of other consumer goods, is the *Trade Practices Act 1974*. This legislation currently prohibits the making of false and misleading representations about the place of origin of goods.

On 23 March 1994, the Trade Practices Amendment (Origin Labelling) Bill was introduced into the House of Representatives. Set down for debate in the House early in May 1994 and in the Senate one month later, the changes that this Bill makes to the law do not come into effect until twelve months after the passing of legislation. The Bill sets the meanings for the following terms:

> 'Product of Australia' and 'Produce of Australia' will mean that each major component or ingredient originated in Australia and that all operations involved in the manufacture or production of the goods happened in Australia.
>
> 'Made in Australia' will mean that the goods acquired their essential character or qualities in Australia. Some or all of the components or ingredients may be imported on goods carrying this label.

The Bill requires that where a label identifies a particular production step which happened in Australia, for example, 'Blended in Australia' or 'Packed in Australia', that the label must also identify the source of the ingredients; for example, 'Packed in Australia from imported ingredients'.

The Bill also requires that where a label carries a picture of an Australian flag, a map of Australia, words such as '100% Australian', or any other words or symbols that are likely to be seen as a claim that the goods originated in Australia, then the label must identify the place where the goods really originated.

As this is Commonwealth legislation, any changes to the food standards that are implemented through State/Territory laws must be consistent with the scheme in the *Trade Practices Act*.

It takes time to implement all the legal procedures necessary for the new labelling to appear where it matters most — on food packaging. In the meantime, the food labelling currently in use is described. With this

Eating within Our Means • 3

and the Buyer's Guides for the various food categories, you should be able to make informed choices now. Many of the following labelling statements will still be relevant as a result of the new legislation.

AUSTRALIAN FLAG

(on pack with no accompanying wording)
Look carefully for the country of origin; this has appeared on food products which state clearly elsewhere on the pack that the food is imported from country X. This is misleading labelling unless the company is Australian-owned.

AUSTRALIAN MADE

(superimposed on outline of Australia)
This is found on a certain house brand of grocery items and it immediately identifies a product as Australian made, but some items could have some imported content.

AUSTRALIAN MADE / PRODUCE OF AUSTRALIA

(under green triangular logo with stylised kangaroo)
These are the official logos of the Advance Australia Foundation, granted under licence. They signify that the product has at least 75 per cent Australian content.

AUSTRALIAN OWNED / OWNED BY AUSTRALIANS

(with individual logos)
Companies that use such logos may not be associated with the Australian Owned Companies Association (at time of writing, anyway). Statements as to the origin of food content are noticeably lacking on some products, but do appear on others.

AUSTRALIAN OWNED — PRODUCT OF AUSTRALIA

(within diamond or triangular logo with boomerang)
This logo signifies that the company is Australian owned, though we have yet to see it on food products.

The right to use the logo is granted under licence from the Australian Owned Companies Association. While the aims of this organisation — to support Australian-owned companies as against those wholly or partly foreign-owned — are commendable, the aim of this book is to support Australian made and produced foods, regardless of the company's ownership, since they provide jobs for Australians. If the company is Australian-owned, so much the better. (See Acknowledgements, page 210, for more information.)

AUSTRALIAN OWNED / PROUDLY AUSTRALIAN

(under Australian flag)
This signifies that the company is Australian owned. The product is usually further labelled with more information about country of origin and ingredients. However, the product could be wholly or partly Australian in content or wholly imported.

MADE IN AUSTRALIA

A product with this logo could be made in Australia with local ingredients or with local and imported ingredients. Some labels give sufficient information, others do not.

MADE IN AUSTRALIA (FROM AUSTRALIAN OR IMPORTED PEANUTS)

This appears on a particular brand of salted peanuts. Imports are often necessary in the peanut industry to make up for shortfalls in local supplies. Because of the costs involved in having to change packaging according to the source of the nuts, this labelling is honest and acceptable.

MADE IN AUSTRALIA FROM X (country) Y (ingredients)

An example: 'Made in Australia from Spanish capers'. Other ingredients, such as vinegar, would be locally sourced. This is honest labelling.

Eating within Our Means • 5

PACKED IN AUSTRALIA USING IMPORTED INGREDIENTS

Honest labelling.

PACKED IN AUSTRALIA USING LOCAL AND IMPORTED INGREDIENTS

Honest labelling.

PRODUCT OF AUSTRALIA / PRODUCE OF AUSTRALIA

(with no official logo)
This usually means what it implies — Australian-produced food processed and packed in Australia. However, there are certain food items carrying this label which mislead the consumer, such as chocolate with cashew nuts. Both the cocoa paste and the nuts are imported, even though the value-adding has been done in Australia with some local ingredients and, of course, the labour. More honest labelling would be: 'Product of Australia using local and imported ingredients'.

QUALITY AUSTRALIAN DRIED FRUIT

(superimposed on outline of Australia)
This is found on some products such as spicy fruit loaf. It is obvious that the bread is made here, but the company wants it known that the dried fruit are locally sourced. This is commendable.

WITH AUSTRALIAN SULTANAS

This appears on certain breakfast cereal packs and is reassuring, since imported sultanas are used in many packaged or prepared foods.

100% AUSTRALIAN ORANGE JUICE

On orange juice containers, this signifies that the juice is a wholly Australian product.

The Australian Vegetarian

Fortunately most vegetarians of today are well informed and have learnt to choose foods which give a balanced, nutritious diet. Combining vegetable proteins such as pulses with grain foods, and having soy drink and other soy products, are now accepted diet regimens, particularly for vegans. But many of these foods rely on imports to make up the shortfall in Australian supplies, particularly soy beans for their by-products. We also need to import a large percentage of other pulses, but local production is gradually increasing.

It is much more Australia-friendly to be an ovo-lacto-vegetarian, that is to use eggs and dairy products along with cereals, grains, pulses, nuts, seeds, vegetables and fruit, especially if locally produced pulses, nuts and seeds are used.

Indigenous Foods

Because they are widely available, only macadamia nuts and their by-products are mentioned and used in recipes. Of course, our excellent seafoods are also indigenous (except for Atlantic salmon and trout), and these are covered also. Native foods show great promise in Australia's culinary future, but they are not under threat from imports. If you would like to explore these foods more fully, I recommend you obtain books on the subject by Jennifer Isaacs and Vic Cherikoff, experts in this fascinating field (see Further Reading, page 209).

Spreading the Word

Having worked as an industry food consultant and food writer for over 30 years, I speak from experience when I say anything is possible when you put your mind to it. Editorial or company policy can encourage more use of Australian food products and less of imported; industry home economists can formulate recipes using as many Australian ingredients as possible, even if the basic food item they promote is imported. Perhaps we need to become less 'purist' in our recipe advice and more responsible towards our primary producers.

The Food Statistics

Figures quoted are from the Australian Bureau of Statistics for 12 months to 30 June, 1993. Any discrepancy between a total for a particular food group quoted from other sources and individual figures given in the Buyer's Guides is due to interpretations of the statistics. For example, some interpretations give a figure of some $470 million worth of fruit and vegetable imports. From the statistics, I have concentrated on the fruits and vegetables which would be used instead of locally produced ones for traditional uses; figures relating to other foods of fruit or vegetable origin are included in chapters such as Pulses, Nuts and Seeds; Pickles, Sauces and Condiments; Jams, Syrups and Honey; and Herbs and Spices.

Figures for individual food groups and foods have been given with practicalities in mind; from these you can determine which changes you can make in your food-buying habits, so that you spend that $20 per month more from your household budget on foods of Australian origin rather than the imported foods you might have purchased previously. (An oblique between food names indicates an alternative name; for example, bean curd/tofu.)

Using the Recipes

It goes without saying that ingredients in recipes must be Australian-produced or made. The word 'Australian' is only used occasionally, such as in 'Australian salmon', as that is what it is called on the can. I have kept imported foods to a minimum, and these are mainly spices, some coconut products, olive oil (we produce some) and some imported pulse alternatives, as we do not produce enough of the popular ones, such as haricot beans, which almost all end up in canned baked beans, and red kidney beans.

Only Australian wines and spirits have been used in testing the recipes; brand names are only given occasionally where it was necessary to do so.

There are quite a lot of do-it-yourself recipes, such as how to make tomato paste, cure olives, 'sun-dry' tomatoes, dry herbs, make yoghurt, pickles, chutneys, jams and jellies. These are for the adventurous, the home-gardener and the cook who is really getting into the spirit of this book. There are also recipes which try to duplicate popular convenience items found in supermarket freezers and on shelves; too often I have heard the comment that imports are purchased because they are cheaper, but this is not always the case. By making some of these recipes, you can save money and spend it on more Australian foods.

There are also many basic recipes for family meals, with variations to show that many recipes are simply variations on a theme — master the basics, then ring the changes. I have also included some hints and other information to help you in the preparation, storage and cooking of Australian foods; these are boxed within relevant chapters to separate them from recipes.

In all, the recipes show the scope and variety that is possible in cooking with Australian foods. Some only serve four, as they are recipes you would only prepare on special occasions; but most serve six or sometimes more, depending on the meal situation or occasion. Only metric mass (weight), cup and spoon measures are used; oven temperatures are given in degrees Celsius and Fahrenheit, because so many cooks have clung to their tried and trusted ovens (as I have). As fan-forced oven temperatures vary between different makes, these have not been given in the recipes. Within the method is a description of the oven heat used; refer to your manual for the temperature of your particular oven. The Weights and Measures section gives further details and conversions for the imperialists amongst you.

Eating within Our Means

Cereals and Grains

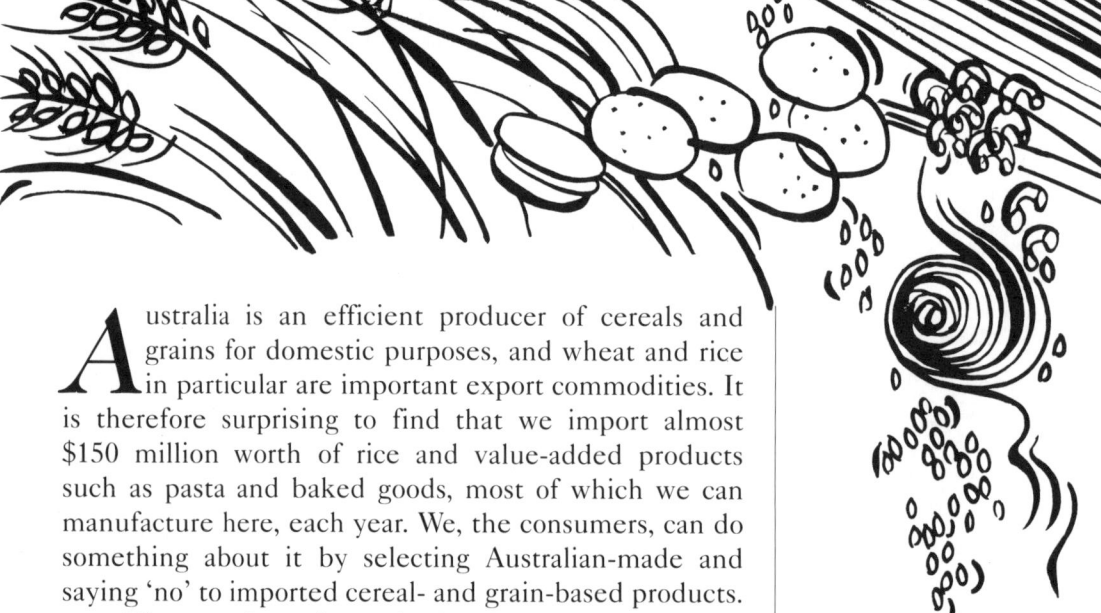

Australia is an efficient producer of cereals and grains for domestic purposes, and wheat and rice in particular are important export commodities. It is therefore surprising to find that we import almost $150 million worth of rice and value-added products such as pasta and baked goods, most of which we can manufacture here, each year. We, the consumers, can do something about it by selecting Australian-made and saying 'no' to imported cereal- and grain-based products.

The cereals, grains and related products covered in the following Buyer's Guide are those more widely used in Australian kitchens, produced locally but competing in the market with similar imports, or imported with little or no local competition.

Local Products Little Affected by Imports

Wheaten and rye flours, barley, oats and oat products, the various brans (wheat, rice, oat and barley), corn meal (polenta), most fresh bakery products (breads, buns and cakes), cake mixes, pastries and pastry mixes are all locally produced and have little competition from imports. They are therefore not listed in the Guide.

Buyer's Guide
CHOOSING AUSTRALIAN CEREAL AND GRAIN FOODS

Product	Australian-produced	Imported	What we can do
WHEAT PRODUCTS			
Burghul/Bulgar (steamed, cracked wheat)	Yes, in fine or coarse grades	Yes, small quantity sold in bulk in specialised markets, also packaged	Buy locally produced packaged burghul; check label.
Matzo meal	Yes	Yes, in small quantities	Check labels for local product.
MAIZE/CORN PRODUCTS			
Cornflour	Yes	Yes, about $1.8 million worth for manufacturing purposes and specialised markets	Check labels if buying from specialised markets.
RICE			
Brown rice — standard and quick-cooking	Yes	Yes, but amount insignificant	No problem in obtaining local product.
Frozen, cooked rice	No	Yes	Don't buy product. For same convenience, see Boiled Rice (page 20).
Glutinous rice — white, red long-grain or black	No	Yes. No Australian equivalent for red long-grain or black varieties	Use sparingly. Calrose can be used for Thai sticky rice — don't wash before cooking.
Instant rice	No, but working on it	Yes	Meanwhile learn to cook Calrose and long grain or use Sunlong rice.
Parboiled rice (golden long-grain)	Yes — Sungold rice	No	Support the product — you can also 'cook' it in the refrigerator.
Polished rice — Arborio, Basmati, Calrose, Jasmine/Thai, long-grain	Yes — Calrose, long-grain, Jasmine; Arborio grown in small quantities	Yes, some $20 million worth including Arborio (Italian), Jasmine and Basmati	Check labels and buy Australian. Use Calrose for risotto, long-grain in place of Basmati.
Rice flour, ground rice	Yes	Yes, rice flour of certain type for rice noodles	No problem in obtaining local product.
Wild rice (not related to rice; the seed of a North American marsh grass)	No	Yes — very expensive	Buy premium Australian rice blend which includes it with local brown rice.

Choosing Australian Cereals and Grains • 11

Product	Australian-produced	Imported	What we can do
VALUE-ADDED PRODUCTS			
Biscuits, savoury — crackers, flat crispbreads, matzo	Yes	Yes, over $13 million worth	Plenty of local products to choose from. Check labels on unfamiliar brands.
Biscuits, sweet — plain, chocolate, cream, gingerbread, shortbread, wafers	Yes	Yes, some $28 million worth	Buy Australian! Plenty to choose from. Check labels, especially on Christmas stock.
Breads, toasted — bagel and pita crisps, breadsticks, rusks, canape bases, croutons, zwieback	Only breadsticks (grisini)	Yes, some $4 million worth	Buy local breadsticks. Make your own toasted breads and croutons; see page 24.
Breakfast cereals (all varieties)	Yes	Yes, some $3 million worth	Check labels for locally made cereals, especially in health food stores.
Cakes, sweet yeast breads (e.g. Panforte, Panettone, sponge flans)	Yes	Yes, large quantities, especially for Christmas trade	Check labels on packaged items or buy from specialised cake shops.
Corn chips, tacos, tortillas	Yes	Yes, particularly tortillas	Check labels for locally made products.
Infant foods — cereal mixes, rusks, formula	Yes	Yes, over $2 million worth	Check labels for local products.
Noodles, instant or quick-cooking	Yes	Yes, see 'Pasta, noodles'	Noodles in locally produced 2-minute noodles made locally; use in place of imports.
Noodles (non-wheat) — rice, transparent, shirataki	Yes, some types	Yes, see 'Pasta, noodles'	Substitute local products for imported noodles.
Pasta, noodles	Yes, Italian pasta and most Asian noodles, including fresh products	Yes, some $37 million worth, including rice noodles	Choose local products; right choice will make a difference.
Pizza bases	Yes, pre-baked and frozen	Yes, pre-baked (cooked but not browned)	Choose locally made bases, pre-baked or frozen.
Rice crackers (wafer-thin savoury crackers)	No, but thick cakes and slices made locally; Rice Growers' Co-operative working on making rice crackers	Yes	Select another type of locally made cracker. Use local rice cakes for gluten-free diets.
Rice mixes (packaged quick-cooking, flavoured)	Yes	No, but rice used in most brands is imported	Check labels; Rice Growers' Co-operative developing strains suitable for such mixes.

Recipes
USING AUSTRALIAN CEREALS AND GRAINS

Porridge

The breakfast bowl of porridge has made a comeback, particularly on cold, wintry mornings. Besides the traditional oatmeal, quick-cooking and instant oats are also available for ease of preparation. Nutritionally, oatmeal is regarded as one of the best breakfast cereals.

Oatmeal Porridge *(Traditional)*
Serves 3–4

1 cup rolled oats
2½ cups boiling water
pinch of salt

1 Put oats in a heavy-based saucepan and pour on boiling water. Stand for 5 minutes. Add salt.
2 Place pan over medium heat and bring to the boil. Reduce heat and boil gently, stirring occasionally, for 10 minutes. Serve with milk and sugar to taste.

Quick-cooking Oats: Use same quantities of quick-cooking oats and cold water (or half water, half milk). Add salt and bring to the boil, stirring occasionally. Boil gently for 1 minute.

Instant Oat Porridge: This comes in single-serve sachets. Follow directions on pack for cooking on stove or in microwave oven. It takes 30 seconds to cook after coming to the boil on the stove; 90 seconds to cook in the microwave oven.

Microwave Porridge

This is a substitute for instant oat porridge, just as convenient and cheaper. Directions are for one serve cooked in a bowl. Semolina can be used in place of the oats, and the porridge is creamier if cooked with milk, preferably low-fat.

Serves 1

¾ cup milk
4 tablespoons quick-cooking oats OR
  2 tablespoons semolina
small pinch of salt

1 Put milk in cereal bowl, sprinkle on choice of oats or semolina in quantities given, add salt and stir well.
2 Microwave on full power for 2½–3 minutes. After 1 minute stir porridge, then stir at 30-second intervals or less as porridge becomes thick. When porridge bubbles up in bowl it is ready. Don't let it boil over.
3 Stand porridge for a minute or so, then serve with hot or cold milk and sugar to taste.

Additions for porridge: Sweeten with white, brown or raw sugar, or honey. Low-fat or skim milk is preferable to full-cream milk or, for a modern touch, serve with natural yoghurt. Oat, wheat or rice bran can be sprinkled on for extra fibre. Canned, stewed, dried or fresh fruit may also be added.

Keeping Weevils and Moths at Bay

If you have problems with weevils and moth grubs thriving in your flours, cereals, rice and pasta during summer, strew some bay leaves or cloves on your pantry shelves. You can also tape a bay leaf to the underside of the lids on your flour containers for a more direct deterrent to these troublesome creatures; cloves are too strongly flavoured for this purpose.
If you have the space, store little-used items in the refrigerator or freezer; it saves you money in the long run.

Short Cut to Shortcrust Pastry

Pastry-making is one of those culinary tasks many cooks avoid. With ready-made and ready-rolled pastries and dry, packaged pastry mixes available, it's easier to use these rather than make pastry from scratch. Puff pastry can be tricky, so go for the convenience product. However, for pies, flans or tarts, home-made shortcrust is so much better, particularly if butter is used.

The following method uses the food processor, and I make no apologies for only giving that method. If you have trouble with pastry-making, you'll find the food processor gives excellent results every time.

Shortcrust Pastry

Makes 1 x 20 or 23-cm pie (bottom and top crust); 2 x 20- or 23-cm flan cases

2 cups plain flour
small pinch of salt
125 g firm butter or margarine
4–6 tablespoons ice-cold water

1 Put flour and salt in bowl of food processor fitted with steel blade. Process for 5 seconds to remove any lumps (saves sifting).
2 Cut up butter or margarine roughly and add to flour. Process for 20 seconds or so until mixture resembles coarse crumbs.
3 With processor running, pour water through feed tube. If, after 4 tablespoons are added, pastry has still not clung together, add another 1–2 tablespoons gradually until dough forms on blades. Keep processing in as brief 'bursts' as possible so that dough does not become warm through friction. Stop and start processor as needed to prevent this.
4 Turn pastry onto a board, knead lightly just to smooth the dough, and flatten into a thick disc. Wrap in plastic film and chill for 30 minutes to rest. Use as directed in recipes.

Variations

Wholemeal Shortcrust Pastry

Replace 1 cup of the plain flour with plain wholemeal flour. Make as above.

Sweet Shortcrust Pastry

Add 2 tablespoons caster sugar with the flour. Beat 1 egg yolk with 2 teaspoons lemon juice and 2 tablespoons ice-cold water. Add at Step 3 and process, adding a little more water if necessary. Use for sweet pies, tarts and tartlet cases.

Using the Pastry

For two-crust pies: After chilling, divide into two portions, one slightly larger than the other. Roll out larger portion on lightly floured board and place in greased pie plate. Add filling and moisten edge of pastry. Roll out remaining pastry, place on top and press edges to seal. Trim and crimp edge.

For open pies and flans: After chilling, divide equally into two portions (see 'Leftover pastry' if you only want one pie or flan). Roll out on a lightly floured board and place in greased pie dish or flan tin. Press lightly into shape of dish, making sure no air bubbles remain under pastry. Trim edge; if pastry is for an open pie, crimp edge with finger tips or press with tines of a fork.

To bake blind: When a partly or fully cooked pastry case is required, this type of pastry needs to be baked 'blind', that is without a filling. Cut a round of grease-proof paper to cover the pastry and grease on one side. Place greased side down onto pastry and weigh down with baking beans or rice (dried pulses or rice kept for this purpose), covering the base and piled up against the sides. Bake in a hot oven, 200°C (400°F), for 10 minutes and remove paper and beans. Return to oven for 5 minutes for a partly cooked case (savoury flans), or 10 minutes for a fully cooked case.

Leftover pastry: If you only want to make one open pie or flan, line another pie dish or flan tin with remaining pastry. Freeze until firm, press some plastic wrap over the surface, then pack into a freezer bag in the dish, seal and return to freezer. Use within two months. Or simply shape remaining pastry into a block, wrap, seal and freeze. Sweet Shortcrust Pastry will keep in the refrigerator for two to three days, wrapped well in plastic film; the egg yolk and lemon juice prevent the pastry turning grey.

Working with Fillo Pastry

Fillo pastry is well and truly installed in the Australian kitchen. It is light and crisp, and fat content can be minimal if you brush the sheets lightly with butter. If you have problems working with fillo, these guidelines might help you to use it more efficiently. While there are a number of ways to use fillo, only the basic uses are detailed.

AUSTRALIAN FLOURS

Our wheat flours are of excellent quality and are milled in such a way that a high proportion of nutrients are retained. Flour from Western Australia is regarded as the best in the world for making noodles; in fact many noodles imported from China are made with Australian flour.

Wheat flours available include plain white and self-raising, unbleached white flour, wholemeal flour (both plain and self-raising), stoneground wholemeal, and three new additions to the range — organic, unbleached plain and self-raising flour (sold under the Tip Top brand or in bulk from health food stores) and organic stoneground flour (Old Grain Mill).

Basic Handling

1 Whether chilled or frozen fillo pastry is to be used, bring to room temperature before attempting to unfold sheets.

2 Melt the butter or margarine (butter is better) and skim off any froth. Milk solids will settle in the base of the pan, and while the clear butterfat should be poured into another pan, you can just dip the brush into the butterfat, leaving the residue in the pan. Salt is effectively removed with the froth, and any remaining salt is left in the residue.

3 Open out sheets on work surface and cover with a thick sheet of plastic. Do not let fillo come into contact with a damp tea towel or pastry sheets will stick together.

Fillo sheets for a large pie:

1 Count out the sheets required and remove from stack. Place on board, leaving remainder of fillo covered.

2 Brush top sheet lightly with melted butter, pick up at corners furthest from you and turn over on top of stack. Don't be concerned if pastry creases as you turn it — just smooth it out with your hand as best you can. Brush top, pick up the top two sheets and turn over onto stack.

3 Complete buttering, picking up an extra sheet each time. Leave top and bottom of stack unbuttered. Place in greased dish, butter top, fill, do another stack and complete pie.

4 Using a Stanley knife, trim edges about 1 cm above top of pie. Brush top with butter, score through top 2–3 sheets into portions required, sprinkle lightly with water to prevent pastry curling, then bake.

Fillo sheets for triangles or rolls:

1 Cut fillo into strips across the length of the pastry, making them twice as wide as required. The length of each strip is the same as the width of a whole sheet; e.g. if pastry is 30 cm wide, strips are then 30 cm long. Cut strips as economically as possible; because length of pastry varies, you might have to cut them a little less than indicated in recipes so that there is minimum wastage. Stack and cover with plastic.

2 For triangles, take a strip, brush lightly with melted butter and fold in half lengthwise. Brush lightly, place filling on bottom corner, fold pastry over filling so that

---

Australian Fillo is No 1

Chris Antoniou began making fillo pastry in Sydney in 1961. He wasn't the first, but he makes the best. He air-freighted his pastry to the UK for two years and, since stores such as Harrods and Marks and Spencer demanded more and more of it, his company now manufactures fillo pastry in the UK. That tells us a great deal about Australian food quality and the expertise of our food manufacturers. A good fillo pastry requires flour with a high gluten content, and Australian wheat growers and flour millers are very good at producing the right flour for the job — for any job for that matter.

base of strip lines up with side, beginning the triangle. Fold straight up, then across in a triangle to other side (just as a flag is folded). Complete folding to end of strip. Place seam side down on greased baking tray and brush lightly with butter.

3 For **rolls**, strips should be wider than for triangles. Butter and fold in half as for triangles. Butter again, place filling along lower end, keeping it in from the sides. Fold over once, fold in sides, roll up to end of strip. Finish as for triangles.

Fillo parcels:
1 Brush a fillo sheet with butter, top with another sheet and butter. Fold sheet almost in half across its length to give a square of pastry. Butter lightly.
2 Place food to be wrapped on one corner, fold over end, turn once, fold in sides and complete wrapping. Finish as for triangles.

To store leftover fillo: Fold up and return to plastic bag, seal with masking tape and place back in its box. Put box in a plastic bag and seal. Store in refrigerator, even for previously frozen fillo pastry. Do not return frozen pastry to freezer. Frozen fillo keeps for 2–3 weeks, chilled fillo for 2–3 months.

Damper

The damper sold in supermarkets and hot bread shops is not the damper of tradition — a yeast dough was never used for this Australian icon. Originally, it was made with unleavened flour because our early white settlers had no yeast. If it is eaten fresh from the fire, you could just bear to eat it; left until cold, it was extremely leaden. With the discovery of the leavening properties of bicarbonate of soda combined with an acidic ingredient, bush damper became indispensable to outback and camp cooks who did not have access to yeast for making bread. Its resemblance to Irish soda bread, which uses sour milk and bicarbonate of soda, was more than co-incidental. However, with the introduction of baking powder and then self-raising flour, damper took on its present, essentially Australian character. It is still popular with camp cooks, but just as popular cooked in the comfort of your kitchen.

Wheat Tortillas

Corn tortillas are flat, soft rounds of corn meal dough, cooked on a griddle. They are the 'bread' of Mexico, and when fried in oil until crisp, then folded, become the tacos familiar to most Australians today. The soft corn tortillas are mostly imported, preserved in flat cans, however Hilroy Foods of Sydney make them for sale through their retail outlet in Randwick, some delicatessens and Mexican food outlets. Wheat tortillas, popular in the north of Mexico, are now available in the refrigerator section of some supermarkets. As tortillas are used to wrap foods similarly to crepes, you can substitute small, wholemeal pita breads, slitting each bread into two rounds, or use the rectangular lavash bread, halving each bread.

Plain Damper

Oven temperature: 210°C (425°F)

Serves 5–6

3 cups self-raising flour
½ teaspoon salt
2 teaspoons caster sugar
¾ cup milk
½ cup water
extra milk to glaze

1 Sift flour, salt and sugar into a mixing bowl. Make a well in the centre.
2 Combine milk and water and pour into centre of flour. Mix lightly and quickly with a round-bladed knife to form a soft, sticky dough.
3 Turn out onto a greased baking tray and shape into a round with a wide spatula. Brush top with extra milk and cut a cross in the centre of the dough with a floured knife.
4 Bake in preheated hot oven for 30–35 minutes until it sounds hollow when tapped. Serve hot with butter and jam, honey, or the very Australian golden syrup.

Herbed Damper Loaves

Makes about 8 loaves

1 Make damper as above. Turn out onto a floured board and dust top lightly with flour. Knead lightly, about 4–5 turns, to smooth out dough a little.
2 Dust board again with flour and roll out dough to a rectangle about 1 cm thick. Brush with 2 tablespoons finely chopped garlic chives, 2 tablespoons finely chopped parsley and 2 teaspoons chopped fresh thyme. Roll up from longer side. Cut into pieces 10 cm long.
3 Place seam side down on a greased baking tray or into greased, small loaf pans. Cut two diagonal shallow slashes in the top of each loaf. Brush with milk or beaten egg and sprinkle with sunflower seeds. Bake in a preheated hot oven for 15 minutes until cooked. Serve hot as an accompaniment to meals.

Boiled Rice

Directions on packs of polished rice call for boiling 8 cups water for 1 cup rice, so that a lot of the starch is removed when the rice is drained. In this age of energy conservation, boiling such a volume of water for 1 cup rice does seem wasteful. The following method is one I use which gives separate, just-firm-to-the-bite rice grains every time. It may be served hot, but this is the rice needed for fried rice and salads. It is also the way to cook rice for freezer storage. Use Calrose for fried rice, either rice for salads.

Boiled Rice

Makes about 6 cups boiled rice

2 cups Calrose or long-grain rice
6 cups water
1 teaspoon salt

1 Put water on to boil.
2 Put rice in a sieve and run cold water through it, moving grains with the fingers to release some of the starch.
3 Add rice and salt to boiling water and return to the boil, stirring to separate grains. Boil, uncovered, for 12 minutes. Test a grain — it should still be firm in the centre.
4 Pour rice and cooking water through a large sieve or colander and run some hot water over the rice to remove more of the starch.
5 Place sieve or colander over empty pan in which rice was cooked. Poke 3 or 4 holes into the rice with the end of a wooden spoon. Place pan lid over the rice to keep in the heat and stand for 10 minutes. Rice grains complete cooking in the stored heat, dry out and remain separate. Serve hot or turn into a container, seal and store in the refrigerator until required. If to be used for fried rice, chill overnight.

Freezing rice: Boil rice as above, up to and including Step 4. Tip drained rice into a baking dish and fluff up with fork. Leave until cool, then pack in meal-sized portions in freezer bags, seal and store in freezer.

Maize and Wheaten Cornflours

While the Buyer's Guide only lists cornflour made from corn (maize), a cornflour made from wheat is also made in Australia. When used to thicken sauces and Asian dishes, I find that maize cornflour retains its thickening properties to a better degree than wheaten cornflour. If you have had problems with cornflour in the past, check your brand to see if it is maize or wheaten.

Flour Paste for Thickening
....
A paste of flour and water is often required for thickening stews, casseroles and gravies, as it gives a smoother texture than a cornflour paste. However, some plain flours have the annoying habit of becoming lumpy when mixed with cold water. To solve the problem, put about 1/3 cup cold water in a jar, add 2–3 tablespoons of plain, white flour, seal and shake vigorously. The resultant thin paste is smooth and can be poured into the simmering liquid. Stir constantly as you pour, until thickened to desired consistency, then boil gently for 1–2 minutes to cook the starch.

To reheat, place required amount in microwave-safe dish, cover and microwave on HIGH for 3–5 minutes. For stove-top reheating, bring 2 cups water to the boil, add rice, return to the boil, boil for 1 minute then drain and serve. For fried rice, add frozen rice to wok or pan with other ingredients and stir-fry until well heated.

Boiled Rice — Absorption Method
Makes 3 cups

1 cup Calrose, long-grain or jasmine rice
2 cups water
1/2 teaspoon salt

1 Rinse rice as for Boiled Rice, Step 1.
2 Bring water to the boil, add salt and rice. Return to the boil, stirring occasionally to separate grains.
3 When boiling, cover tightly with lid, reduce heat to low and cook without stirring for 15–18 minutes, until water is absorbed.
4 Remove from heat and leave covered for 5–10 minutes. Fluff up with fork and serve hot as an accompaniment to meals. This rice is also good for serving with Asian dishes.

Note: If 2 cups rice is required for cooking, only add 3 1/2 cups water. As a general rule, reduce water by half a cup for each additional cup of rice cooked.

Boiled Brown Rice
As for Boiled Rice, using 8 cups water for 2 cups rice and boil, uncovered, for 35–40 minutes. Test a grain; it should be almost tender. Drain, rinse with hot water and finish as for Boiled Rice. This may also be prepared for freezer storage; follow directions for Frozen Rice.

Boiled Brown Rice — Absorption Method
Same as for Boiled Rice — Absorption Method. When rice returns to the boil, simmer, tightly covered, on low heat for 40–45 minutes until water is absorbed and grains are tender. Leave covered, off the heat, for 10 minutes.

Quick-cooking brown rice: Prepare as for Boiled Brown Rice, cooking for 15–18 minutes. To cook by absorption method, add 1 cup rice to 1 1/2 cups boiling, lightly salted water, return to boil, reduce heat, cover and simmer for 25 minutes. Stand off the heat for 10 minutes.

Parboiled long-grain rice (Sungold): Use absorption method and add 1 cup rice to 1 cup boiling, lightly salted water. Return to boil, reduce heat, cover and simmer for 12 minutes. Stand, covered, for 5 minutes.

To prepare this rice without cooking, place required amount in a casserole dish or container with lid to fit, pour on an equal quantity of boiling water, cover and place in the refrigerator for a minimum of 1 hour until water is absorbed. Rice can remain in the refrigerator for several hours or overnight. This gives perfect rice for rice salads and fried rice. It can be heated in the microwave oven or steamed in a colander over boiling water if required hot. It is important that this rice be refrigerated for the 'cooking' process in the interests of food safety. Any cooked rice should never be left at room temperature for long periods.

Microwave rice cooking: All packs of Australian rice carry microwave cooking directions. Use the right-sized container to avoid boil-over.

Fried Rice
Serves 6

4 tablespoons peanut oil
2 eggs, beaten
pinch of salt
1 teaspoon grated fresh ginger
1 clove garlic, crushed
1 cup chopped spring onions
1 cup sliced fresh mushrooms
6 cups Boiled Rice (page 20) using Calrose rice
1 cup chopped cooked chicken
½ cup chopped ham
1 cup cooked green peas
1 tablespoon dry sherry
1 tablespoon soy sauce

1 Heat 1 tablespoon oil in a large frying pan or wok. Beat eggs with salt, pour into pan and cook into a thin omelette. Remove to a plate and chop in small squares. Keep aside.
2 Add remaining oil to pan with ginger and garlic and cook gently for a few seconds, add spring onions and mushrooms and stir-fry on medium heat for 2–3 minutes. Increase heat.
3 Add rice and stir often until heated, add chicken, ham and peas and cook for 2–3 minutes, stirring often.

Australian Rice

All rices used in the rice cooking directions are Australian. Our rice industry is constantly looking to fulfil the needs of Australians, introducing quick-to-cook rices and developing new strains such as jasmine, popular in Asian cooking. Brown Calrose rice, with its outer bran layers and germ, has a higher nutritional value, but takes longer to cook. Quick-cooking brown rice has been partly steam-cooked to enable this nutritious grain to be cooked more quickly. Parboiled long-grain rice (Sungold) is actually steamed under pressure, forcing the bran into the grain, and contains 60% of the soluble nutrient content of brown rice, which gives the rice a golden colour. Besides being able to 'cook' it in the fridge, it also cooks quickly by traditional means.

Mix sherry and soy sauce and sprinkle over rice with chopped omelette. Toss well over heat and serve hot as a light meal.

Variations

Fried Brown Rice
Replace boiled Calrose rice with 6 cups boiled brown rice and proceed as in above recipe.

Vegetarian Fried Rice
Replace boiled Calrose rice with 6 cups boiled brown rice. Omit chicken and ham. Prepare 1 cup chopped green and red pepper and add with spring onions and mushrooms. Complete as above.

Perfect Pilaf

This is based on the absorption method of cooking rice. The basic method may be turned into plain boiled rice simply by not using the butter and replacing the chicken stock with water. However, most cooks would want to flavour the rice in some way.

Basic Pilaf
Serves 6

2 cups long-grain rice
3 tablespoons butter
3½ cups chicken stock
salt to taste

1 Place rice in a sieve and rinse until water runs clear. Leave aside to drain for about 30 minutes.
2 Melt butter in a medium-sized saucepan, add drained rice and cook over medium heat, stirring often, until rice begins to look opaque.
3 Add chicken stock and salt, stir well and bring to the boil. Reduce heat to low, cover pan and cook for 20 minutes or until rice is just tender to the bite and liquid is absorbed.
4 Place a white paper towel over the rim of the pan, cover tightly with lid and leave aside for 5–10 minutes. Fluff up with fork and serve hot.

Variations

Fruit and Nut Pilaf

At Step 2, lightly brown ¼ cup slivered almonds in the butter. Remove with a draining spoon and keep aside. Add rice and continue to step 3. Use 3 cups chicken stock and ½ cup orange juice, and add ¼ cup each dried apricots and currants and the grated rind of 1 orange. Complete cooking. Fluff up with fork, turn out into serving dish and sprinkle on lightly browned almonds. If desired, blanched shreds of orange rind may also be used as a garnish. Serve with chicken, pork or lamb. Any left over makes an excellent stuffing for roast chicken.

Vegetable Pilaf

At Step 2, cook 1 chopped onion and ½ cup each chopped green pepper and celery in the butter until onion is transparent. Peel and chop 2 medium-sized ripe tomatoes and add to pan with the rice. Continue with Step 3, adding 3 cups water in place of the 3½ cups chicken stock. Add 1 tablespoon chopped parsley, season to taste with salt and pepper and complete cooking. Serve with beef, lamb or chicken.

Toasted, Crisped Breads

With such a large baking industry, it is surprising that crisped breads are not manufactured to a significant extent in Australia. With their excellent keeping qualities, and being low-fat into the bargain, they are a very popular snack food. One popular line of imported bagel and pita crisps (not so low in fat) works out at triple the price of the fresh product; what's more, most of the pack contents are broken pieces! Prepare your own crisped breads, croutons and canapé bases, supporting the local bread industry and saving yourself money into the bargain. This is also an excellent way to use up stale breads, besides using them for crumbs.

Cooking Pasta

Pasta strands have the annoying habit of sticking together during cooking. Use a large boiler or saucepan and bring water to the boil. Add about a tablespoon each of vegetable oil and salt. If cooking spaghetti, leave it in the long strands and place in the boiling water, fanning out the bundles of strands as they are added. Gradually ease into the water as the strands soften, with the aid of a long wooden fork or spoon. Once it is immersed, stir the pasta now and then until the water returns to the boil. Allow to boil, with lid half on the pan, until cooked *al dente* — that is, just firm to the bite. The oil prevents the pasta water boiling over and the movement of the pasta in the early stages of cooking prevents the strands sticking together. Add about a cup of cold water and drain immediately into a colander. All pasta should be cooked in the same way, moving it in the water as the strands or pieces soften, to separate them and prevent sticking.

Making Breadcrumbs

For soft breadcrumbs, bread should be stale. If from an unsliced loaf, trim off crusts on three sides, leaving crust on one side. Hold the crust side and grate on shredder section of grater.

If you have a food processor, remove crusts from bread piece or slices, break up bread and process in batches with steel blade until crumbed. Fresh bread can also be crumbed in this way.

For dried breadcrumbs, use sliced bread, including crusts, and dry out in a moderate oven for 10–15 minutes until crisp. Reduce to fine crumbs by rolling on a board with a rolling pin, or break into pieces and process in batches in food processor. Store in an airtight container.

Preparing the Breads

Canapé Bases: Select a long French bread stick, choosing one which is of small diameter. Leave in its bag at room temperature for a day or so. Freeze until just firm and cut with a sharp knife into 1-cm slices.

Croutons: Use stale slices from a toast loaf of bread. Trim off crusts and cut bread into approximately 1.5-cm cubes. Partial freezing of the bread will make cubing easier.

Bagel Crisps: Select small bagels and partially freeze. Cut each bagel into circles, slicing as thinly as possible.

Pita Crisps: Select medium-sized, 25-cm pita bread or the small, 15-cm breads, either white or wholemeal. Slit around edge of each bread to separate into two rounds. Cut larger breads into eight even wedges, quarter the small breads.

Crisping the Breads

Place prepared breads — canapé bases, croutons, bagels or pitas — in a single layer on baking trays. Preheat oven to moderate, 180°C (350°F), and cook breads for 12–15 minutes until crisp and lightly golden. Cool and store in an airtight container.

Flavouring the Breads

Garlic Croutons: Pour 1/4 cup sunola oil in a large baking dish and add 2 halved cloves of garlic. Heat in oven for 2 minutes. Add prepared croutons, toss in the oil and cook until crisp, stirring croutons occasionally to brown evenly. Drain on kitchen paper and store when cold, discarding garlic.

Garlic and Herb Bagel and Pita Crisps: Soften 125g butter and mix in 1 crushed clove garlic and 1 tablespoon finely chopped parsley. Spread lightly on one side of prepared bagel or pita slices (spread the soft, inner surface of the pita bread). Place on baking trays, buttered side up, and cook until crisp and lightly golden. Any leftover butter mixture can be covered and refrigerated for later use.

• Use canapé bases with a variety of savoury toppings as finger food or serve with dips, spreads or cheese. Top with shredded gruyère cheese, place under grill until cheese melts and float on top of French onion soup.

- Add croutons to pea or cream soups, or use in salads such as Caesar Salad.
- Serve bagel and pita crisps with dips, spreads or cheese, or break into pieces and add to salads or soups.

True-blue Pizzas

••••••••••••••••••••••••••••

For pizzas to have almost all local ingredients means pizzas without olives and anchovies, unless you have cured your own olives, or have been able to purchase Australian cured olives and tracked down the West Australian anchovies.

Oven temperature: 190°C (375°F)

Serves 5–6

1 x 30-cm pre-baked pizza base
½ cup Tomato Pasta Sauce, page 136
Topping mixtures (see below)
1½ cups shredded mozzarella or pizza cheese
1 tablespoon grated Parmesan cheese

1 Place pizza base on a large baking tray. Spread on sauce. If pizza base has its own sauce already spread on it, you can use less of the tomato sauce.

2 Cover with desired topping mixtures and top with mozzarella or pizza cheese. Sprinkle Parmesan cheese on top.

3 Bake in a preheated, moderately hot oven for 20–25 minutes until top is bubbly and lightly browned. Serve hot.

Topping Mixtures

Beef and pepperoni: Cook 200 g minced beef in a heated pan, stirring until crumbly and lightly browned. Mix with ½ cup sliced pepperoni sausage, ½ cup each chopped green pepper and mushrooms and 1 small sliced onion. Spread over pizza and sprinkle with ¼ cup chopped, sun-dried tomatoes. Add cheese topping.

Ham and Pineapple: Use only ¼ cup of the sauce to spread on the pizza base. Drain a 440-g can of pineapple pieces and mix with ¾ cup chopped, double-smoked ham. Top with mozzarella or pizza cheese and omit the Parmesan cheese.

Storing Bread

••••••••••••••••••

If you have a large household, storing bread in a bread box or crock would probably be suitable. However, if you find that it takes a few days to get through a loaf of sliced bread, store it in the freezer, well sealed in its bag. Remove frozen slices as required.

Do not store bread in the refrigerator unless you like it stale. The refrigerator is an evaporator and removes moisture from food as it is chilled. That is why we use so much plastic film! With bread, the moisture migrates from the crumb, leaving it dry. Actually it is a good means of 'staling' bread for crumbing!

Eggplant and Kumara (vegetarian): Cut a small, oval eggplant in 1-cm cubes, place in a colander and sprinkle with 2 teaspoons salt. Toss and leave for 30 minutes, rinse, drain and dry cubes in a cloth. Prepare 1 cup cubed kumara (orange sweet potato) and boil or microwave until just tender; drain. Heat 1 tablespoon sunola oil in a frying pan, add 1 sliced onion and cook gently until soft. Increase heat, add eggplant and cook, stirring often, until lightly browned. Mix in sweet potato. Spread mixture over the tomato sauce, sprinkle with 1 tablespoon chopped fresh basil and add 12 halved cherry tomatoes. Top with cheeses. As a special treat, replace cheeses with 100 g sliced chèvre (goat's cheese).

Focaccia

This delicious Italian bread has been enthusiastically adopted into our kitchens. It is a popular item in fast food outlets, with fillings or toppings somewhat removed from Italian origins. Serve as a light meal or snack, but the bread should be very fresh. If you don't intend using focaccia on the day of purchase, store in a sealed freezer bag in the freezer. As focaccia breads vary in size, the quantity is given in portions; buy whatever amount of focaccia you consider adequate for your needs.

Oven temperature: 180°C (350°F)

Serves 6

6 portions fresh focaccia bread
Salad Oil, page 80
selected fillings and toppings, see below

1 Leave bread portions whole or slit according to method of serving.
2 Brush top or cut sides of bread with oil. Top or fill and bake in a moderate oven for 10 minutes until heated through. Serve hot.

Which Bread?

It is all a matter of taste. Any bread is good for you — it does not *have* to be wholemeal or whole grain or high fibre. Certainly breads with a high fibre content are valuable in the diet if you do not have enough other fibre-rich foods such as cereals, pulses, fruits and vegetables. Just be aware that, while the vitamin and mineral content of wholemeal and whole grain breads is higher than in white bread, such breads contain phytic acid which, together with the high fibre content, inhibits absorption of these nutrients by the body.

Focaccia with Caramelised Onions and Red Peppers

4 large brown onions
3 tablespoons butter
24 pieces Marinated Roasted Red Peppers, page 143
salt
freshly ground black pepper

1   Halve onions and cut in 5-mm thick slices across onion to give half-moon shapes.
2   Melt butter in a large frying pan with lid to fit, add onions and cook on gentle heat, with lid on, for 15 minutes, stirring occasionally. When softened, remove lid and continue to cook slowly for further 20–25 minutes until onion is golden brown, with a caramel-like aroma. You can hasten the caramel effect by sprinkling on a teaspoon of sugar.
3   Divide onions onto 6 of the slit focaccia portions, top each with 4 marinated pepper pieces and season with salt and pepper. Top with remaining focaccia and heat in oven for 10 minutes. Serve hot. If bread is very fresh, there is no need to heat it in the oven.

Focaccia with Prosciutto and Mozzarella

12 paper-thin slices of prosciutto
12 slices mozzarella cheese
½ cup chopped, sun-dried tomatoes or 3 fresh tomatoes
¼ cup shredded fresh basil leaves
salt
freshly ground black pepper

1   Prepare slit focaccia; place 2 slices each prosciutto and mozzarella cheese on 6 portions, sprinkle with sun-dried tomatoes or top with tomato slices. Sprinkle with basil, salt and pepper.
2   Top with remaining focaccia and bake in oven for 10 minutes until cheese melts. Serve hot.

Focaccia with Chicken, Avocado and Cheese

12 slices cooked chicken
3 ripe avocados
lemon juice
salt
freshly ground black pepper
2 cups pizza cheese

Falwasser Crispbread

For a special accompaniment to cheese, try Falwasser crispbread, made by Peter Freeman at Surfer's Paradise. He uses Australian ingredients as far as possible, except for pepper and caraway seeds. The delicious, wafer-thin, round crispbreads come in various flavours — Mexican chilli, caraway, cheese and onion, cracked pepper and chives, poppy seed, sesame, and dried tomato.
Qantas and Ansett airlines use them on cheese platters for first-class service; that is recommendation enough for the quality of the product. But you don't have to fly first class to try them — they are available at gourmet food halls and delicatessens and some green grocers.

Warming Pita Breads

....

The number of brands of pita breads on the market is a testament to their popularity. It is often necessary to warm them for serving with certain foods. As they can lose moisture easily, it is better to wrap the required number in foil in a stack, so that they remain moist. Use the foil with the dull side out (the shiny surface deflects the heat), wrap and seal, and heat in a moderate oven. If required at the barbecue, place package on the barbecue grid and turn occasionally.

1 Do not slit focaccia. Top each piece with 2 chicken slices.
2 Prepare and slice avocado and place slices on top of chicken. Sprinkle with lemon juice, salt and pepper.
3 Sprinkle 4 tablespoons shredded cheese on top of avocado. Heat under a moderately hot grill until cheese melts and browns lightly. Serve hot.

Marvellous Muffins

●●●●●●●●●●●●●●●●●●●●●●●●●●●●●●

These are fast replacing hot scones as the quick-to-prepare treat to serve with that cuppa. Basically, muffins consist of a dry mixture to which a wet mixture is added. As for a good scone, mixing must be light and brief; don't be concerned if mixture is lumpy, as long as the dry ingredients are moistened. Once you have a basic recipe, all kinds of variations are possible. If you like to bake healthier treats, replacing half the white flour with wholemeal increases fibre and nutritive value and gives a delicious, nutty flavour. If made entirely with wholemeal flour, muffins are heavier in texture.

Basic Muffin Mix
Oven temperature: 200°C (400°F)

Makes 12 x 8-cm muffins or 20 x 5-cm muffins

Dry mixture
2 cups self-raising flour
¼ cup caster sugar
¼ teaspoon salt

Wet mixture
1 egg
1 cup milk
¼ cup melted butter or margarine

1 Grease muffin pans with butter; if using non-stick bakeware, it is not necessary to grease them. Preheat oven.
2 Prepare dry mixture: Sift flour and salt into a bowl, mix in sugar and make a well in the centre.
3 Prepare wet mixture: In another bowl, beat egg with milk and warm melted butter.

Using Australian Cereals and Grains • 29

4 Pour wet mixture into centre of dry mixture and mix quickly and lightly with a fork until dry ingredients are moistened.

5 Spoon into prepared muffin pans to two-thirds fill each pan. Bake in preheated moderately hot oven for about 20 minutes for large, 8-cm muffins, 12–15 minutes for 5-cm muffins. To test if cooked, insert a fine skewer into the centre of a muffin; it should come out clean. Turn out onto a wire cake rack when cooked. Serve warm with butter and jam, honey or golden syrup.

Variations:
In the following, adjustments are made to the basic dry and wet mixtures to give a range of popular muffins.

Berry Muffins
Make as above, increasing sugar in dry mixture to 1/3 cup. Pour in wet mixture, mix a little, then add 1 cup fresh blueberries, mulberries or blackberries, complete mixing and finish as above. Use 8-cm muffin pans for preference, baking for 20–25 minutes. Serve warm or cold with butter.

Orange and Pecan Muffins
For dry mixture, replace 1 cup of the flour with 1 cup self-raising wholemeal flour and add 1/2 cup chopped pecan nuts. To wet mixture, add 1 teaspoon grated orange rind, reduce milk to 1/2 cup and add 1/2 cup fresh orange juice. Finish as above, using 8-cm muffin pans and bake for 20–25 minutes. If desired, top each muffin with a pecan half. Serve warm or cold, either plain or with butter or cream cheese spread.

Banana and Raisin Muffins
For dry mixture, replace 1 cup of the flour with 1 cup wholemeal self-raising flour and sift with 1/2 teaspoon bicarbonate of soda. Stir in sugar as in Step 1. For wet mixture, reduce milk to 3/4 cup, use 1/4 cup macadamia or canola oil in place of the melted butter and beat in 1/2 cup mashed, ripe banana. Add to dry mixture with 1/2 cup raisins and complete as in basic recipe, using 8-cm muffin pans. Bake for 20–25 minutes. Serve warm or cold, either plain or with butter.

Savoury Herb and Cheese Muffins
For dry mixture, replace 1 cup of the flour with 1 cup wholemeal self-raising flour and reduce sugar to 2 teaspoons. Stir in 3 tablespoons chopped fresh herbs (pars-

PANCAKES AND PIKELETS

Pancake shake mixes in plastic containers are a clever marketing ploy (along with muffin and cake shakes). It seems such fun in the television commercials, and the children love doing it, but think of all those plastic containers requiring disposal! These popular batter cakes are just so easy to make from scratch, and cheaper too. The same mixture is required for both; the pancakes are simply large versions of pikelets.

Put 1 1/2 cups self-raising flour in a bowl, add 2 tablespoons caster sugar, 1 egg, 2 tablespoons bland vegetable oil and 1 cup milk. Stir to a smooth batter with a balloon whisk. Use about 1/4 cup of the mixture for each pancake, or a generous tablespoonful for each pikelet, cooking them in a well-greased frying pan or on a griddle. When bubbles appear over the surface, turn and complete cooking.

ley, thyme and chives), a pinch of chilli powder and ³/₄ cup shredded cheddar cheese. Add wet mixture as for basic recipe, spoon into 8-cm muffin pans and sprinkle a teaspoon of shredded cheese on top of each muffin. Bake for 20–25 minutes. Serve hot or warm.

Basic Butter Cake

One cake mix — lots of different cakes. My method varies a little from the norm; if you add one of the eggs when creaming the butter and sugar, the mixture becomes light and fluffy much more quickly. After remaining eggs are beaten in, complete the mixing by hand for a light result.

Oven temperature: 180°C (350°F)

250g butter
1 cup caster sugar
3 eggs
2 teaspoons vanilla essence
2 cups self-raising flour
½ cup milk
Glacé Icing of choice, page 33

1 Grease and flour a deep 23-cm cake pan, fluted ring mould or tube cake pan.
2 Place soft butter and sugar in large bowl of electric mixer. Beat until combined, add 1 egg and vanilla and beat until light and fluffy. Beat in remaining eggs and remove bowl from mixer.
3 Sift flour and fold in alternately with milk. Turn into prepared cake pan and spread mixture evenly.
4 Bake in preheated moderate oven for 55–60 minutes until cooked when tested. Stand 5 minutes then turn onto a wire rack, invert right side up on another rack (round cake only) and leave until cool. Dust with icing sugar or top with icing of choice.

Variations

Orange Cake
Add 2 teaspoons grated orange rind instead of vanilla and replace ¼ cup of the milk with fresh orange juice. Top with Orange Glacé Icing (page 34) when cold.

Chocolate Cake
Sift 4 tablespoons cocoa with the flour and add an extra ¼ cup milk. Complete as above. It may also be cooked in 2 × 23-cm layer cake pans for 40 minutes and sandwiched with whipped cream, lightly sweetened and flavoured with vanilla essence. Dust top with icing sugar or spread with Chocolate Glacé Icing.

Apple Cake
Use half the mixture and place in a greased 23-cm layer cake pan. Peel 2 small apples (Granny Smith or Golden Delicious) and cut into quarters. Remove core and cut almost through rounded side in thin slices. Place quarters lightly on top of batter, rounded side up, and sprinkle with caster sugar and cinnamon. Bake in moderate oven for 40 minutes. Dust with icing sugar and serve warm with cream for a dessert or cold as a cake. Make patty cakes with remaining mixture.

Patty Cakes
Put heaped tablespoons of mixture into paper cases or greased patty cake pans to two-thirds full; if using paper cases, place in ungreased patty cake pans so that cakes keep their shape. Bake in a moderately hot oven, 190°C (375°F), for 15–20 minutes. When cold, ice as desired. To make butterfly cakes, scoop out a circle from the top of each cake with a pointed knife. Fill cavity with whipped cream. Cut circle of cake in half and place on each side of cream, angling pieces upwards like wings. Dust with sifted icing sugar and top each with a strawberry if desired. Makes about 30 cakes.

Lamingtons
Bake cake in a greased 28- × 18-cm lamington tin for 30–35 minutes. Cool and store in a sealed container for two days. Cut into approximately 4-cm squares. Make a double quantity of Chocolate Glacé Icing (page 34) and stir in an extra 3–4 tablespoons of boiling water to give a thin cream consistency. Stand bowl in a pan of hot water to keep icing liquid. Using two forks, dip each piece of cake into the icing then drop into a dish of desiccated coconut. Roll in coconut to coat and place on a wire rack to set.

Loaf Cakes
Basic mixture makes 2 loaf cakes in 20- × 9-cm loaf pans. Second cooked cake may be stored, properly wrapped, in freezer for up to 2 months.

Quick Scones

Sift 2 cups self-raising flour into a bowl with 1 teaspoon baking powder and a pinch of salt. Melt 30 g butter. Pour ¾ cup milk into flour, add melted butter and stir to a soft dough with a round-bladed knife. Turn onto a floured board, dust top with flour and knead lightly for 4–5 turns to smooth the dough. Shape into a round about 2 centimetres thick and lift onto a greased scone tray. With a floured knife, cut almost through into eight wedges. Brush top with milk and bake in a very hot oven, 250°C (500°F), for 12–15 minutes. To test if cooked, tap base of tray under the scone round — it should sound hollow. Serve hot or warm.

Apricot and Walnut Loaf Cakes
Omit vanilla from basic recipe. Before folding in flour, stir in ½ cup chopped, dried apricots and ¼ cup chopped walnuts. Bake loaves for 40–45 minutes.

Fruit Loaf Cakes
Sift 1 teaspoon mixed spice with the flour. Fold in flour and milk alternately with 1 cup mixed dried fruit or sultanas. Bake loaves for 45–50 minutes.

Banana Loaf Cakes
Add ¾ cup mashed banana alternately with flour. Use ⅓ cup milk and dissolve ½ teaspoon bicarbonate of soda in it. Fold into cake batter at end of mixing. Bake loaves for 45–50 minutes.

Glacé Icing

1 cup icing sugar
2 teaspoons butter
about 1 tablespoon boiling water

1 Sift icing sugar into a bowl, add butter and pour about 1 tablespoon boiling water onto butter.

2 Stir to a smooth, creamy consistency, adding more water, drop by drop, if necessary.

3 Place bowl over simmering water and stir until icing melts and becomes glossy — do not overheat. Alternatively, place bowl in microwave oven and heat on high for 5–6 seconds until icing melts. Remove and stir.

4 Pour immediately over cake, and spread quickly with spatula. Leave to set before cutting cake.

Variations

Vanilla Glacé Icing
Add ½ teaspoon vanilla essence with the water. Colour a pale pink if desired with 1–2 drops food colouring. If using on patty cakes, sprinkle with hundreds and thous

Orange Glacé Icing
Add ½ teaspoon grated orange rind and use very soft butter. Use fresh orange juice instead of boiling water. Complete as above.

Chocolate Glacé Icing
Sift 1 tablespoon cocoa with the icing sugar and add ½ teaspoon vanilla essence with the boiling water.

Passionfruit Glacé Icing
Use the pulp of 1 passionfruit in place of the water. Depending on size of passionfruit, it may be necessary to add a little more icing sugar if it is too soft before melting.

Refrigerator Biscuits

We tend to forget some of yesterday's fads. Refrigerator biscuits were very popular years ago, and have made something of a comeback in a related form through a new freezer-stored convenience product. In its original form, the biscuit dough is shaped into logs, suitably wrapped and stored in the refrigerator until you fancy some freshly baked biscuits. Of course, this had to be used within a week. It makes much more sense to be able to store the dough in the freezer for a longer period. It is important, however, that the measures be as accurate as possible; if too much flour is added (easy to do in hot weather when mixture is softer), then you could have difficulty slicing the dough straight from the freezer.

Basic Refrigerator Biscuits
Oven temperature: 180°C (350°F)

Makes about 80 biscuits

250 g butter
1¼ cups caster sugar
2 teaspoons vanilla essence
2 eggs
3¼ cups plain flour
2 teaspoons baking powder

Is the Cake Cooked?

How does one know when a cake is cooked? You can try the skewer test — the cake is cooked when the skewer comes out clean. When the cake shrinks from the sides of the pan is another indication. Or listen to it! Hold cake up to your ear — if it sizzles softly, it needs more cooking; if there is no sizzle, it is cooked. If there is fresh or dried fruit in the cake, these sizzle even when the cake is cooked, so try one of the other tests.

1 Beat butter and sugar with vanilla essence and eggs until light and fluffy.

2 Sift flour and baking powder and stir into creamed mixture to form a soft dough. Press with finger — if dough doesn't stick, it is right, otherwise add a little more flour.

3 Turn onto a lightly floured board, shape into a flat round, wrap and chill for 1 hour to make shaping easier. Divide dough into four and roll each portion into a cylinder about 4 cm in diameter; flatten ends of rolls.

4 Wrap each roll in plastic film. If required on day of making, chill in refrigerator for 2–3 hours until firm, or in freezer for 1 hour. Otherwise, store wrapped rolls in a freezer bag or sealed container in the freezer for up to three months.

5 With a sharp knife, cut chilled or frozen dough in 6-mm slices and place 3 cm apart on greased baking trays.

6 Bake in preheated moderate oven for 12–15 minutes until lightly golden. Cool on wire rack and store in an airtight container.

Note: If edge of frozen dough crumbles when sliced, stand at room temperature for 5–10 minutes to slightly soften outside of roll.

Variations

Sugar or Nut-topped Biscuits
Before baking, glaze tops with a little milk and sprinkle with granulated sugar or cinnamon sugar. To make Nut-topped Biscuits, glaze and lightly press some slivered almonds or half a pecan nut on top of each. Use different toppings so that you have a variety of biscuits from the one batch.

Passionfruit Biscuits
Omit vanilla from basic recipe and replace 1 egg with $1/3$ cup passionfruit pulp at Step 1. Increase flour to $3 1/2$ cups. Complete as above. If desired, when biscuits have cooled, sandwich in pairs with passionfruit icing: Sift 1 cup icing sugar into a bowl, beat in 1 tablespoon soft butter and the pulp of 1 passionfruit. Sandwiched biscuits may be dusted lightly with icing sugar for serving.

Pecan Biscuits
Use brown sugar in place of caster, packing it in firmly when measuring. Add $1/2$ cup chopped pecans with the

flour in Step 2. Complete as for basic recipe. Rolls may be squared off after shaping; press roll with a long palette knife to make four flat sides, wrap and chill. When sliced, biscuits will be square.

Anzac Biscuits

These traditional Australian biscuits should be back in favour as they contain good-for-you rolled oats. However, you can change the basic formula in line with today's advice to reduce saturated fat intake. While butter is the traditional fat, and coconut must be used for the sake of authenticity, both these ingredients contain saturated fats. You can reduce this by using a polyunsaturated or mono-unsaturated table margarine in place of the butter.

Oven temperature: 180°C (350°F)

Makes about 48 biscuits

1 cup plain flour
1 cup rolled oats
1 cup desiccated coconut
¾ cup caster sugar
125 g butter or table margarine
2 tablespoons golden syrup
1 teaspoon bicarbonate of soda
2 tablespoons boiling water

1 Mix dry ingredients in a bowl and make a well in the centre.
2 In a medium-sized saucepan, heat butter or margarine and golden syrup, stirring well. Mix soda into boiling water and stir into butter mixture. When it froths up, pour into dry ingredients and mix with a wooden spoon until combined.
3 Drop heaped teaspoonfuls onto greased baking trays, leaving space for biscuits to spread. Bake in preheated moderate oven for 15 minutes until golden brown. Leave on trays for 5 minutes, then remove to a wire rack to cool. Store in a sealed container.

Note: If you like biscuits to be evenly round in shape, roll heaped teaspoonfuls of mixture into balls and place on trays. Flatten lightly with fingers.

Variations (for all-Australian versions)

Peanut Anzac Biscuits
In place of the coconut, use 1 cup coarsely chopped, roasted peanuts. Freshly shelled, Australian roasted peanuts give the best flavour, in preference to ready-chopped peanuts which could be imported.

Almond Anzac Biscuits
In place of the coconut, use 1/2 cup ground almonds and 1/2 cup lightly crushed, flaked almonds.

Oat and Raisin Cookies

A popular grocery line is the soft, American-style cookie using high-fibre ingredients and polyunsaturated oil. These are rather expensive, and do contain some imported ingredients, even though they are made locally. The following are easy to make, cost a fraction of the bought version, and are all-Australian. Use a mono-unsaturated or polyunsaturated oil.

Oven temperature: 190°C (375°F)

Makes about 36 cookies

1 cup self-raising flour
1/2 cup wholemeal self-raising flour
1 teaspoon cinnamon
1/2 cup quick-cooking rolled oats
1 tablespoon oat bran
1/2 cup raisins, chopped
1/2 cup chopped, unblanched almonds or pecans
1 large egg
1/2 cup macadamia or sunflower oil
1/2 cup brown sugar, firmly packed
2 tablespoons golden syrup
1/4 cup milk

1 Sift flours and cinnamon into a mixing bowl, returning husks from sifter to flour. Add oats, bran, dried fruit and nuts and mix well with a wooden spoon.
2 In another bowl, beat egg with a balloon whisk and beat in oil, sugar, golden syrup and milk. Pour into dry mixture and mix to a soft dough.
3 Drop tablespoonfuls onto lightly greased baking trays, spacing mounds. If mixture is stiff and dough

stands high, press each cookie lightly with fingers to flatten slightly.

4 Bake in preheated moderately hot oven for 12 minutes until golden brown. Remove to a rack and cool. Store in a sealed container.

Variation

Oat and Apricot Cookies: Replace raisins with ½ cup chopped, dried apricots.

Pulses, Nuts and Seeds

The total cost of pulse, nut and edible seed imports is over $165 million a year, and some 55 per cent of this is spent on nuts and nut products alone. A little self-denial would not go amiss for some nuts, and substituting Australian-grown nuts for imported could help the situation.

Pulses

Even though we now grow a large proportion of our requirements, some $70 million worth is imported, with soy beans and derivatives accounting for almost three-quarters of pulse imports. Kidney beans — borlotti, cannellini, Great Northern, haricot, lima, pinto and red — both dried and canned, account for another $12 million worth of imports. More pulses are now being grown in Australia, with quantities and varieties set to increase in the near future.

Nuts

Nut production in Australia could become one of our most important tree crop industries. The problems faced include finding the right varieties for certain growing conditions, as with hazelnuts and cashew nuts; developing means to further process nuts such as chestnuts; producing sufficient to warrant the costs involved in setting up cracking plants, as for walnuts and hazelnuts. Pine nuts are labour intensive to process, but it could be possible to produce them in the future. Our success with growing and processing our native macadamia nuts and the introduced pecan nuts augurs well for the production of other nuts, particularly if they also have export potential. The Buyer's Guide gives more details of nut production in Australia.

Seeds

Australian edible seed production is limited to sunflower seeds and seeds used for sprouting; all other seeds are imported. It is unlikely that we would produce sufficient sesame seeds, but attempts are being made. (Other seeds are covered in the chapters on Oils, Fats and Spreads and Herbs and Spices.)

Buyer's Guide
CHOOSING AUSTRALIAN PULSES, NUTS AND SEEDS

Product	Australian-produced	Imported	What we can do
PULSES			
Adzuki beans	Yes, with some exported	Yes, over $1 million worth	Used mostly in Asian recipes; most local beans used in salad sprout mixes.
Black beans — salted Chinese	No, but some products using them made locally	Yes	Limit use of black beans. See Pickles, Sauces and Condiments for local products.
Black-eyed beans	Yes, about 75% of our needs, also exported	Yes	Local product easy to buy; check label anyway
Blue peas — dried	Yes, with production increasing	Yes, over $2.5 million worth, including split peas, mostly from NZ	Check labels for local product.
Borlotti beans — dried and canned	Yes	Yes, small quantity	Check labels on dried and canned beans for local product.
Broad beans — dried	Yes, also exported	Yes, very small quantity	Local product easily obtained.
Cannellini, Great Northern* — dried and canned	Small quantity	Yes, most of those on the market	Limit use or substitute haricot or black-eyed beans.
Chick peas/garbanzos — dried and canned; Bengal gram (small brown chick peas)	Yes, both types; Bengal gram skinned and split and exported as channa dhal	Yes, small quantity of Bengal gram and canned chick peas	Large chick peas are local product as imports are not permitted; check canned chick peas for local product.
Haricot/navy/pea beans — dried and canned, including baked beans	Yes, large quantity, mostly for canned baked beans	Yes, to fulfil demand for baked beans and general sale	Check labels for local product, including baked beans.
Lentils, brown and red — dried and canned	Production of brown lentils increasing; red lentils also being grown in small quantities	Yes, over $1 million worth	Substitute yellow split peas for red lentils; check labels on canned lentils. Local lentils used for sprouting.
Lima beans, large and small — dried and canned	Yes, small quantity, mostly used in canned bean mixes	Yes, dried and canned	Most dried limas are imported; use less of them.
Mung beans — dried, and canned sprouts	Yes, also exported; local beans used for sprouting	Yes, small quantity; also canned sprouts	Check labels for local beans. Use fresh sprouts, not canned.
Pinto beans — dried and canned (refried beans)	No	Yes, dried and canned refried beans	Substitute borlotti beans in recipes; see Refried Beans, page 49.

Choosing Australian Pulses, Nuts and Seeds • 41

Product	Australian-produced	Imported	What we can do
Red kidney beans — dried and canned	Yes, small quantity	Yes, mostly dried	Check labels on cans for local product.
Soy beans — dried, canned, sprouts, bean curd/tofu, soy drink, textured vegetable protein, flour	Yes, but insufficient to meet demand for locally made bean curd, soy drink (popular because of 'no cholesterol' tag)	Yes, some $50 million worth of soy beans and by-products, most for manufacturing purposes	Check labels on packs and cans; avoid imported bean curd products, canned sprouts. Use less fresh bean curd. A cow's milk alternative to soy drink is available (see page 72).
Split peas — dried green and yellow	Yes, both types	Yes, see Blue peas	Use yellow split peas as red lentil substitute.
Tic/ful/ful medamis — dried whole, and skinned and split (called fulia)	Yes, whole; skinned and split, grown and processed locally. Also exported	Yes, whole only	Usually sold in bulk; some labelled properly in health food stores; buy fulia from Lebanese food stores.

NUTS

Product	Australian-produced	Imported	What we can do
Almonds — in shell, shelled, blanched, slivered, flaked, ground, salted etc.; confectionery, marzipan	Yes, about 55% of our needs and production increasing; self-sufficiency envisaged by year 2000	Yes, some $10 million worth, mostly shelled; some almond confectionery and all marzipan imported	Almonds in shell are mostly local product. Check labels on packs of all types of almonds for local product.
Brazil nuts — in shell, shelled and toffeed	No, and not likely to be	Yes, about $1.5 million worth	Substitute macadamias or almonds. Toffeed Brazil nuts prepared locally.
Cashew nuts — shelled, raw, roasted, salted	Production in progress in NT and Qld. Local nuts in marketplace, 1994	Yes, over $21 million worth	Support local product as it comes onto market. Use almonds in Asian dishes.
Chestnuts — fresh and dried; canned whole, pieces and purée; whole glacé	Yes, fresh — more than demand, available in autumn; working on canning chestnuts	Small quantities of dried; fresh imports not allowed. All canned products and glacé chestnuts imported	Use more fresh product. Avoid using dried chestnuts. Learn to prepare whole peeled and purée from fresh chestnuts, page 55.
Chestnuts, water — canned	No	Yes, amount not available	Water chestnuts cannot be substituted. Use imported product sparingly.
Coconut — fresh, desiccated, shredded, coconut milk, cream and dried coconut milk	Yes, some fresh from North Queensland	Yes, over $13 million worth of coconut, amount of milk etc. not known	Use less if possible — better for your health.
Hazelnuts — in shell and shelled	Yes, small quantity, industry in infancy; nuts in shell readily available	Yes, over $5 million worth, mostly shelled; rancidity can be a problem	Buy local product in shell and crack them; they are fresher. Use less of shelled nuts.
Macadamias — in shell, shelled, salted and confectionery	Yes; important export commodity too	No	Use them in place of Brazil nuts in recipes.

Product	Australian-produced	Imported	What we can do
Nut pastes — peanut butter/paste, almond, brazil, cashew, hazelnut, macadamia, pistachio	Yes, using local or imported ingredients; well-known brands of peanut butter use local peanuts	Yes, pastes containing hazelnuts and chocolate	Select well-known brands of peanut butter. Other nut butters available at health stores; select those processed locally.
Peanuts — in shell, shelled, salted, peanut confectionery	Yes, about 70% of requirements, although this varies according to availability of local nuts	Yes, some $8.5 million worth	Check labels for local products or buy in shell. Buy well-known brands of salted nuts and confectionery.
Pecan nuts — in shell, shelled and confectionery	Yes; also exported. Occasionally local supply supplemented with imports	Yes, some $2 million worth, plus some pecan confectionery	Use shelled pecans in place of shelled walnuts. Cheaper to shell your own pecans.
Pine nuts	Not yet; some prospects in far-distant future	Yes, quite a lot; amount not available	Use slivered or ground almonds as substitutes.
Pistachio nuts — fresh, in shell (mostly salted), shelled	Yes; locally grown pistachios first marketed in early 1994. Grown in the Murray Valley, NSW; look for Pioneer Pistachios — also sold fresh in March–April	Yes, over $4 million worth	Fresh pistachios worth trying when in season (early autumn); look for local roasted and salted pistachios; limit use of shelled pistachios.
Walnuts — in shell, shelled and canned	Yes, in shell. Season begins in May	Yes, almost $13 million worth, mostly shelled	Buy in shell and crack them yourself for best flavour.
SEEDS			
Poppy seeds	Yes, grown in Tasmania	Yes, small quantity	Use local seeds if possible.
Pumpkin seeds/pepitas, in shell and shelled	Whole seeds, not shelled	Yes, in shell and shelled (pepitas)	Substitute sunflower seeds in recipes calling for pepitas.
Sesame seeds, tahini/sesame seed paste, sesame confectionery	Yes, grown in Qld; amount small but increasing. Local and imported seeds processed locally for tahini; imported for tahini, halva and sesame bars	Yes, over $8 million worth of seeds, also tahini	Limit use until local seeds available; smooth peanut butter can substitute for tahini in some recipes. Buy local tahini, halva and confectionery.
Seeds for sprouting — alfalfa, red clover, fenugreek	Yes, sufficient for needs	No	For economy, sprout seeds yourself — very easy to do.
Sunflower seeds	Yes, sufficient for needs	Yes, very small quantity	Use in place of sesame seeds on baked goods, salads, vegetarian dishes.

* Cannellini and Great Northern beans are both white kidney beans; the former are from Italy, the latter from the USA. Great Northern beans are sold as cannellini in Australia; there is a small difference in shape only.

Choosing Australian Pulses, Nuts and Seeds • 43

Recipes
USING AUSTRALIAN PULSES, NUTS AND SEEDS

Pulses — Basic Cooking

Pick over pulses to be cooked, removing any small stones and damaged seeds. Place in a bowl and add cold water. Stir, then remove any that float as these could be damaged. Drain, and rinse again. Split peas and lentils do not require soaking and can be cooked after rinsing. To soak other pulses, follow either of these methods.

Slow-soak method: Put pulses in a bowl and add about 3 cups cold water to each cup of pulses used. Soak in a cool place such as the refrigerator for several hours. This prevents pulses from fermenting, one cause of digestive problems associated with these foods. They can be held in the refrigerator for 2–3 days if meal plans have changed. Drain and add fresh water for cooking. If using soaked pulses for making Middle Eastern patties such as Felafel, use this method for soaking, as they should not be cooked until mixed with other ingredients.

Quick-soak method: Put the rinsed pulses in a large saucepan, add cold water as above and bring to the boil. Boil for 2 minutes, remove from heat and cover pan. Leave off the heat for 1–2 hours until plump. No need to drain, unless specified for a particular pulse.

To cook pulses: Bring to the boil, reduce heat and simmer until tender. Time varies according to pulse and soaking method used. Slow-soaked pulses take a little less time than quick-soaked. If cooking any of the kidney beans (see Cooking Times), boil rapidly for at least 15 minutes at some stage during cooking.

To store cooked pulses: They will keep in a covered container in the refrigerator for 3–4 days. For longer storage, and for quicker meal preparation, place in a freezer container with some of the cooking water, leaving head room. Seal and freeze. When required, defrost in microwave oven or place in a saucepan and thaw over heat.

Cooking Times

Pulses listed are those available, whether local or imported, in the hope that we might one day grow all of these. For locally grown pulses, see Buyer's Guide, page 41. Times given vary somewhat from those on packs. For example, certain packs of chick peas indicate boiling for 30 minutes; in practice this takes some 2 hours. Times can vary according to the source of the pulse, so are only approximate. Pulses should be soft when cooked, with no resistance to the bite. With any of the kidney beans (borlotti, cannellini, Great Northern, haricot, lima, red or pinto), boil rapidly for 15 minutes during cooking time to denature anti-nutritional enzymes these contain, then boil gently or simmer for remainder of cooking time. This instruction is given for the relevant beans.

Cooking Times

Black-eyed beans:
1 hour.
Blue peas: 1 hour.
Borlotti beans:
1½–2 hours
(boil 15 minutes).
Broad beans:
2–2½ hours.
Cannellini, Great
Northern: 1–1½ hours
(boil 15 minutes).
Chick peas:
2–2½ hours.
Haricot/navy/pea beans:
1–1½ hours
(boil 15 minutes).
Lentils, brown: 1 hour.
Lentils, red:
30 minutes.
Lima beans:
1–1½ hours
(boil 15 minutes).
Pinto beans:
1½–2 hours
(boil 15 minutes).
Red kidney beans:
1–1½ hours
(boil 15 minutes).
Soy beans:
3–3½ hours.
Split peas, yellow and
green: 1 hour;
2–3 hours for soup.
Tic/ful/ful medamis:
2 hours; 3–3½ hours
to make the Ful
Medamis of Egyptian
cooking.

Felafel

These dried bean patties are a very popular item at Lebanese fast food outlets and restaurants, particularly with those seeking vegetarian foods. While dried broad beans, soaked and skinned, are normally used, All Gold Foods of Leeton, NSW, processes the Australian-grown tic bean, skinning and splitting it. In this form it is known as 'fulia', is creamy white and looks like a large, roughly shaped split pea. The tic bean is a small relative of the broad bean and is, to my mind, better in flavour. Look for fulia at Lebanese or health food stores.

Makes about 36

¾ cup fulia (skinned and split tic beans)
1 cup dried chick peas
water
1 medium-sized onion, roughly chopped
2 cloves garlic, chopped
½ cup chopped flat-leaf parsley
½–1 teaspoon chopped fresh chilli
1 teaspoon ground coriander
1 teaspoon ground cumin
1 teaspoon bicarbonate of soda
1 teaspoon salt
freshly ground black pepper to taste
sunola oil for deep frying

1 Pick over fulia and chick peas and remove any that are discoloured. Place fulia in a bowl. Rinse chick peas and add to bowl. Add 6 cups cold water, cover and soak in the refrigerator for 24 hours.
2 Drain fulia and chick peas well and place in food processor with steel blade fitted. Process to a coarse paste, add remaining ingredients and process to a fairly fine paste — it should have some texture. Taste and add more salt if necessary.
3 Transfer to a bowl and stand for 30 minutes. Take tablespoonfuls of the mixture and shape into 4-cm patties, using moistened hands. Place on a tray and allow to stand for further 30 minutes.
4 Deep fry in hot, not fuming, oil, 6–8 at a time, cooking them for 5–6 minutes. Turn in the oil to brown evenly. Remove with a draining spoon and drain on paper towels. Care must be taken that felafel cook through without burning on the outside. Check one of the first batch — it should be of even colour in the centre, indicating that beans are cooked.

Note: The fulia and chick peas are only soaked to soften them. They are not cooked. If cooked beans are used, they disintegrate when fried.

Felafel with Broad Beans

If you cannot obtain fulia, soak 1 cup dried broad beans in 3 cups water for 48 hours in refrigerator. Drain beans and remove skins; slit skin with fingernail then press so that bean pops out. Discard skins and use beans in place of the fulia above. Soak the chick peas separately for 24 hours.

Chick Pea and Burghul Salad

Serves 6–8 as an accompaniment, 4 as a main meal

2 × 310-g cans chick peas or 1 cup dried chick peas
½ cup burghul
1 green pepper
2 firm, ripe tomatoes
1 red onion
2 tablespoons chopped flat-leaf parsley
1 tablespoon chopped fresh mint
3 tablespoons Salad Oil, page 80
1 tablespoon white wine vinegar
1 tablespoon lemon juice
salt
freshly ground black pepper

1 Australian canned chick peas are available, but are more likely to be found in delicatessens and health food stores than in supermarkets; drain, rinse lightly and drain again. Otherwise use dried chick peas, soaked and cooked according to directions on page 44; cool in the cooking water, then drain.
2 Put burghul in a sieve and run cold water through it. Turn into a bowl and add chick peas.
3 Halve peeled onion and slice in slender wedges. Wash and seed pepper and remove white membrane. Cut into short, thin strips. Halve tomatoes and remove seeds, then dice. Add prepared vegetables to chick pea mixture with spring onions, parsley and mint.
4 Beat oil with vinegar, lemon juice and salt and pepper to taste. Pour over salad, toss well, cover and chill for 1 hour. Serve chilled.

Storing Pulses, Nuts and Seeds

Nuts need careful storage, especially in hot weather; they contain a high proportion of oil, which can turn rancid in a warm kitchen. Seal nuts in plastic bags or jars and store in refrigerator. Store seeds such as sunflower in the same way.
While pulses do not contain oil (except for soy beans), they are susceptible to insect infestation during the warmer months. If you keep a large supply on hand, store in sealed plastic bags in the refrigerator or freezer.

AUSTRALIAN SESAME SEEDS

The Huile Trading Company of Melbourne saw a need to produce sesame seeds in Australia. They are grown in Queensland, mechanically harvested and shipped to Melbourne for hulling. It took five years, in conjunction with the CSIRO, to find the right strain for cultivation. Yield at time of writing is some 300 tonnes, a fraction of the 4000 tonnes we import annually. Australian-grown sesame seeds are larger, lighter in colour and sweeter in flavour than imported seeds. Oil content is also higher, and the hulling process is chemical-free (unlike imported seeds). Local seeds are used in the baking industry and some is processed into tahini. It will be some years before production is sufficient for all our needs, but it is an industry with excellent potential in the long term. In the meantime, keep reading packs of sesame seeds, tahini, sesame seed confectionery and halva until you find the magic words: 'Product of Australia' or 'Made in Australia with Australian sesame seeds'.

Hommos with Peanut Butter

Hommos is traditionally made with tahini, a sesame seed paste. Although tahini is made here, most seeds are imported. Peanut butter is a perfectly acceptable substitute in many recipes, although there are those who would disagree.

Makes about 2 cups

2 cups cooked chick peas
3 tablespoons smooth peanut butter
2 cloves garlic, chopped
4 tablespoons lemon juice
1 tablespoon canola oil, cold pressed if possible
3–4 tablespoons liquid from chick peas
salt to taste

1 Cook your own chick peas or use Australian canned chick peas (2 x 310-g cans). Although it is traditional to remove the skins, an acceptable hommos can be made if the skins are left on. Put drained chick peas into food processor bowl or blender jar, retaining about ½ cup of the chick pea liquid.

2 Add peanut butter, garlic, lemon juice and canola oil. Process until smooth, gradually adding chick pea liquid to facilitate processing and to make a soft purée.

3 Add salt to taste, and if necessary, add a little more lemon juice. Turn into a bowl, cover and chill until required. Serve with pita bread, savoury crackers or crisp vegetable pieces. To serve traditionally, spread purée in a small, oval plate, pour about 2 tablespoons olive oil over the purée and sprinkle with paprika. Use also in pita bread sandwiches with sliced roast lamb or felafel, tabouli, cos lettuce and sliced tomato.

Bean and Tuna Salad

Serves 6

2 x 460-g cans borlotti beans
¾ cup chopped spring onions
¼ cup chopped flat-leaf parsley
2 x 185-g cans tuna in canola oil
⅓ cup Italian Dressing, page 81
salt and freshly ground black pepper

1 Drain beans, rinse lightly, then leave to drain thoroughly. Place in a salad bowl with spring onions and parsley.

Using Australian Pulses, Nuts and Seeds

2 Drain tuna and flake any large chunks. Add to bean mixture.
3 Pour dressing over salad and toss lightly, adding seasoning to taste. Cover and chill. Serve with crusty bread.

Italian Bean Soup
Serves 6

1½ cups dried haricot or cannellini beans
6 cups water
2 tablespoons Salad Oil, page 80
60 g pancetta or 2 bacon rashers, chopped
1 large onion, chopped
1 cup chopped celery, including some leaves
410-g can tomatoes, chopped
1 teaspoon sugar
freshly ground black pepper
salt
1 tablespoon chopped parsley

1 Wash beans and place in a pan with the water. Bring to the boil, boil 2 minutes, remove from heat and stand for 1 hour until beans are plump.
2 Put oil in a large pan with chopped pancetta or bacon, onion and celery. Fry gently until onion is transparent. Add beans with their liquid, cover and boil gently for 1 hour.
3 Add tomatoes and their liquid, sugar and pepper. Cover and cook for further 30 minutes until beans are tender. Add parsley and salt to taste, cook 5 minutes, then serve with crusty bread.

Mexican-style Beans
Mexican food is particularly popular with vegetarians and those who like their food with a zing. Beans are a staple in Mexican cuisine. We don't have the range of beans available here to duplicate their recipes faithfully, but that doesn't matter at all. Of the Australian-grown beans, borlotti or red kidney may be used in place of the usual pinto, pink or black beans of Mexico. They all belong to the same family and are native to the Americas. Borlotti beans are recommended as they have a 'hammy' flavour, with the right colour and texture; Australian red kidney beans may be difficult to obtain. Use canned beans to save on cooking time.

SOME TIPS ON PULSES

• Do not add bicarbonate of soda to hasten cooking as this destroys some of the B-group vitamins.
• Do not add salt until pulse is soft.
• Use filtered water, particularly in hard-water areas, as the minerals in the water can slow down cooking.
• Hold back acidic ingredients such as wine and tomatoes as these also slow down cooking; add them half-way through cooking time.

Pulse Nutrition

Pulses are an excellent source of plant protein, a valuable source of thiamin and niacin, and contain iron, calcium, zinc and other mineral trace elements. They are rich in complex carbohydrates and dietary fibre, but low in fat (except for soy beans). To obtain the full nutritional benefit, especially if you have little or no animal foods in your diet, all pulses (again except for soy beans) should be eaten with another grain or cereal food, such as bread, tacos, cornbread or rice. The proteins lacking in the pulse are found in the cereal or grain food, and together make up the proteins found in foods of animal origin, known as complete proteins.

The iron, calcium and zinc contained in pulses are not as easily used by the body as they are when they come from animal sources; however, iron absorption is improved if a food containing vitamin C, such as tomato, citrus juice, green or red pepper, is taken at the same meal.

Serves 6

125 g bacon bones (optional)
2 × 460-g cans borlotti beans
  OR *2 × 450-g cans red kidney beans*
1 large onion, finely chopped
2 tablespoons maize or canola oil
2 tablespoons chopped fresh coriander
freshly ground pepper to taste

Accompaniments
hot or mild pickled peppers
sour cream
finely chopped spring onions

1 Rinse bacon bones if used and place in the base of a heavy-based saucepan. If using borlotti beans, or for the vegetarian version, omit this step.

2 Pour choice of beans and their liquid into the pan.

3 In a frying pan, cook onion in oil until lightly browned. Add to beans with pepper to taste. Cover and simmer for 30 minutes. Stir in coriander and cook for further 10 minutes.

4 Remove ½ cup of beans to serving bowl and mash well with a fork. Add remaining beans from pot to bowl, discarding bacon bones if used. Stir well, sprinkle with additional coriander and serve with accompaniments arranged in small bowls. Each diner adds accompaniments to taste to their bowl of beans. Serve with crusty bread.

Refried Beans

Mash Mexican beans and heat in a pan in 1–2 tablespoons oil. Add 1 teaspoon ground cumin and heat, stirring often, until thick and hot. Pile into serving bowl and serve in tacos with choice of shredded lettuce, chopped spring onions, sliced tomatoes, shredded cheddar cheese, sour cream and Mexican Chilli Sauce (page 178) arranged on a platter and in bowls, to be added according to individual taste. May also be served cold as a dip with corn chips.

Pea and Ham Soup

An old-fashioned soup which has not lost its appeal. While it does not take long to put together, it does need long, slow cooking. I like to make a large pot of it; either store leftover soup in the refrigerator for up to 5 days, or store in the freezer for up to 3 months.

Serves 8–10

bones from leg ham or 2 ham hocks
1 large onion, chopped
1 stick celery, chopped
2 medium-sized carrots, chopped
8 cups water
500 g green or yellow split peas
freshly ground black pepper
salt to taste

1 If you purchase ham bones from the butcher, you'll need about 750 g, or use bones from the Christmas ham which you might have stored in the freezer. If using hocks, have butcher saw them in half.

2 Rinse ham bones or hocks and place in a large boiler. Add chopped vegetables. Add water and rinsed split peas. Bring to a simmer, skim froth from top, add pepper and cover with lid. Simmer on low heat for 3 hours without stirring — this prevents the peas from sticking to the base of the pan.

3 When cooked, remove bones or hocks to a plate and check that there are no loose bones in the soup. Trim ham from bones, discarding any fat and skin. Chop the ham. You can purée the soup if you like — use a hand-held food processor if you have one, but a good stir is usually enough. Add ham and salt to taste, heat through and serve hot with crusty bread or croutons.

Vegetarian Pea Soup

Omit ham bones or hocks. Prepare vegetables, adding some celery leaves with the celery for extra flavour, and 1 finely chopped clove garlic. Heat 2 tablespoons oil in boiler, add vegetables and garlic and cook slowly for 10 minutes until onion is soft. Add water and split peas and proceed as for Pea and Ham Soup.

AUSTRALIAN PISTACHIO NUTS

In the Murray Valley, straddling the New South Wales and Victorian borders, pistachio trees are now thriving after years of experimentation to produce trees that crop well. Trial plantings were begun in 1984, with the first commercial crop of around 80 tonnes mechanically harvested from March, 1994. At time of writing, two producers were supplying the market, Kyalite Pistachios at Kyalite, and Pistachio Producers at Robinvale. These producers share a hulling, drying and grading facility and market their nuts as Pioneer Pistachios. By the year 2000, it is estimated that annual production will be 600 tonnes, a little over half the amount imported at present. The industry holds great promise.

In March to mid-April, fresh pistachios are available at better greengrocers and produce markets. Still in their green husks, they are small, oval-shaped fruit about the size of an olive. Slip away the soft covering to reveal the nut, with the shell already split. The nut itself is covered with a speckled pink and green skin; when fresh, this comes off easily. If covered with boiling water and left to steep for a minute or so, the skin comes away more easily and the green colour is accentuated, making for more attractive presentation. Skin dried pistachio nuts in the way way. Use skinned, unsalted pistachios, fresh or dried, in stuffings, terrines, pasta dishes, sauces, fruit desserts, ice creams, pastries and biscuits. Serve in the shell on cheese boards; use salted for nibbling.

When you do purchase fresh pistachios, store them in the refrigerator; they will keep for a week or so.

Split Pea Patties

I used to make these with red lentils, but have changed to split peas as these are locally grown; local red lentils are in short supply, but should be available in the not-too-distant future.

Serves 6

1½ cups yellow split peas
3 cups water
1 medium-sized onion, finely chopped
1 cup canned corn kernels, drained
1 small egg, beaten
3 tablespoons finely chopped green pepper
1 tablespoon chopped parsley
salt
freshly ground black pepper
flour for coating
1 egg extra, beaten
dried breadcrumbs
oil for shallow frying

1 Rinse split peas and place in a heavy-based pan with the water. Bring to the boil, skim off froth, then turn heat to low, cover and simmer gently for 45–60 minutes until peas are soft and water has evaporated. Do not stir during cooking or peas will stick. If peas are soft and there is still water in the pan (check by tilting pan), cook on slightly higher heat with lid off.

2 Stir peas to a purée and turn into a mixing bowl. Cool, or cover and refrigerate until next day if necessary.

3 Mix onion, corn, green pepper and parsley into peas. Add egg, salt and pepper to taste. Stir well and chill for 2 hours to firm mixture (not necessary if peas are already chilled).

4 Shape heaped tablespoons of mixture into thick patties with moistened hands. Coat with flour, dip into beaten egg and coat with breadcrumbs. Place on a tray and chill for 30 minutes.

5 Shallow fry in hot oil for about 3 minutes each side, turning with spatula. Drain on paper towels and serve hot with vegetables or salad.

Black-eyed Bean Stew

Black-eyed beans are quick to cook compared with other dried beans, and have a delicious, sweetish flavour; besides they are one of the few dried beans we produce in abundance. This is an excellent recipe for vegetarians.

Serves 6

2 cups black-eyed beans
6 cups water
1 large onion, chopped
1 clove garlic, crushed
4 tablespoons Salad Oil, page 80
2 medium-sized carrots, chopped
1 small parsnip, chopped
1 cup chopped celery
2 tablespoons chopped celery leaves
1/4 cup tomato paste
1 teaspoon sugar
salt
freshly ground black pepper
finely chopped parsley for serving

1 Pick over beans, removing any damaged ones. Rinse well and place in a large pan with the water. Bring to the boil, boil 2 minutes, cover, remove from heat and stand for 1 hour until beans are plump.

2 In another pan, cook onion and garlic gently in oil until onion is soft. Add carrot, parsnip and celery and cook for further 5 minutes. Add beans and their liquid, celery leaves, tomato paste and sugar and bring to the boil.

3 Reduce heat, cover and simmer for 1 hour until beans are tender. Add salt and pepper to taste and serve in deep plates sprinkled with chopped parsley. Serve with crusty grain bread and a tossed green salad.

Note: The black eye on the beans darkens the colour of this stew. I prefer to use the soaking water as it contains some of the water-soluble vitamins. However, if you do not like the colour, drain and measure the water drained, adding that amount to the beans.

BLANCHING ALMONDS

For economy, shell almonds yourself or purchase unblanched almonds. Place shelled almonds in a bowl and pour on boiling water to cover. Leave for 3–4 minutes and drain. When cool enough to handle, press almond between fingers and nut will pop out of its skin. Use immediately; if to be stored, dry at room temperature or in a slow oven if very moist (depends on how long they were left in the water). Store in a plastic bag in the refrigerator.

Almond Pesto

As pine nuts are imported, I tried this popular Italian pasta sauce with almonds, efficiently produced in Australia (and less expensive too!). While ground almonds have been used, you can grind your own using blanched almonds. Process ½ cup whole almonds before beginning the pesto.

Makes about 2 cups

2 cups tightly packed basil leaves
3 cloves garlic, chopped
½ cup ground almonds
½ cup grated Parmesan cheese
⅓ cup grated pecorino cheese
¼ teaspoon salt
freshly ground black pepper
½ cup virgin olive oil
½ cup canola oil

1 Rinse bunch of basil well and shake off excess moisture. Remove leaves, discarding any damaged ones. Roll loosely in a tea towel to absorb excess moisture. Measure required amount and place in food processor or blender.
2 Add garlic and process to a coarse purée, adding a little of the oil to facilitate processing.
3 Add ground almonds, cheeses, salt and freshly ground pepper to taste. Continue to process, gradually adding remaining oils. Serve tossed through hot pasta. Almond Pesto may be stored in refrigerator in a sterilised, sealed jar.

Note: When basil is not in season, use the same quantity of flat-leaf parsley for an equally delicious sauce.

Variation

Macadamia Pesto: Use macadamia nuts in place of almonds and replace canola oil with macadamia oil.

TO SKIN HAZELNUTS

Hazelnuts may be eaten raw, but their flavour is improved if skinned. If you shell your own hazelnuts, you are more than likely to have Australian-grown nuts, as most of our imports are shelled. Even if you break some nuts when shelling, these can be included for skinning. Place nuts on a baking tray and put in a preheated moderate oven for 5–6 minutes, stirring nuts once. Put the hot nuts in a clean cloth. Bundle up and rub nuts against each other. Open out cloth and pick out skinned nuts, repeating process until nuts are skinned.
To roast the nuts, leave in oven for 8–12 minutes, stirring occasionally. Take care not to burn them; test one towards end of roasting time. Skin as above.

Using Australian Pulses, Nuts and Seeds

Macadamia Shortbread

Here's a recipe to Australianise our Christmas/New Year tables. No more Scottish shortbread — bring out the Australian version!

Oven temperature: 170°C (325°F)

Makes 24 pieces

250 g butter
¼ cup caster sugar
1¾ cups plain flour
¼ cup rice flour
1 cup coarsely chopped, toasted macadamia nuts

1 Cream butter and sugar until light — do not over-beat.
2 Sift flours and stir into butter mixture with macadamia nuts.
3 Turn dough onto a lightly floured board and knead lightly. Press into a greased 18- x 28-cm lamington pan. Roll top of shortbread with a straight-sided tumbler to even it. Prick surface evenly with a fork and score surface into finger lengths or squares of even size.
4 Bake in preheated, moderately slow oven for 40–45 minutes. Shortbread should remain pale in colour. Stand 10 minutes, cut through score marks into pieces while in pan, leave until cool.
5 Remove pieces with the aid of a palette knife and store in a sealed container until required.

Macadamia Pie

Oven temperature: 200°C (400°F), reducing to 180°C (350°F)

Serves 6–8

1 uncooked 23-cm pie case, page 16
1½ cups toasted macadamia nuts
3 eggs
pinch of salt
½ cup caster sugar
½ cup golden syrup
1 teaspoon vanilla essence
2 tablespoons plain flour
3 tablespoons melted butter

1 Make pie case according to directions, using Sweet Shortcrust Pastry recipe and prepare a pie case as detailed. Place in refrigerator while making filling.

Shell Your Own Nuts

If you buy almonds, walnuts, hazelnuts, pecans or macadamias in the shell, not only are you more certain of buying Australian nuts, you can also save at least half the cost of shelled nuts. Almonds, walnuts and hazelnuts only need a sharp tap with a hammer, or use a nut cracker. Pecans may be cracked in the same way, with a lighter touch, but you might be able to find the special pecan sheller, with directions for use on its packaging — unfortunately these are imported. Macadamias are a hard nut to crack, and a favoured method is to place the nut in the groove of a brick, to prevent it rolling away, and hit with a heavy hammer. Another method is to put a few nuts in an old, clean sock and hammer away. No flying nuts!

AUSTRALIAN CHESTNUTS

Chestnuts have been growing in Australia for over 100 years. After years as a cottage industry, chestnut growing became a commercial operation in the mid-eighties.

Most of the chestnuts are grown in the Dandenongs and the north-eastern region of Victoria; Tasmania; the Adelaide Hills; the central and southern tablelands of New South Wales; and the south-western corner of Western Australia. The average plantation has 200–300 trees, with larger plantations of 7000 trees or more. Hand-gathering of the nuts is the most common method of harvest, although larger plantations use a vacuum machine. At the time of writing, the harvest yielded 500 tonnes of chestnuts; by the year 2000 it is predicted that 3500 tonnes will be produced.

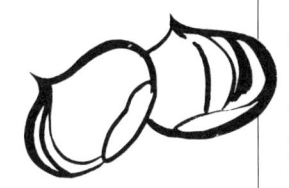

2 Lightly beat eggs with salt just until whites and yolks are thoroughly mixed — the salt helps to break down the whites. Do not beat until frothy.

3 Add sugar, golden syrup, vanilla, flour and melted butter and stir until smooth. You can use a balloon whisk for stirring as it helps to break up any flour lumps, but do not beat.

4 Pour into prepared pie case and strew the macadamia nuts on top. Bake in preheated hot oven for 20 minutes, reduce to moderate and bake for further 20–25 minutes until a knife, inserted halfway between centre and edge, comes out clean. Cool and serve with whipped, lightly sweetened cream.

Variation

Pecan or Walnut Pie

Make as above, using 1½ cups pecan nuts or walnut halves in place of the macadamias. Because these nuts are lighter than macadamias, beat the eggs with the sugar, golden syrup and vanilla until thick and foamy, then stir in flour and melted butter — the nuts rise to the top of the egg mixture during cooking. Arrange nuts in the base of the pie case and pour egg mixture on top. Bake as above. You can also use a mixture of pecans and walnuts if you like.

Chestnuts

In a good season, there are ample supplies of fresh chestnuts. Unlike other nuts, they are low in fat, and should be used more frequently in Australia. There is considerable experimentation in progress to preserve the nuts through canning or freezing techniques, which will make Australian chestnut products available year-round.

Fresh chestnuts appear on the market from March to June. They should be glossy and yield slightly when pressed. Avoid dull nuts with brittle shells. Store in a paper bag in the refrigerator for up to 10 days.

You should also take the time to prepare and freeze chestnuts so that they may be used throughout the year, particularly at Christmas for the festive turkey.

Shelling Chestnuts

Basic preparation: Cut a cross on the flat side of the shell of each nut. This prevents nuts from exploding as they cook and facilitates peeling.

Peeling: Put prepared nuts in a saucepan and cover with cold water. Add 1 teaspoon salt per 500 g chestnuts — this helps to remove inner skin of nut. Bring to the boil, and boil 1 minute. Remove from heat. Remove one chestnut at a time and strip off shell and inner skin (pellicle). Wear rubber gloves to protect fingers. Any which are difficult to skin may be returned to the pan of chestnuts and left to be skinned later — reboil if necessary.

Boiling: Rinse skinned chestnuts, cover with water and boil for 20 minutes or until tender. Drain in a colander and use in recipes.

Microwave Preparation: Prepare chestnuts and place in an even layer in a large microwave-safe pie plate. Microwave on HIGH for 5–6 minutes, stirring several times so that they heat evenly. Stand for 5 minutes then shell, remove inner skin and either eat hot or use in recipes or for freezer storage.

Freezing: After boiling, arrest cooking by holding colander of chestnuts under cold, running water, drain well and spread out on paper towels to dry. Pack in freezer bags, seal and freeze — will keep for up to 12 months. For microwaved chestnuts, cool after peeling, pack and store as for boiled chestnuts.

Roasting: Prepare whole chestnuts and place in a large, cast-iron frying pan. Roast on an open fire or a barbecue until shells split open, stirring chestnuts occasionally. Peel and eat while hot. They may also be cooked on the barbecue grid, turning them, or roasted in a baking dish in a moderate oven. Any roasting takes about 20 minutes.

Chestnut Purée

Shell and peel chestnuts, then boil in fresh water until soft. Drain, reserving some of the liquid. Place chestnuts in food processor and process to a thick purée, adding a little of the reserved liquid if necessary. Use as directed in recipes — 1½ cups purée is equivalent to a 440-g can of unsweetened chestnut purée. Purée may be packed in rigid containers and frozen for later use.

To Toast Almonds

Put whole, blanched, slivered or flaked almonds in a frying pan and place over moderate heat. Stir nuts occasionally until golden. When desired colour is reached, tip out immediately onto a plate as the stored heat in the pan will burn the nuts.

To Toast Macadamia Nuts

The flavour of macadamia nuts improves when toasted. Spread the unsalted nuts on a scone tray and place in a moderate oven for 15–20 minutes. Stir now and then so that they brown as evenly as possible. When golden brown, tip out onto a plate to cool.

Clockwise from top — Orange Cake, Apple Cake, Butterfly Cakes (see Patty Cakes), all variations of Basic Butter Cake (page 31)

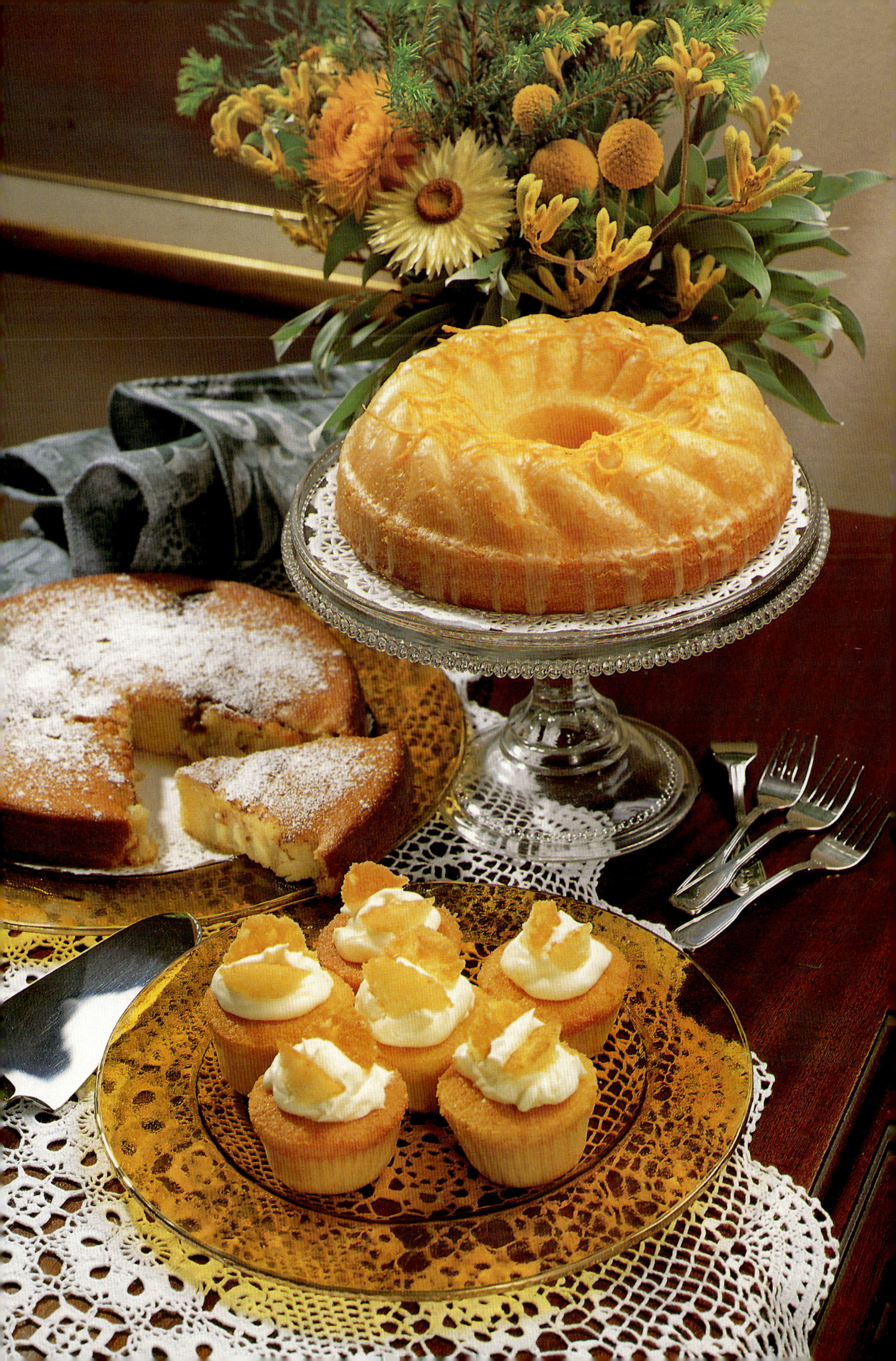

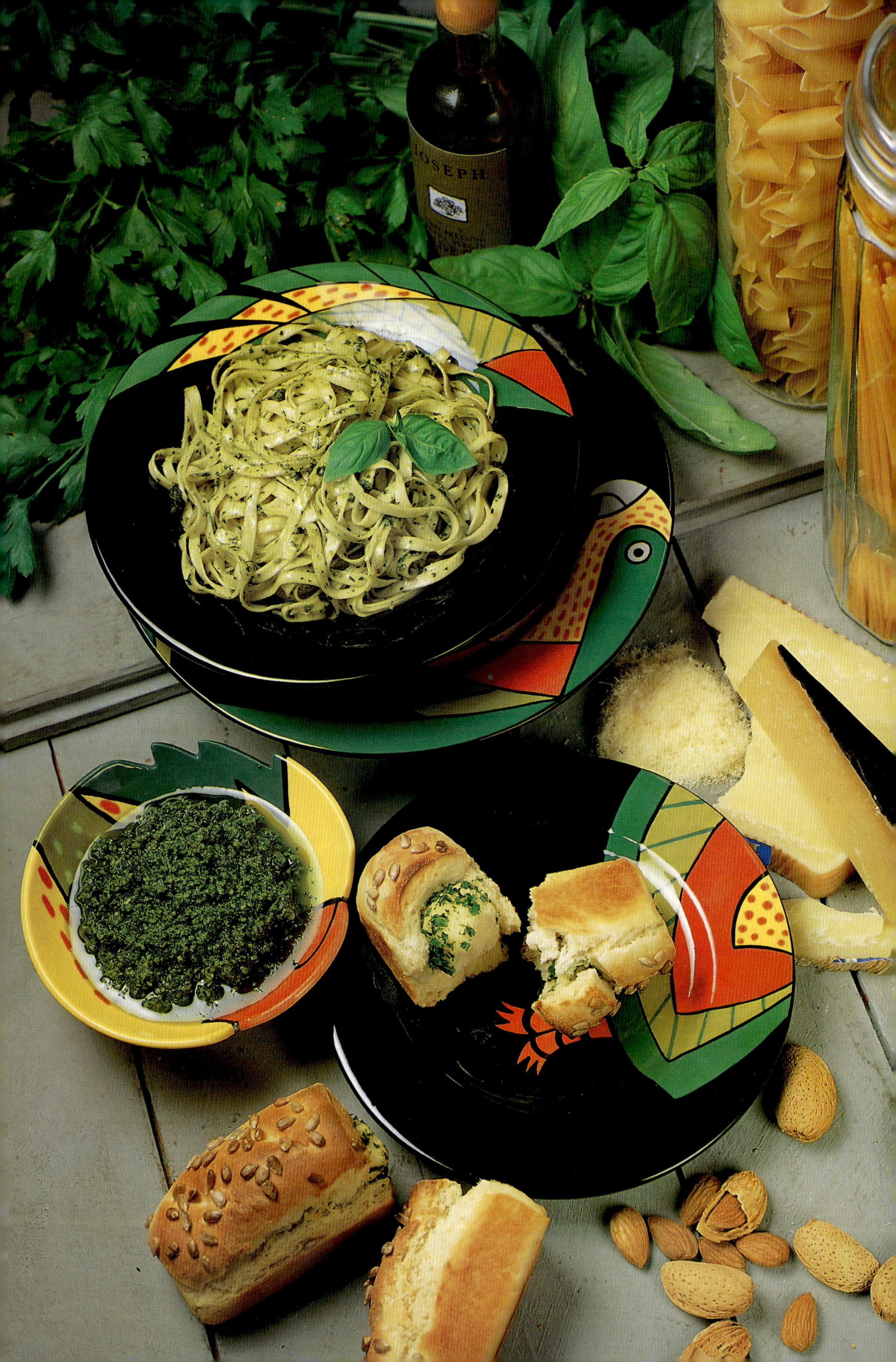

CHOPPING MACADAMIA NUTS

It is very difficult to buy chopped macadamia nuts for cooking; in the cracking process, only about 15% of the nuts are broken, and these are snapped up by food and confectionery manufacturers.

You may be able to find packaged, unsalted macadamias containing whole and halved nuts; these are a little less expensive than whole macadamias. If toasted, chop them to the desired consistency in a food processor; if raw, they seem to get a life of their own in the processor, flying around the bowl and clinging all over it, and are even hard to control when tipping them out. It seems that the combination of the plastic processor bowl and the raw nuts creates static electricity.

The alternative is to place raw nuts in a strong plastic bag and hit them with a rolling pin or mallet. You can try chopping them with a knife, but you will soon find out why I haven't given this method. Oh, for ready-chopped macadamias!

Almond Pesto (page 53) served on fettucine, Herbed Damper Loaves (page 19)

Chestnut and Chocolate Dessert Cake

A delicious dessert cake which requires no baking. Of course, the chestnuts take some preparation, but if you have stored some in the freezer during the chestnut season, all you have to do is thaw them. The rest is easy, and can be almost all-Australian in content, except for the cocoa. If you have some brandied kumquats on hand, you can use the kumquat brandy instead of the locally made orange curaçao (see page 203).

Serves 8–10

250 g unsalted butter
1½ cups unsweetened chestnut purée, page 56
1½ cups icing sugar
2 tablespoons cocoa
4 egg yolks
24 large sponge fingers
2 tablespoons Seagram's orange curaçao liqueur
2 tablespoons water
300 ml thickened cream
2 tablespoons caster sugar
½ teaspoon vanilla essence
grated chocolate or toasted almond slivers to decorate

1 Have butter at room temperature and beat in large bowl of electric mixer until light. Sift icing sugar and cocoa and beat into butter with chestnut purée and egg yolks. Continue beating until fluffy.

2 On a large, square serving plate, arrange 8 sponge fingers in two rows of 4 to give a squarish shape. Dilute orange curaçao with water and brush some of this liquid onto the sponge fingers.

3 Spread half the chestnut cream over the sponge fingers. Top with another 8 sponge fingers, brush with liqueur mixture and spread with remaining chestnut cream. Top with last of sponge fingers and brush again with remaining liqueur mixture.

4 Cover cake and chill overnight in refrigerator.

5 Whip cream until stiff and fold in caster sugar and vanilla. Spread over top and sides of cake. Decorate top with swirls of whipped cream if desired, grated chocolate or toasted almond slivers. Cake may be returned to refrigerator for 1–2 hours before serving.

Dairy Foods

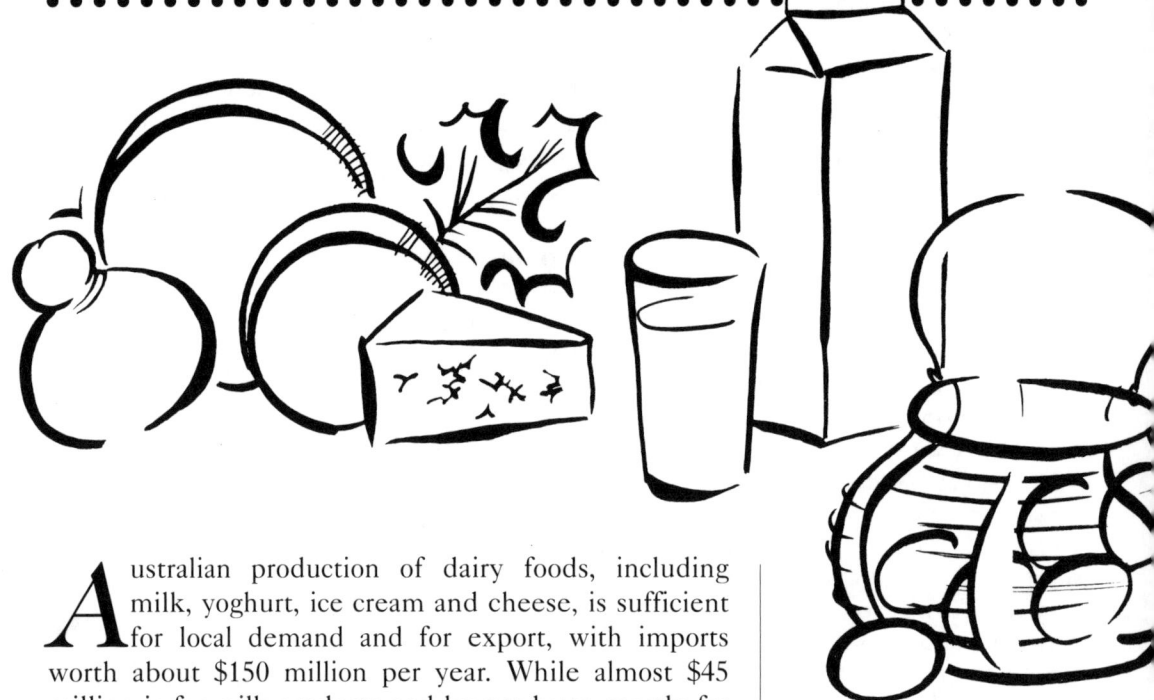

Australian production of dairy foods, including milk, yoghurt, ice cream and cheese, is sufficient for local demand and for export, with imports worth about $150 million per year. While almost $45 million is for milk products and by-products, mostly for manufacturing purposes (and most of which the Australian industry can supply), the remainder is for cheese. For the twelve months to June 1993, cheese consumption in Australia was 9.05 kilograms per head; Australian cheeses account for 84 per cent of this, but when one considers what the 16 per cent cost us, we should be aiming for 100 per cent.

Cheesemaking in Australia has a long and interesting history. In recent times, the variety of cheeses made is astounding; not only are they made from cow's milk, but from goat's and sheep's milk as well. There are a few popular cheeses we don't make, but we do make very good substitutes; for example, we cannot make blue vein cheeses called roquefort, stilton or gorgonzola as these names are protected. But we do make excellent blue vein cheeses, some of which are made in these styles.

The Buyer's Guide covers cheeses in basic categories. However, there are some unique Australian cheeses that are worthy of special mention or do not quite fall into any of these categories. Because they are really worth trying they are listed separately. If a particular favourite is not listed, it is simply because there are so many wonderful Australian cheeses available today that to list them, and their attributes, would take an entire book. (See Further Reading, page 209.) When purchasing cheese in a specialty shop, ask about Australian cheeses in stock.

Some Special Australian Cheeses

Blue Brie: an innovative brie made by two of Australia's leading cheesemakers — Lactos's true blue and King Island's Lighthouse blue brie. As the names suggest, both are brie-style cheeses with blue veins rippling through the creamy centre.

Jumbunna: from Top Paddock Cheeses at Bena in the Gippsland district of Victoria, jumbunna is styled on the English blue wensleydale, which, in England, is regarded as a rival to stilton. If you fancy stilton, use jumbunna instead.

Mersey Valley Vintage Club Cheese: developed in Burnie, Tasmania, by Milan Vyhnalek, founder of Lactos, a company now owned by the French cheese manufacturer, Bongrain. It is a blend of aged cheddar, edam and gouda, aged for 2 years. Available plain and with peppercorns, it is a tangy, crumbly cheese with a smooth texture.

Mungabareena: from Swissfield, a subsidiary of Haberfields in Albury, New South Wales, this cheese is brie-like in texture, matured with gum leaves to give it a unique and subtle Australian bush flavour. A 'must' for an Australian cheese board.

Pastorello: made by United Dairies of Sydney, pastorello is only produced in Australia. Developed by Italian-born Dr Daniele Lostia at United Dairies, it is a soft cheese with a firm texture and pale brown rind with a lattice pattern from the baskets in which the curd is drained. It is mild and buttery in flavour and can be used as a table cheese or as a melting cheese in cooking.

Port of Sale: from Maffra Farmhouse, Tinamba, Victoria, this cheese is Australia's answer to port salut, an excellent cheese. Look for some of their other cheeses too — gruyère, cheshire and Riverslei red (a leicester-style cheese) to name only a few.

Royal Victorian Blue: from the Tarago River Cheese Company, the makers of the well-known Gippsland blue. Royal Victorian blue is a blue-veined cheese made with a mixture of creamy curds and deep orange-coloured curds similar to red leicester — a colourful and very tasty cheese.

Tilba Blue Club: an unusual club cheese combining blue-vein with sweet cheddar, and sometimes including walnuts. Tilba also make a reduced-fat club, plain or flavoured with herbs, and the acclaimed Tilba club vintage.

Goat's and Sheep's Milk Cheeses

Goat's milk cheeses (chèvres): brands to look for are Kervella from Gidgegannup, Western Australia; Hellenic Cheese Farm and Milawa Cheese Company, both in Victoria; and Jindabyne Cheesemakers, New South Wales; but be guided by your cheese supplier as there is a growing band of goat's milk cheesemakers emerging in the industry. Hellenic Cheese Farm also makes a goat's milk feta which is reduced in fat and salt for the health-conscious. The Sydney company, Attiki, makes goat's milk feta at their plant in New Zealand for sale in Australia.

Sheep's Milk Cheeses: a developing industry, with much of the sheep's milk used for yoghurt rather than cheese. However, Meredith Dairy, Victoria, also makes a sheep's milk camembert and a roquefort-style blue-vein, which is the closest one could get to the imported roquefort, traditionally made with sheep's milk. Milawa also makes sheep's milk cheeses.

Feta is traditionally made with sheep or goat's milk; for a sheep's milk feta, try the Hellenic Cheese Farm feta made in the traditional way by Jim Conas, and his gourmet feta, marinated in olive oil, herbs and spices; both are excellent. There is also the Jumbuck gourmet feta from the Riverina region of New South Wales, first released in early 1994.

While pecorino is made by a number of cheese-makers using cow's milk, traditionally pecorino is made with sheep's milk. As a substitute for the imported pecorino romano, use Hellenic Cheese Farm's merino gold. They also make kasseri, graviera and kefalotiri in the traditional Greek style, and claim that their matured graviera is a good substitute for the imported grana padano, of the same genre as Parmesan.

Goat's and sheep's milk cheeses can be found at gourmet delicatessens and cheese shops, and at many health food stores.

Note: In the following Buyer's Guide, dollar values of imports fall short of the figure given at the beginning of the chapter. This is because other cheese types of less popular appeal are not listed.

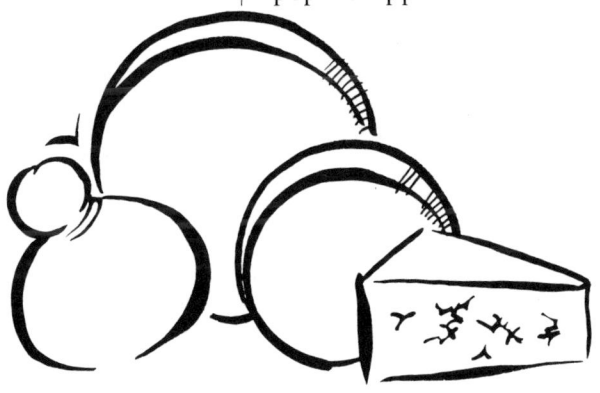

Buyer's Guide
CHOOSING AUSTRALIAN DAIRY FOODS

Product	Australian-produced	Imported	What we can do
CHEDDAR CHEESE TYPES Mild, matured, tasty, vintage; colby, cheshire, gloucester, leicester, low-fat, processed, portions etc.	Yes, almost 90% of requirements — all of types named	Yes, over $30 million worth	Check labels or ask for local product. Try Bass River red or Maffra Farmhouse in place of imported leicester.
ROUND-EYE TYPES Edam, emmental, fontina, gouda, gruyère, havarti, jarlsburg, raclette, samsoe, swiss, tilsit	Yes, almost 50% of requirements — all of types named except for jarlsburg	Yes, some $17 million worth; all jarlsburg and most emmental is imported	Check labels or ask for local product. Use St Claire, Swissfield or Heidi emmental instead of imported emmental or jarlsburg.
STRETCHED CURD TYPES Bocconcini, haloumy, mozzarella, provolone, scarmorza	Yes, over 90% of requirements — all of types named	Yes, almost $5 million worth	Check labels or ask for local product, which is in plentiful supply.
HARD GRATING TYPES Parmesan, pecorino, pepato, romano	Yes, 88% of requirements — all types named, including grated Parmesan, romano and mixtures	Yes, some $7.5 million worth	Check labels or ask for local product. Grated Parmesan, etc., convenient to use.
FRESH CHEESE TYPES Baker's, cottage, cream, mascarpone, neufchatel, quark, ricotta, stracchino	Yes, all of requirements	No	Full-cream and low-fat varieties available.
MOULD-RIPENED TYPES *Surface mould-ripened* Brie, camembert, double and triple cream	Yes, 62% of requirements — all types named and of excellent quality	Yes, some $9.5 million worth	Check labels or ask for local product. Very easy to buy local cheeses.
Internal mould-ripened Blue-vein, blue castello, gorgonzola, roquefort, stilton	Yes, 25% of requirements. Many can substitute for imported blue-vein cheeses	Yes, some $5 million worth	Substitute Lactos true blue for blue castello; Milawa blue for gorgonzola; Tarrago River blue orchid or Meredith Dairy blue for roquefort, jumbunna for stilton.

Product	Australian-produced	Imported	What we can do
GOAT AND SHEEP'S MILK CHEESES Feta, goat's cheeses (chèvres), kashkaval, kasseri, pecorino, romano	Yes, a growing industry. See separate entries on these cheeses, page 60	Yes, almost $7 million worth of goat's and sheep's milk cheeses	If you cannot find local cheeses using these milks, use cow's milk feta and pecorino instead. In place of kashkaval and kasseri, use Hellenic Dairy's kasseri.
CREAM Cream, thickened cream, clotted, sour etc.	Yes, with variable fat content	No	Choose a cream to suit purposes; check fat content.
DAIRY DESSERTS Custard, fromage frais, mousse, frozen desserts	Yes, a fast-growing industry	No, but many of the additives, such as fruit, are imported	Convenient desserts, but check kilojoule count if dieting.
ICECREAM AND ICE CONFECTIONS Full cream, low fat, low-Joule ice confections, icecream bars, blocks etc.	Yes, in many flavours and types; manufacturers offering a wider range of reduced fat, lower kilojoule icecreams and ice confections	Yes, over $12 million worth	Buy local product only; check labels of unfamiliar brands. Icecream bars emulating chocolate bars (Snickers etc.) imported — buy local icecream treats.
MILK Fresh, condensed, evaporated, long-life, powdered, full cream, reduced-fat and skim varieties	Yes; industry very aware of consumers' needs. There is also a milk with mono-unsaturated canola oil and no cholesterol	Yes, some $28 million worth, mainly for manufacturing purposes	Choose from range to suit requirements. Fat-modified, no-cholesterol milk is a good substitute for soy drink — see page 72.
YOGHURT Natural, low-fat, skim milk, flavoured; sheep's and goat's milk yoghurts	Yes, in many styles and of excellent quality, including sheep's and goat's milk yoghurts	Yes, over $2.7 million worth	Buy local product only; imported product cannot possibly be better.

Choosing Australian Dairy Foods

Recipes
USING AUSTRALIAN DAIRY FOODS

Savoury Flans

• •

The popularity of savoury flans or quiches has not diminished, and real men do eat them. A look at the frozen food section in your supermarket shows they are still as popular as ever. As manufactured foods often have a proportion of imported ingredients, sometimes quite high, it can help if we learn to make more of the popular foods at home. The method below does not include the pre-baking of the pastry case (baking blind), but it does work well and saves time and effort.

Cheese and Bacon Flan

Oven temperature: 200°C (400°F), reducing to 180°C (350°F)

Serves 4–6

½ *quantity Shortcrust Pastry, page 15*

Cheese and Bacon Filling
3 bacon rashers, trimmed and chopped
2 teaspoons butter
6 spring onions, chopped
3 eggs
1 teaspoon prepared French mustard
1 cup cream
½ cup milk
salt
freshly ground black pepper
1 cup shredded Swiss or cheddar cheese

1 Grease and line a 23-cm flan tin with rolled-out pastry. Press into shape of tin and trim top even with rim. Chill until needed. Preheat oven.
2 Put chopped bacon into a heated frying pan and cook until lightly browned. Add butter and spring onions and cook for 2–3 minutes. Remove pan from heat.
3 Beat eggs and mustard in a bowl and stir in cream, milk and salt and pepper to taste.

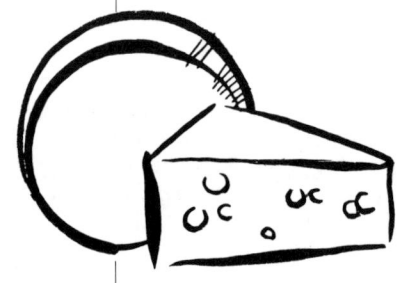

Grating Hard Cheese

....

Many cooks prefer to grate their own cheese rather than to buy the cheese ready-grated. There are various cheese graters on the market, but they all require some effort on your part. While food processors come with shredding disks, handy for shredding softer cheeses such as cheddar, few have a grating disk.
However, you can use your food processor for grating hard cheese. Simply cut the cheese in small dice, and using the steel blade, process until very fine. It might not be as fine as traditional grating, but it gives a satisfactory result. To prevent cheese jamming under the blade, drop the diced cheese into the bowl with motor running.

4 Spread half the cheese in the base of the flan case, top with bacon and onion mixture. Pour in egg mixture over the back of a spoon so that filling is not displaced. Sprinkle on remaining cheese.

5 Place flan in preheated hot oven and cook for 15 minutes, reduce to moderate and cook for further 15–20 minutes until filling is puffed, golden and set when tested with the point of a knife. Stand for 5 minutes, cut in wedges and serve hot with a tossed salad.

Variations

Pumpkin Flan

Pumpkin Filling:
1 large onion, thinly sliced
1 tablespoon butter
1 cup firmly packed, shredded pumpkin
3 eggs
salt
freshly ground black pepper
1 cup cream
1/4 teaspoon grated nutmeg
1/2 cup shredded cheddar cheese
1 tablespoon snipped chives

1 As for Cheese and Bacon Flan.
2 Put onion in a frying pan with butter and cook gently until soft. Add pumpkin and cook, stirring often, for 2–3 minutes to soften it. Remove from heat and cool.
3 Beat eggs, stir in salt and pepper to taste, cream, nutmeg and cheese. Stir in cooled pumpkin mixture and pour into flan case. Sprinkle chives on top and complete as in Step 5 above.

Zucchini Flan

As for Pumpkin Flan, replacing pumpkin with equal quantity of shredded zucchini. Cook with onion until moisture evaporates.

Spinach Flan

As for Pumpkin Flan, replacing pumpkin with 1 cup cooked, chopped and well-drained leaf spinach. Cook with onion to evaporate excess moisture. Sprinkle top with 1 tablespoon grated Parmesan cheese in place of chives.

Fillo Pastry Triangles

Read section on Handling Fillo Pastry, page 16, and refer to this when making triangles. I have given various fillings, followed by general instructions for all triangles.

Each filling is enough for 60 triangles.

Cheese Filling

1 cup crumbled feta cheese
½ cup cottage or ricotta cheese
½ cup shredded tasty cheddar cheese
¼ cup chopped parsley
¼ teaspoon grated nutmeg
freshly ground black pepper
1 large egg

Mix all ingredients together. Use 1 heaped teaspoon filling for each triangle.

Salmon Filling

1½ cups poached, flaked Atlantic salmon, page 88
1 cup ricotta cheese
¼ cup finely chopped spring onions
1–2 teaspoons chopped fresh dill
3 teaspoons lemon juice
salt
freshly ground black pepper
1 egg

1 Poach and flake salmon as directed — you will need about 400 g fresh salmon.
2 When salmon is cool, mix with remaining ingredients, adding dill, salt and pepper to taste. Use heaped teaspoons of filling for each triangle.

Note: Ocean trout may be used in place of Atlantic salmon.

Spinach Filling

1 cup cooked, well-drained leaf spinach, page 135
½ cup finely chopped spring onions
2 teaspoons butter
2 tablespoons chopped parsley
¼ teaspoon grated nutmeg
½ cup ricotta cheese
½ cup shredded tasty cheddar cheese

Use-by Dates

The use-by dates on dairy products are a guide to the storage life of the produce under recommended storage conditions. If products such as milk, cream, sour cream, cream cheese and other cheeses have passed their use-by date, check the product before throwing it out. Milk would taste sour, but if you are not sure, simply heat a small amount. If it curdles, throw it out, otherwise use it. Any cream develops a bitter taste or mould when it goes 'off'; if there is no visible mould, taste it, and if there is no trace of bitterness, it is safe to use. Likewise with cream cheese. If mould develops on hard or semi-hard cheeses, simply cut off the mould; the cheese is still safe to eat.

EGG STORAGE

Eggs do not appear in any Buyer's Guide simply because imports are negligible. However, it is worthwhile giving a little information on egg purchasing and storage. When buying eggs, choose eggs with a use-by date as far advanced as possible — at least three weeks ahead. Leave in the carton and store in the body of the refrigerator — not in the egg holder in the door of the refrigerator. By storing in this way, the eggs remain at a more constant temperature, and are less likely to crack because of door movement.

If your stored eggs have passed their use-by date, check them before throwing them out. Place eggs carefully in a bowl of tap water. If they stay near the bottom of the bowl, they are still fresh; if half-way up, they are still safe to use, but the whites will be more liquid (they can be used in custards, cakes or scrambled). If they float near the top, they are stale and shouldn't be used. Dry the usable eggs with a cloth, return to the carton, refrigerate and use as soon as possible.

2 tablespoons grated Parmesan cheese
1 egg
salt
freshly ground black pepper

1 Finely chop the spinach and place in a bowl.
2 Cook spring onions in butter until soft and add to spinach.
3 Mix in remaining ingredients, seasoning to taste with salt and pepper. Use heaped teaspoons of filling for each triangle.

To make triangles:

1 You will need 12–18 sheets pastry, depending on size of sheets used. Cut in 12-cm wide strips. Butter and fold pastry to give 6-cm wide strip, fill and shape as directed on page 17.
2 Place on greased baking trays, brush tops lightly with butter and bake in a preheated, moderately hot oven, 190°C (375°F), for 15 minutes until puffed and golden. Serve hot.

Fillo Rolls

Make any of the fillings for triangles. Use pastry strips cut 20–24 cm wide, butter and fold. Using a tablespoon of filling for each roll, fill and shape as directed on page 18. Bake as for triangles. Each filling makes about 40 rolls.

Easy White Sauce

This is a low-fat version of white sauce for preparing in the microwave oven. Use basic sauce or variations as indicated or in recipes.

Makes about 1 cup

1 cup milk
2 tablespoons plain flour
2 teaspoons butter
salt
freshly ground pepper

Using Australian Dairy Foods • 67

1 Put milk in a microwave-safe jug and whisk in flour with a balloon whisk until flour is well mixed into milk. Add butter.
2 Microwave on HIGH for about 3 minutes. Whisk after 1 minute, then each 20–30 seconds until thickened and bubbling up in jug.
3 If sauce is thicker than desired, add a little more milk and microwave for 20 seconds or so. Season with salt and pepper to taste. Use as indicated in recipes.

Variations

Mornay Sauce
Add 1/2 cup grated tasty cheddar cheese to sauce when it is cooked. Stir until smooth. Use for dressing vegetables such as cauliflower, chokoes and broccoli, and for mornays.

Parsley Sauce
Stir in 2 tablespoons finely chopped parsley and 1/2 teaspoon prepared English mustard after sauce is cooked. Serve on hot corned beef. Omit mustard, add a squeeze of lemon juice and serve on steamed fresh or smoked fish.

Making Yoghurt

The yoghurt industry has been most successful; we can't seem to do without yoghurt and keep consuming more each year. Making your own is considerably cheaper. You don't have to invest in a yoghurt maker — if you have one, use it, but directions are for the old-fashioned method with some modernisation for better food handling. By the way, you cannot make yoghurt in the microwave oven as you need very gentle, constant warmth for a long period, impossible to achieve in the microwave.

The starter: Choose a commercial natural yoghurt you like, either for flavour (very tangy such as Lebanese yoghurt, mildly tangy such as Greek country-style, or something in between), or for the additional cultures it contains, such as Lactobacillus acidophilus (claimed to have more health benefits). If you are making a low-fat yoghurt, you can use any type of natural yoghurt as a starter.

Calcium in the Diet

This important nutrient is necessary for strong bones and teeth, and can prevent osteoporosis. Milk is a rich source of calcium, better absorbed by the body than the calcium from other sources. Many milks are calcium-enriched and fat-reduced, making it easier to choose a milk suitable for your particular needs. Yoghurt and cheese are other excellent sources. Non-dairy sources are soy drink, bean curd, almonds and hazelnuts, but their calcium content is not as readily absorbed.

The milk: For a full-bodied yoghurt, use full-cream milk and full-cream milk powder; for a low-fat yoghurt use reduced-fat milk and skim milk powder.

Equipment: A large saucepan for the milk; a clinical thermometer kept for this specific purpose; 3 sterilised glass jars, 2-cup capacity, with plastic lids (boil the lids); large boiler; large blanket or two beach towels.

Making the yoghurt:

1 Combine 6 cups milk of your choice with ³/₄ cup milk powder of your choice in a saucepan, stirring powdered milk in thoroughly. Bring slowly to the boil and when almost at boiling point, remove from heat.

2 Set aside and let milk come down to a little above blood temperature — 45°C on thermometer. Stir occasionally to prevent skin forming.

3 Blend ¼ cup of the warm milk with ¼ cup of the chosen starter. Gently stir starter into milk and pour immediately into jars. Seal jars with lids.

4 Stand jars in a boiler and add water to come up to neck of jars.

5 Heat until water temperature reaches 50°C and remove boiler from heat onto doubled blanket or the two towels. Bring wrap over to cover boiler entirely and leave undisturbed for 3 hours.

6 Screw lids firmly on jars and remove from water. Store in refrigerator. This yoghurt keeps for over a week. You can use some as a starter for the next batch, but after making four batches, buy fresh yoghurt for your next starter.

Yoghurt Serving Suggestions

1 Use one of the fruit purées given on page 150 and stir amount to taste into yoghurt; use a fresh purée for immediate eating, a cooked purée if you mix a batch and leave it in the refrigerator for family snacks.

2 Drizzle the yoghurt with honey and add a spoonful or two of chopped, mixed nuts, almonds, walnuts or pecans.

3 Serve on your breakfast muesli or other cereal in place of milk.

4 Serve with fresh fruit salad instead of cream or ice cream, using a natural yoghurt. You can drizzle on a little honey if you like.

Using Australian Dairy Foods

5 Use in place of sour cream in savoury dishes or on baked potatoes. Add a spoonful onto each serving of food rather than stir it into the cooked dish.

Yoghurt and Cucumber Sauce or Dip

You will find this in tubs at your supermarket or delicatessen. It is one of the easiest sauces to make, so if you want to save money in one area, and spend it on other Australian-produced food, then here is a recipe.

Makes about 3 cups

2 cups thick yoghurt
2 Lebanese cucumbers
2 teaspoons salt
1 clove garlic, crushed
1 tablespoon chopped fresh mint
1 tablespoon olive oil (optional)
freshly ground black pepper

1 If possible purchase the thick, country-style yoghurt available at delicatessens and specialty food stores. If ordinary or fat-free yoghurt is preferred, strain about 500 g in cheesecloth for a few hours. An easy method is to line a plastic or stainless steel strainer with cheesecloth, set it over a bowl, tip yoghurt into strainer and cover top with a plate. Place in refrigerator and leave overnight.
2 Peel cucumbers and shred coarsely into a bowl. Mix in salt and leave for 30 minutes. Drain in a strainer and press pulp with the back of a spoon to extract excess moisture.
3 Tip into a clean bowl, stir in thick yoghurt, mint, olive oil if used and pepper to taste. Serve as a dip with crusty bread, raw vegetables or crackers, or as a sauce for fried, grilled or steamed fish, or as directed in recipes.

Stirred Custard

While packaged custard powder makes a quick stirred custard, this particular custard is very quick to make, and is much easier than the delicate English stirred custard made in a double boiler.

STORING CHEESE

If cheese is not properly wrapped, the flavour can migrate to other foods in the refrigerator. If cheese is packed in its own plastic sleeve, return cheese to pack, fold down open end, keeping it in place with a rubber band. Leftover camembert and brie, once removed from their packs, should be wrapped in plastic film — they keep for about a week. Hard cheeses, cheddars, blue-vein and round-eye types may be wrapped in greaseproof paper and overwrapped with foil; this allows the cheese to 'breathe' without drying out. Remember the greaseproof paper first, as the salt in the cheese could corrode the foil.

Cooling Custards and Sauces

Custards and milk-based sauces, if not to be used immediately, form a thick surface skin while cooling unless stirred occasionally. An alternative is to press a piece of plastic film directly onto the surface; this prevents a skin forming. For custards, another alternative is to hold back a couple of teaspoons of the sugar; when custard is poured into the bowl, sprinkle surface with remaining sugar. This melts on the hot surface, preventing a skin forming, and can be stirred into custard when it is cool.

Makes about 2 cups

2 egg yolks
2 cups milk
2 tablespoons cornflour
3 tablespoons sugar
pinch of salt
1½ teaspoons vanilla essence

1 Put egg yolks into a bowl with ½ cup of the milk, cornflour, sugar and salt. Beat with a balloon whisk until thoroughly mixed.
2 In a heavy-based stainless steel or enamelled saucepan, bring remaining milk almost to boiling point. Pour into egg mixture, stirring continuously. Return to pan.
3 Place pan over moderate heat and stir with balloon whisk until thickened and beginning to bubble. Continue to stir and boil gently for 30 seconds.
4 Remove from heat, stir in vanilla and pour into bowl. Serve hot if desired, or cover surface with a piece of plastic wrap to prevent skin forming and leave until cool. Chill until required if necessary.

Variations

Custard Cream
Mix chilled, Stirred Custard with an equal quantity of whipped cream. Alternatively use prepared custard from a carton. Serve with canned, poached or stewed fruits, fruit pies, fruit crumble or any other pudding served with custard.

Brandied Custard Cream
Serve this with your Christmas pudding. For serving 10–12, mix 1 quantity Stirred Custard or 2 cups prepared vanilla custard from a carton with 2 cups whipped cream and 3 tablespoons brandy or to taste. Cover and chill until required. This is quick and easy to make, and much lighter than the traditional Hard Sauce or Brandy Sauce. If children are to be served, remove some of the custard cream to a separate jug before adding the brandy.

Baking a Custard

When using the oven for your main meal, it takes very little effort to put a baked custard together. Once you master the basic recipe, other variations are possible.

Baked Custard

Oven temperature: 180°C (350°F)

Serves 6

3 eggs
pinch of salt
2½ cups warm milk
¼ cup caster sugar
1 teaspoon vanilla essence
grated nutmeg

1 Lightly grease a 4–5 cup deep pie dish or casserole dish with butter.
2 In a large bowl, beat eggs with salt until well mixed but not frothy. Stir in warm milk, sugar and vanilla essence.
3 Strain into prepared dish and sprinkle top with grated nutmeg.
4 Place dish in a baking dish of hot water and bake in preheated oven for 35–40 minutes until set. Test with a knife blade inserted into centre — it should come away clean. Take care that custard does not overcook.
5 Remove set custard from water bath and leave to cool. Serve warm or chilled with cream and canned or stewed fruit if desired.

Variations

Baked Pumpkin Custard

Make basic Baked Custard mixture, reducing milk to 2 cups. Beat in ½ cup smooth butternut pumpkin purée and 3 tablespoons sultanas or raisins. Pour into prepared dish, sprinkle with ground nutmeg and bake as above. Pumpkin does separate a little in cooking, giving custard a two-toned effect. Serve warm or chilled with cream.

Bread and Butter Custard

Butter 3 slices white bread with crusts on. Halve slices diagonally and arrange, slightly overlapping, in base of prepared dish. Sprinkle with 3 tablespoons sultanas and

SOY DRINK SUBSTITUTE

Who would have thought that a drink made from a plant would be competition for naturally produced milk! But sadly, this is the case — sadly because, to keep up with the demand for a product with no cholesterol, we need to supplement our own soy bean supply with substantial imports. Fortunately the dairy industry has come up with a milk for those who feel that it is necessary to have foods with no cholesterol (see glossary for more information). The result is a cholesterol-free milk with its fat modified, that is replaced with mono-unsaturated canola oil. Marketed as Farmers Best, it is available in all states and the ACT, but not in the Northern Territory. Similar, no-cholesterol milks are Dairy Wise (Queensland) and Dairy Choice (Victoria). There are other fat-modified milks available, but only the milks named above are cholesterol free. Fat content is a low 1.35 per cent; compare this to low-fat soy drink, and if you have no other reason for using soy drink (such as allergy or lactose-intolerance), then try one of these milks for Australia's sake.

strain basic custard mixture over bread. Sprinkle top with ground cinnamon or nutmeg. Bake as for Baked Custard. Serve warm with cream.

Queen of Puddings

Use 4 yolks in custard mixture in place of the 3 whole eggs, reserving egg whites. Use custard to make the Bread and Butter Custard above, sprinkle with ground cinnamon and bake. When set, remove from oven and spread top with 3 tablespoons warmed apricot or berry jam. Beat egg whites until stiff and gradually beat in ½ cup caster sugar. Pile meringue onto custard, spreading it to edge of dish. Replace hot water in dish with cold water, add dish of custard and return to oven for 8–10 minutes until meringue is set and lightly browned. Serve warm with cream.

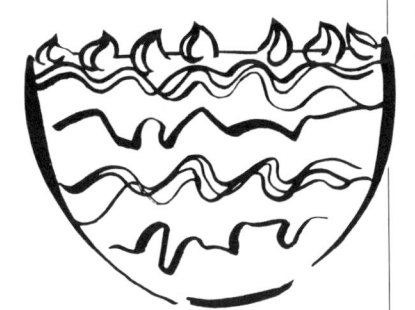

Australian Trifle

The trifle of England has undergone many changes in the Australian kitchen, and still remains one of those old-fashioned puds fondly remembered from the halcyon days of our childhood. For speed use ready-made custard, or make your own. Raspberry jam is traditional, or use plum or apricot.

Trifle
Serves 6

1 packet raspberry, port wine or strawberry jelly crystals
1 day-old sponge cake
2–3 tablespoons raspberry, plum or apricot jam
2–3 tablespoons sherry
2 cups prepared, cooled custard
300 ml thickened cream
1 tablespoon caster sugar
2 tablespoons toasted, slivered almonds
halved strawberries to decorate (optional)

1 Make jelly according to packet directions and set in a lamington tin in refrigerator.
2 Split cake in half, spread with jam and sandwich halves together. Cut into 3-cm cubes and place a layer of cubes in a glass serving bowl. Sprinkle with some of the

Using Australian Dairy Foods

sherry and cover with a layer of custard. Repeat layers of sherry-sprinkled cake and custard, finishing with custard. Cover and chill until required for serving.

3 Whip cream and fold in sugar. Spread a layer of cream over the custard and pipe a border of cream rosettes around edge. Cut jelly into cubes and pile in centre (you may only require half the jelly). Sprinkle almonds onto cream rosettes and place strawberries between rosettes if desired.

Peach Trifle
Add a layer of sliced, well-drained, canned peaches over sherried sponge before adding custard.

Lemon Cheesecake

Crumb Crust
2 cups sweet biscuit crumbs
90 g butter, melted
2 teaspoons hot water

Filling
2/3 cup very hot water
1 packet lemon jelly crystals
185 g packaged cream cheese
1 cup caster sugar
grated rind and juice of 1 lemon
375-ml can evaporated milk, chilled

1 Mix biscuit crumbs with melted butter and hot water and press onto base and sides of a 20-cm springform tin. Chill until required.
2 Pour hot water onto jelly crystals and stir well until dissolved. Leave aside to cool thoroughly.
3 Beat cream cheese and sugar until light and fluffy then beat in cooled jelly, lemon rind and juice.
4 Whip chilled evaporated milk until thick and fold into cream cheese mixture. Pour into prepared crumb crust and chill until set. Release from springform tin and serve in wedges with whipped cream.

Handy Hint: Springform Tin

If you want to present a cheesecake or other crumb- or pastry-crusted tart without the base of the springform tin, the crust is often damaged when trying to remove it. Before putting crumb or pastry into your tin, invert the base in the ring. When required for serving, release sides and run a long palette knife between the crust and the base to loosen it. Slide onto serving plate.

Pantry-shelf Icecream

Tinned milks and creams are handy pantry items, ideal for adding to all kinds of recipes. This recipe uses these products and is so quick to put together that it will become a family favourite.

Makes about 2 litres

225-g can reduced cream
375-ml can evaporated milk
415-g can sweetened condensed milk
2 teaspoons vanilla essence

1 Shake can of reduced cream thoroughly before opening. Combine the milks and the cream in a bowl, stir in vanilla essence, cover and chill for 1–2 hours.
2 Churn method: Put into icecream churn and churn for 20–25 minutes until thick. Turn into a clean, chilled icecream container, seal and store in freezer for 24 hours before using.
Beating method: Put mixture in large bowl of electric mixer and place in freezer. Put beaters in freezer as well.
3 When icecream mixture is frozen almost to the centre, break up with a wooden spoon, then beat on high speed on mixer until double in volume. Turn into chilled container, seal and return to freezer.

Variations

Mango Icecream
Omit vanilla essence. Purée the flesh of 2 large, ripe mangoes and mix into milk mixture. Finish as above.

Butternut Crunch Icecream
Prepare icecream as in basic recipe. When churned or beaten, fold in 1 cup coarsely crushed vanilla almonds or other toffeed nuts.

Raspberry Ripple Icecream
Make a raspberry purée according to directions on page 150, reducing it over heat. Cool and chill. Make icecream, omitting vanilla from basic recipe. When icecream is churned or beaten, turn half into storage container, add half the raspberry purée and swirl it through the icecream with the handle of a wooden spoon. Add remaining icecream and purée and repeat swirling. Seal and store in freezer.

Oils, Fats and Spreads

In the past two decades or so there has been a vast change in our attitudes to oils and fats. Where oil was once spurned except by the adventurous and the initiated, we now use far more of it than traditional fats such as butter, dripping and lard. There are some benefits in that our intake of saturated fats has been reduced, but as a whole we consume the same amount of oils and fats as before, contrary to the urging of health advisers to cut down on total fat intake.

Other changes have also increased oil consumption. Australians of southern European and Asian background are large users of oils for cooking and dressing foods, and the increase in fast food outlets with their high percentage of fried foods has also added to oil usage and intake. Margarines have eroded butter's place in the Australian diet to the extent that we now consume more than twice as much margarine as butter, and margarines (spreads and for cooking) contain a high percentage of vegetable oils.

As a consequence we imported over $180 million worth of oils and oilseeds, in the twelve months to June 1993, to fulfil demand, or because a processor or importer wanted to source a cheaper product. Australian processors of edible oils and margarines endeavour to source oil seeds and other products within Australia, importing when there is a shortfall in a particular oil seed, or because we do not produce a certain product in Australia. But this is not so with all suppliers of oils for general sale or food manufacturing.

The Buyer's Guide shows where you can make changes to reduce oil and fat imports. The predominant type of fat is given for each item — saturated, mono-unsaturated or polyunsaturated.

Buyer's Guide
CHOOSING AUSTRALIAN OILS AND FATS

Product	Australian-produced	Imported	What we can do
OILS			
Canola oil — standard and cold pressed (mono-unsaturated)	Yes, both types; cold-pressed (Australian Country Canola), available from health food stores, some supermarkets and delicatessens	Yes, small amount of canola oil, and seeds for processing locally	Use in place of light olive oil as it has the same, if not better, nutritional advantages (contains Omega 3). Cold-pressed canola has a nutty flavour; use where such a flavour is required.
Coconut oil/copha butter (highly saturated)	No, but is further processed locally	Yes, some $7 million worth	Use less of it. Avoid using solid vegetable frying fats. Also used in some vegetable margarines.
Cotton seed oil (polyunsaturated)	Yes	Yes, very small amount	Difficult to buy as an oil. Used in oil blends, margarines and cooking fat blends.
Grapeseed oil (polyunsaturated)	No, but it should be a by-product of our wine industry	Yes (amount not known)	Avoid buying it; use other locally made oils instead.
Hazelnut oil (mono-unsaturated)	No	Yes (amount not known)	Use cold-pressed canola or macadamia oil.
Macadamia oil (mono-unsaturated)	Yes, various brands	No	Excellent for dressings and baking; use in place of imported nut oil and olive oil.
Maize/corn oil (polyunsaturated)	Yes	Yes, almost $1 million worth	Check labels for local product. A good oil for cooking.
Olive oil — extra virgin, virgin, pure, extra light (mono-unsaturated)	Yes, very small quantity of extra virgin — Joseph, McLaren Vale, Foothills, Ferrari are some of the brands available as production slowly increases	Yes, over $50 million worth	Use canola or sunola oil in place of extra light olive oil. For way to save on imports, see Salad Oil, page 80.
Palm and palm kernel oil (highly saturated)	No, but processed locally into margarine and frying fat blends	Yes, almost $60 million worth, mainly for food processing	Not available for general sale, but used in some margarines and frying fat blends, such blends favoured in food industry and fast foods as they remain more stable. Reduce intake of fried snack foods (such as potato crisps) and fried fast foods (such as fish and chips).

Choosing Australian Oils, Fats and Spreads • 77

Product	Australian-produced	Imported	What we can do
Peanut oil (mono-unsaturated)	Yes	Yes, small amount	Use mainly for Asian cooking.
Safflower (polyunsaturated)	Yes, also used in table margarines	Yes, with sunflower, over $7 million worth	Good for general cooking purposes but not deep-frying. Check labels for local product.
Sunflower (polyunsaturated)	Yes, also used in table margarines	See previous item	As for previous item.
Sunola oil (mono-unsaturated)	Yes; previously imported, locally grown and processed since August 1994	No	Excellent for frying as it remains more stable through repeated heating. Use in place of light olive oil; also see Salad Oil, page 80.
Sesame oil (polyunsaturated and mono-unsaturated)	No	Yes, over $2.6 million worth	Use only in very small amounts for flavouring foods; use cold-pressed canola or macadamia oil in recipes requiring large amounts of sesame oil.
Soy bean oil (polyunsaturated)	Yes, used mostly in oil blends and margarines, some oil for direct sale	Yes, some $18 million worth	Use another polyunsaturated oil which requires fewer imports to fill demand, although canola is better.
Vegetable blend oils (mono-unsaturated and polyunsaturated)	Yes, with some of imported product further processed locally	Yes, some $16 million worth	Check labels on vegetable oil blends for local product.
Walnut oil (polyunsaturated)	No	Yes (amount not known)	Use macadamia or cold-pressed canola oil for nutty flavour.
FATS AND SPREADS			
Animal fats — dripping and lard (saturated)	Yes	Yes, small amount	Avoid using for health's sake. Use less of commercially made biscuits, cakes and pastries. Also used in frying fat and shortening blends.
Butter, including low-salt and unsalted (saturated)	Yes, with sufficient for export	Yes, almost $4 million worth, used mainly in food industry	Use butter as a spread to reduce reliance on imports because of increased demand for margarines. Neither spread should be used in excess. Both contain same kilojoules.
Butter blends — dairy blend and reduced-fat butter spread (less saturated than butter)	Yes; dairy blend contains vegetable oil, reduced-fat spread has about half the fat content of butter	No	Use as an alternative to butter; use dairy blend for spread and cooking, reduced fat butter spread as spread or on vegetables.

Product	Australian-produced	Imported	What we can do
Ghee (pure butter fat) (saturated)	Yes	No	Use in small quantities for light frying as it does not burn easily.
Margarine — cooking (saturated and mono-unsaturated)	Yes	No, but some ingredients for manufacture are imported	Use butter or table margarine instead for cooking. Some cooking margarine high in saturated fats.
Margarine — reduced-fat spread (mono-unsaturated and polyunsaturated)	Yes, contains half the fat content of table margarine	No, but some ingredients for manufacture could be imported	Use as an alternative to table margarine as it is lower in fat. Do not use in cooking, but can be used on cooked vegetables.
Margarine — table (levels of saturated, mono-unsaturated and polyunsaturated fats vary)	Yes, available using various vegetable oils, including olive oil in one brand	No, but some ingredients for manufacture may be imported	Use sparingly as a spread and in cooking; choose those with a higher ratio of polyunsaturated or mono-unsaturated fats to saturated fats. Check labels.
Shortening, solid — used for frying etc. (highly saturated)	Yes	No, but many of the ingredients are imported	See Palm and Coconut oils. Don't be misled by 'low cholesterol' tag on 100% vegetable oil shortenings. Avoid using them.
Suet (saturated)	Yes	No	Use occasionally, such as for Christmas pudding.

Choosing Australian Oils, Fats and Spreads • 79

Recipes
USING AUSTRALIAN OILS, FATS AND SPREADS

Olive Oils

• •

Some detail is given in the Buyer's Guide, but a little more explanation is required for a commodity we import in such quantities. Flavours of oils vary greatly; extra virgin oil is from the first pressing, and can be very fruity in flavour, mildly fruity, or even peppery (some Italian oils from Tuscany and Australia's Joseph extra virgin). There are oils from Greece, Kalamata in particular, which, while not extra virgin, have a delightful fruity flavour at much less cost. I mention these only because they are cheaper than premium Italian, French and Australian oils and some Spanish oils.

Extra virgin, pure and extra light olive oils vary in flavour according to source, but extra light olive oil, a close second to the biggest selling pure olive oil, is bland. Olive oil is in favour because health educators have convinced us that we now need to include more mono-unsaturated oils in our diet. Australian-produced canola and sunola oil are mono-unsaturated oils that have almost the same structure of fatty acids. Canola is actually better because it contains Omega-3 fatty acids. When you want light olive oil, use canola or sunola instead; for an olive-flavoured oil, prepare the following as a means to reducing imports. I have named it Salad Oil, but its uses can go beyond salads.

Salad Oil
Use a recently emptied oil bottle and do not wash. Mix equal quantities of extra virgin or fruity-flavoured olive oil with canola or sunola oil and use in dressings and on foods requiring a flavoursome olive oil. Use as directed in recipes.

FRYING OIL

Oil that is used for deep frying can be used 3–4 times with care. Recommended oil is sunola, a mono-unsaturated oil. Factors which cause oils to oxidise quickly are moisture and overheating. Dry foods such as potatoes thoroughly before frying to reduce amount of moisture. After food is fried, leave oil on medium heat until bubbles stop rising to the surface (these are small bubbles of moisture), but do not let oil overheat. Remove, cool and strain through a fine sieve into a clean, dry container or bottle. Store in a cool, dark place.

You can re-use the oil a few times; it is wasteful and an environmental problem to dispose of deep-frying oil after only one use as is often recommended. When oil has broken down (become unstable), you can tell by the way it cooks foods — if the bubbles are largish, clear and sparkling, the oil is still good; if the bubbles are small and frothy-looking, the oil has broken down and should be discarded. Food cooked in such oil will absorb more of the oil; the oil itself also forms oxidised products because the vitamin E content (an antioxidant) is considerably reduced.

Salad Dressings

Bottled salad dressings are popular convenience items, but it is much cheaper to make these up yourself, particularly if you wish to ensure maximum use of Australian products. The bottled dressings look attractive with bits of red and green pepper, herbs etc. floating in them, but many of the dressings don't require these additions. Make your own favourite dressings in large quantities and store in bottles or jars for convenience.

Italian Dressing
Makes about 1¼ cups

1 cup Salad Oil, page 80
3 tablespoons lemon juice
1 clove garlic, crushed (optional)
salt and freshly ground black pepper

1 Put oil into a clean jar, add lemon juice.
2 If using garlic, crush, and using the tip of a knife, mix to a paste with a little salt. Add to jar with pepper to taste. Seal and shake well.
3 Leave in jar or pour into a clean bottle. Seal and store in refrigerator. Shake well before using as required. Keeps for up to 2 weeks.

Note: Oils could become cloudy when chilled (the term is 'winterised'), but will clear on standing at room temperature. This is of little concern when used on a salad.

French Dressing
Makes about 1¼ cups

1 cup Salad Oil, page 80
1 clove garlic, halved
4 tablespoons white or red wine vinegar
1 teaspoon prepared French mustard
½ teaspoon caster sugar
½ teaspoon salt
freshly ground black pepper to taste

1 Combine oils in a clean, screw-top jar. Add garlic and leave to steep for 2–3 hours, then remove and discard.

Using Australian Oils, Fats and Spreads

2 Add remaining ingredients, seal and shake well until thoroughly mixed.
3 Leave in jar or pour into a clean bottle, seal and store in a cool, dark place (refrigeration is not necessary). Shake again before using.

Australian Nut-flavoured Dressing
Makes about 1 1/4 cups

1 cup cold-pressed canola oil or macadamia oil
3 tablespoons cider vinegar
1/2 teaspoon powdered mustard
1/2 teaspoon caster sugar
1/2 teaspoon salt
freshly ground white pepper to taste

1 Combine ingredients in a clean, screw-top jar, seal and shake well.
2 Pour into a clean bottle or leave in jar and store in the refrigerator. Shake just before using.

Mayonnaise
Makes about 2 cups

yolk of 1 hard-boiled egg
2 raw egg yolks
1 teaspoon French mustard
1 teaspoon salt
2 tablespoons lemon juice
3/4 cup canola or sunflower oil
3/4 cup pure olive oil
freshly ground white pepper

1 Press cooked egg yolk through a sieve into a bowl. Add raw egg yolks, mustard and salt and stir with a balloon whisk until smooth.
2 Beat in half the lemon juice. Combine oils in a jug and gradually add, a few drops at a time, whisking constantly.
3 As mayonnaise begins to thicken, add oil in a steady stream, continuing to whisk constantly.
4 When oil is added, whisk in remainder of lemon juice and pepper to taste. Cover bowl and leave at room temperature until required. Mayonnaise may be stored in the refrigerator, but bring to room temperature before attempting to serve, otherwise it could separate.

DISPOSAL OF COOKING OILS AND FATS

Never pour oil or fat down the kitchen sink, or have too much on pots and pans before washing them. Even if in the washing-up water, or poured straight down the plug hole, fats and oils play havoc with our sewerage disposal systems and are major pollutants.
If disposing of meat or bacon fat, allow it to set, scrape onto newspaper and wipe pan with a wad of newspaper before washing up. Dispose of paper in the garbage.
If you have used oil, the oil must be disposed of safely.
An enterprising Australian came up with just such an idea. He produced a product called Oilsorb. It is simply a waxed container the size of a 1-litre milk carton, filled with an absorbent mineral called attapulgite, with disinfectant and deodorisers added.
The idea is to pour in cool, used oil (it takes about 600 ml), and when full, staple it closed and use it as a fire starter for open or slow-combustion fires (it burns cleanly). The attapulgite and ash can then be dug into the garden, as the mineral is used in some potting mixes. Unfortunately supermarkets have

stopped carrying the product, but it is available from Amway distributors. The idea is one that is too good to lose, as domestic cooking oil disposal is a major problem.

Fortunately you can purchase attapulgite from a pet store, as it is also used in fish tanks and as pet litter. You need the one without any additives as these might differ from those in Oilsorb, and you have to be sure that there are no dangerous emissions if you burn it at home. Check with the manufacturer if using a pack labelled as pet litter. Completely open top of a waxed milk or juice carton, rinse and drain well. Add attapulgite to within 3 cm of the top ridge where container folds. Add *cool*, used oil to it until no more can be absorbed. Betweentimes, keep top closed with a bulldog paper clip and store out of sight.

When full, staple carton closed. Even if you don't have a fireplace or heater, the carton can be disposed of in the garbage. Remember to wipe out any oily pan with paper before you wash it! Attapulgite is mined in abundance in northern Queensland and Western Australia — it is not imported.

Variations

Garlic Mayonnaise

Crush 4 cloves garlic, then mix to a smooth paste with the salt. Add to egg yolks, omit French mustard and proceed as for Mayonnaise. Serve as a dip with raw vegetable pieces, or as a sauce with cold poached fish, cooked prawns or lobster.

Tartare Sauce

To 1 cup mayonnaise, add 1 teaspoon finely chopped gherkins, 1 tablespoon finely chopped parsley, 2 teaspoons finely chopped chives and 1 teaspoon finely chopped capers or Pickled Nasturtium Pods (page 175). Serve with fried or grilled fish or shellfish.

Seafoods

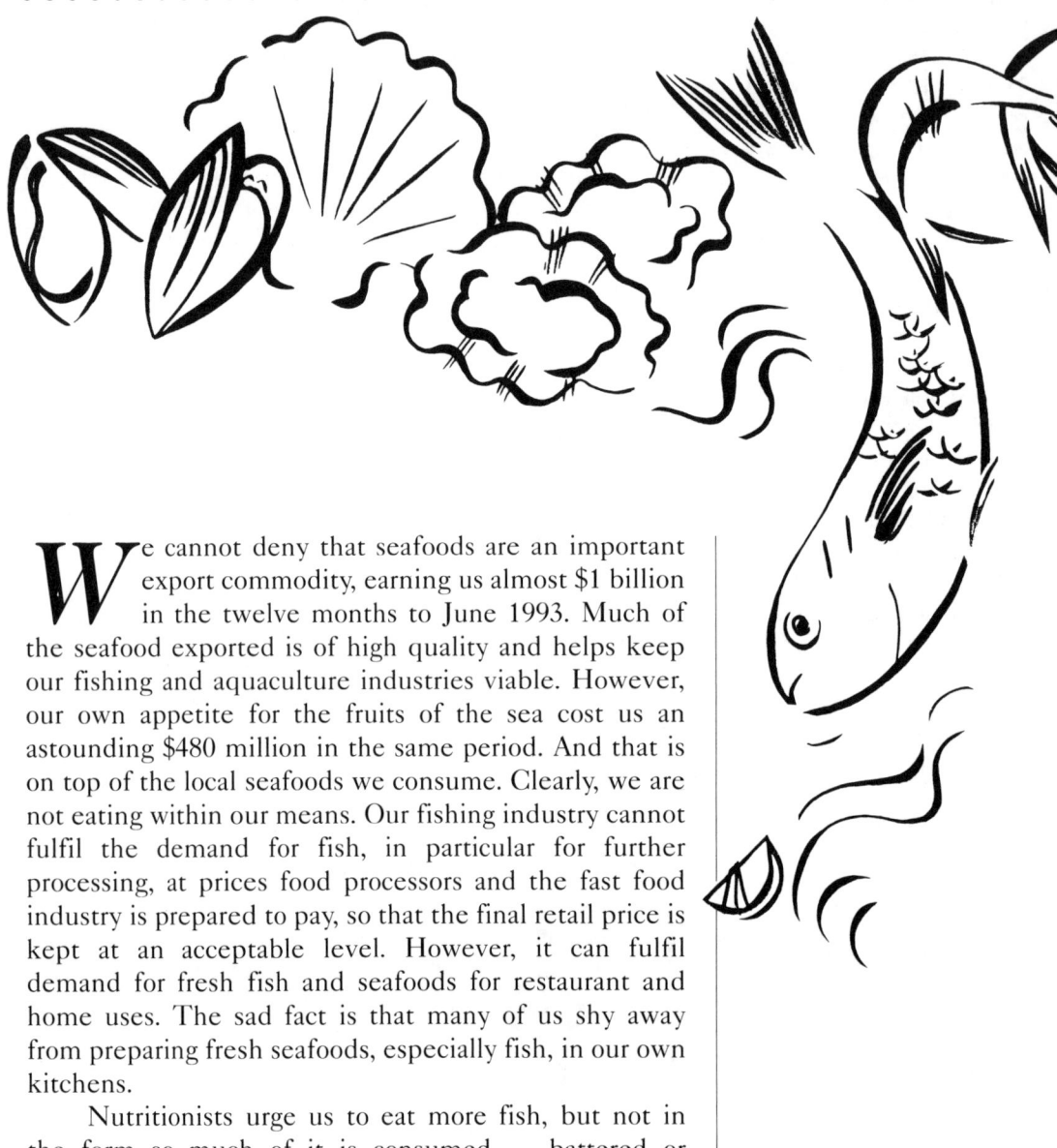

We cannot deny that seafoods are an important export commodity, earning us almost $1 billion in the twelve months to June 1993. Much of the seafood exported is of high quality and helps keep our fishing and aquaculture industries viable. However, our own appetite for the fruits of the sea cost us an astounding $480 million in the same period. And that is on top of the local seafoods we consume. Clearly, we are not eating within our means. Our fishing industry cannot fulfil the demand for fish, in particular for further processing, at prices food processors and the fast food industry is prepared to pay, so that the final retail price is kept at an acceptable level. However, it can fulfil demand for fresh fish and seafoods for restaurant and home uses. The sad fact is that many of us shy away from preparing fresh seafoods, especially fish, in our own kitchens.

Nutritionists urge us to eat more fish, but not in the form so much of it is consumed — battered or crumbed and fried. The same goes for prawns and calamari (squid). As these are usually frozen, processed or fast foods, they are mostly prepared from imports.

Fish and other seafoods preserved in cans and jars and smoked fish are included in the figure given above. We need to look at our seafood-eating habits and make changes to reduce our dependence on imports. The Buyer's Guide gives suggestions on what you can do.

Because there are so many varieties of fish, it is impossible to list them by species. Familiarise yourself with the Australian fish species available in your particular state, and buy these rather than imported fish. Until national legislation compels retailers to label fresh and smoked imported fish with country of origin, the consumer is going to find it difficult to make the right choices.

Australian Canned Fish

Canned tuna and salmon: Our tuna industry is fighting for survival because of competition from imports. The local industry should be supported because it has made every effort to supply the types of product we demand today; besides tuna in brine, there is tuna in spring water, with reduced salt and no added salt, and tuna in canola oil, so there is no excuse for purchasing imported Italian tuna in oil, or other imported tunas for that matter.

The Australian salmon that is canned is not related to the Atlantic salmon now farmed in Tasmania (which is not canned); it is best used in cooked dishes such as fish cakes and mornays.

Anchovies and sardines: These have always been imported, but there is now an alternative. Mendolia Seafoods of Fremantle, Western Australia, catches and processes anchovies and sardines. The quality is excellent, though the anchovies are packed not in canola or other Australian oil, but in imported olive oil. Anchovies are available in jars (called Auschovies) and cans (called Bella del Tindari Anchovies), and salted sardines are bulk-packed in salt in 4-kg cans, like those imported from Italy and Greece. Look for them at delicatessens and gourmet food stores.

COST COMPARISON

Local Atlantic salmon and imported canned red salmon: Canned red and pink salmon add a lot to our import bills. Poached or steamed local Atlantic salmon is a viable alternative. The local product works out cheaper than the best quality imported red salmon, is on a par with a lower grade of red salmon, and is a little dearer than a generic medium red salmon. See Poaching Fish, page 88, and Simply Salmon, page 89.

Buyer's Guide
CHOOSING AUSTRALIAN SEAFOODS

Product	Australian-produced	Imported	What we can do
FISH			
Fresh	Yes, ample supplies available	Yes, some $10 million worth; e.g. sole, flounder, sardines, snapper, whitebait	Insist on local fish, even when eating out. Cook your own fish meals rather than using frozen fish meals.
Frozen — fast foods and manufactured frozen fish products (crumbed or battered fish, fish fingers, fish dinners etc.)	Yes, some local fish used, but mostly imported, particularly in manufactured frozen fish products	Yes, over $120 million worth	If buying fish and chips from fish shop, ask for a local fish to be cooked. Limit use of frozen fish products, or at least buy locally made products.
Canned or jar-packed — anchovies, herrings, mackerel, pilchards, rollmops, sardines, tuna	Yes; tuna, Australian salmon, anchovies — more details on page 85	Yes, some $140 million worth; canned salmon accounts for about 40% of this amount	Buy local tuna only; use Australian salmon for cooking; cook Atlantic salmon for mousses, dips, in place of canned red salmon. Try the WA anchovies. Use less imported canned fish in general.
Salted, salted and dried, dried — Bombay duck, cod, sardines, shark fins and other Asian fish products	Yes, sardines; see page 85	Yes, $7.5 million worth	Try the WA sardines; other salted fish an acquired taste, particularly dried cod and Asian fish.
Smoked — cod, eel, gemfish, haddock, herrings, mackerel, salmon, tailor, trout	Yes, Atlantic salmon, blue-eyed cod, eel, gemfish, herrings, mackerel, tailor, trout (herring imported but smoked locally)	Yes, almost $10 million worth of cod, eel, haddock, herrings, salmon	Use local product only. Local smoked salmon is excellent, as is other smoked fish listed.
PRAWNS			
Fresh — in shell, green or cooked	Yes, for local use and export	Yes, small quantity	Easy to purchase local product.
Frozen — shelled green and cooked; crumbed cutlets	No, labour costs prohibit shelling and crumbing	Yes, over $120 million worth of frozen and all other prawn products listed below	A little too much to ask you not to buy crumbed prawns, but you could make them yourself. Don't choose prawn dishes at low-cost restaurants.
Canned, shelled — whole or pastes; potted in jars, Asian prawn products	No	Yes, all of those listed	Try to use fresh product; limit use of canned or bottled prawn preparations.

Product	Australian-produced	Imported	What we can do
LOBSTER			
Fresh, cooked and live	Yes, always available	Yes, but not a great deal	Use local product.
Frozen, cooked and uncooked	Yes, whole or tails	Yes, about $2 million worth	Ask for local product.
CRAB			
Fresh — cooked and live	Yes	No	Use local product, a number of varieties available.
Frozen — cooked in shell	No; plenty of fresh available	Yes, but not in large quantities	More likely to be used in restaurant trade than retailed.
Preserved — canned, pastes etc.	No	Yes, but not in large quantities	Use fresh cooked crab in place of canned in recipes.
Seafood sticks — made mostly from minced fish (used to be known as crab sticks)	No	Yes, some $7 million worth	Avoid these. They are dyed to look like crab but are a kind of fish 'sausage'. Used also in marinara mixes at retail outlets.
SHELLFISH			
Oysters and mussels — fresh and frozen	Yes, mainly fresh in shell or bottled	Yes, about $5 million worth, mostly frozen	Ask for local product. We do not have the greenlip mussel of NZ in our waters.
Oysters, mussels and other molluscs (abalone, clams, etc.) — frozen, canned, pickled, smoked, in sauce, etc.	No	Yes, about $27 million worth	Use fewer of these if possible. Large variety in Asian food stores — replace with fresh. Some end up in marinara mixes.
Scallops — fresh	Yes, a number of varieties	Yes, small quantity	Ask for local product.
Scallops — frozen	No	Yes, over $4 million worth	Use fresh product. Ask if they are local when eating out. The waiter might be honest!
CEPHALOPODS			
Squid/calamari — fresh (whole), rings (frozen), plain and crumbed	Yes, fresh whole squid	Yes, some $15 million worth, mostly frozen although plain rings sold as fresh	Buy fresh product and prepare it yourself (see page 97). Avoid crumbed calamari in fast food and low-cost restaurants.
Octopus — fresh, frozen and preserved	Yes, fresh	Yes, only small quantity of frozen and preserved	Use local product, although frozen is sold as fresh.
FISH ROES			
Caviar, lumpfish roe, tarama (cod roe), salmon roe	Yes, salmon roe; salted and dried mullet roe	Yes, almost $2 million worth	Use local salmon roe; local salted and dried mullet roe makes excellent Taramosalata (recipe, page 92).

Choosing Australian Seafoods

Recipes
USING AUSTRALIAN SEAFOODS

Poaching Fish

Often recipes call for poached fish; to do this, use a large frying pan with lid to fit so that fish can be added in a single layer. Add about 2 cups water (or enough to cover fish), a little lemon juice, 2 sprigs parsley, salt to taste and a few peppercorns. Bring to the boil. Slide in fish fillets, steaks or cutlets, cover and simmer very gently for 3–7 minutes, depending on thickness of fish. Test with the point of a knife; when it flakes, fish is cooked. Serve as directed in recipes.

If fish is to be prepared further, cool in covered pan so that it does not dry out, remove to a plate and remove skin and bones if necessary. Use as indicated in recipes.

Atlantic Salmon Mousse

Salmon mousse is one of those versatile dishes that may be served as a pâté with crusty French bread or savoury crackers, set in individual moulds and served with salad greens as an entree, or star as the main course for a summertime lunch. The following recipe uses our local fresh salmon in place of the usual imported canned red salmon.

Serves 12–15 as a starter, 8–10 as an entree, 6 as a light meal

2 Atlantic salmon steaks, poached, see above
2 tablespoons finely chopped white onion
½ teaspoon finely chopped fresh chilli
2 teaspoons butter
2 tablespoons lemon juice
1½ tablespoons gelatine
¼ cup strained poaching liquid
2 teaspoons tomato paste
1 cup cream, whipped
¼ cup mayonnaise
salt to taste
freshly ground white pepper
1 egg white

Fruit and Nut Ring (page 155), Nut Chocolates (page 196), Macadamia Shortbread (page 54)

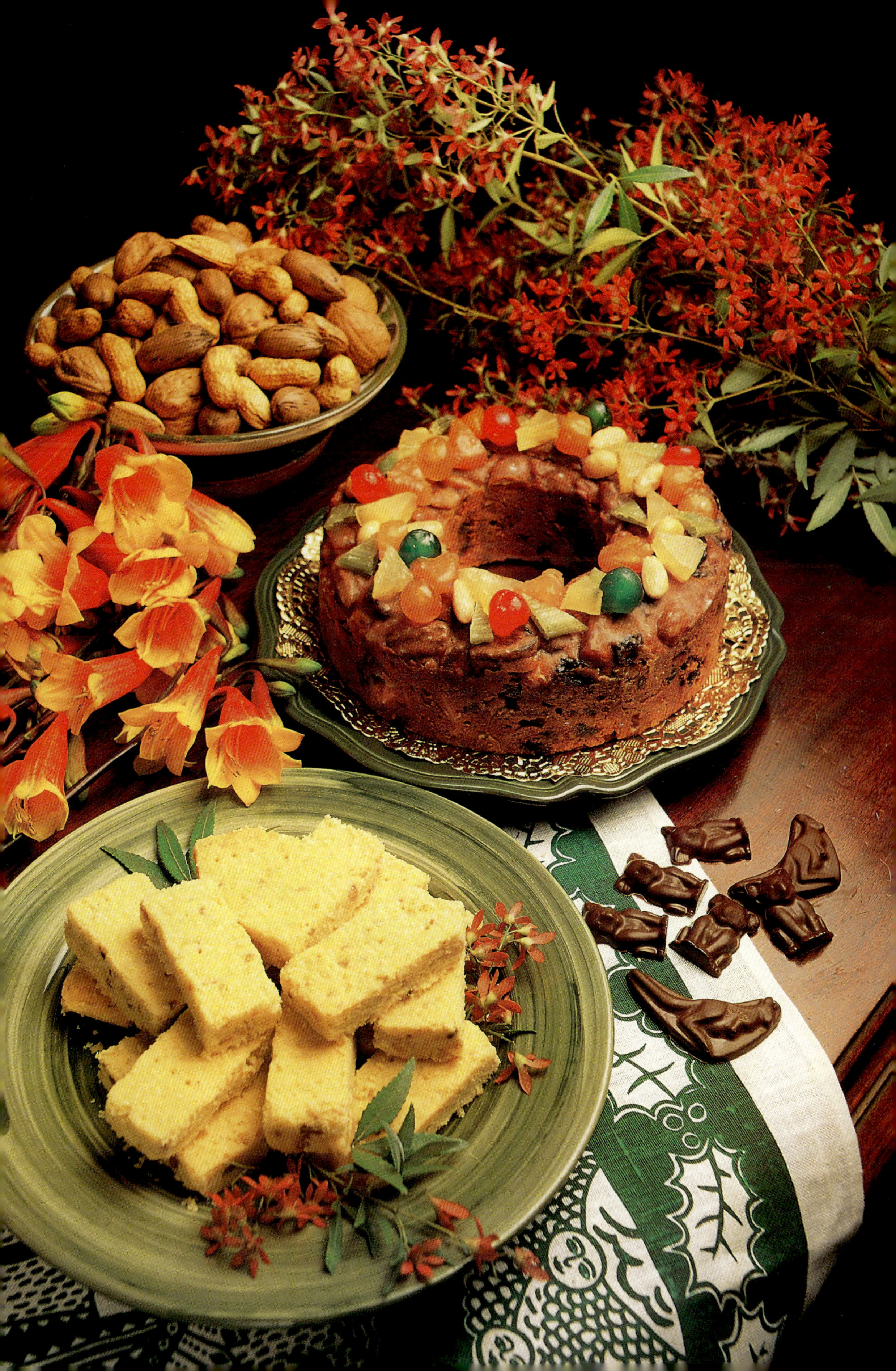

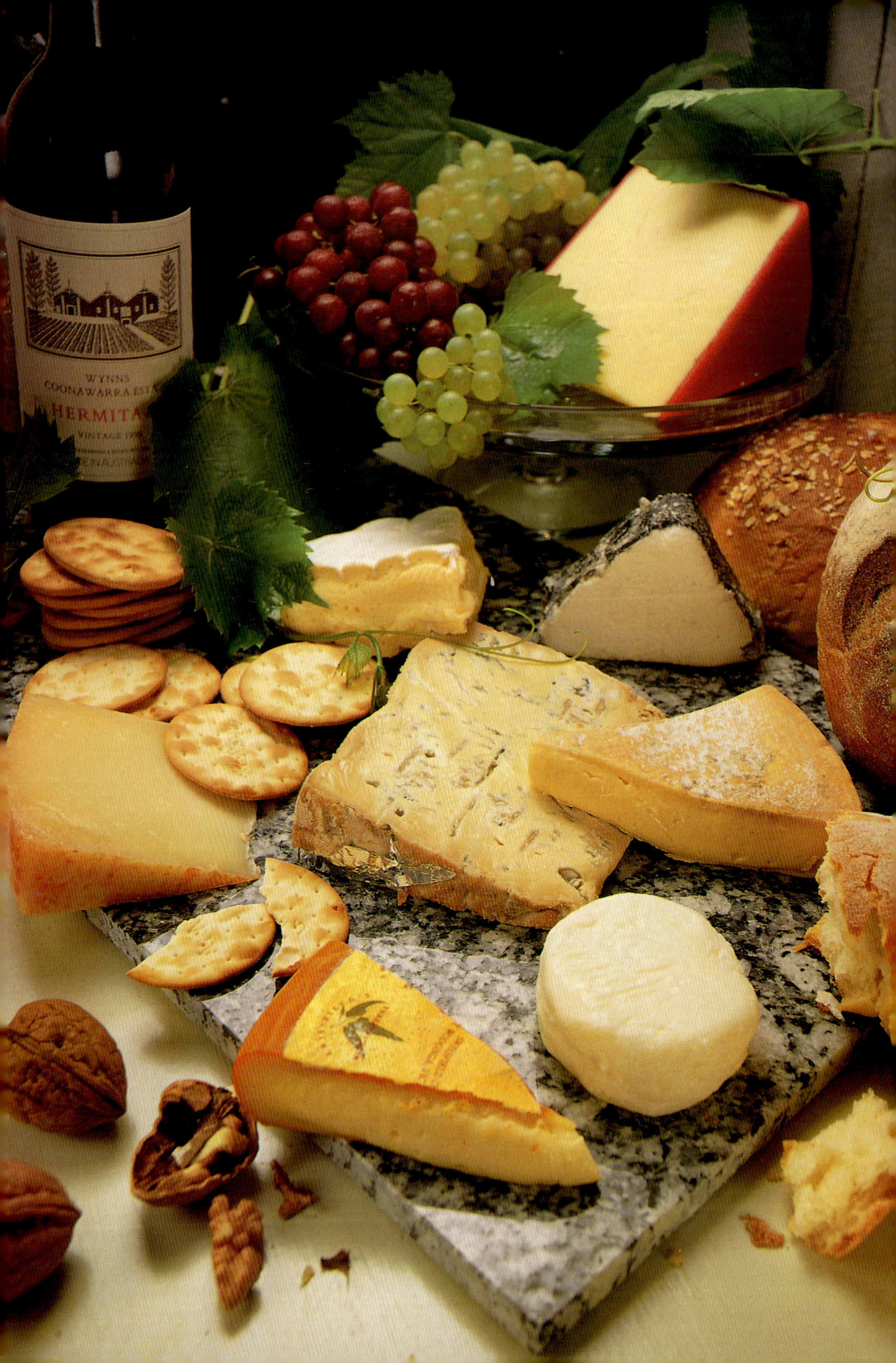
WYNNS
COONAWARRA

Omega-3 Fatty Acids

....

These fatty acids can reduce blood fats, decrease blood pressure and prevent blood clots from forming, thus reducing the risk of heart disease. Oily fish contain omega-3 fats, making them an important addition to the Australian diet. Australian fish with valuable amounts of omega-3s are — Atlantic salmon, blue-eyed cod, gemfish, mackerel, mullet, orange roughy/sea perch, sardines and sea-run trout.

Australian Cheese Platter: Clockwise from top — King Island Surprise Bay cheddar, Milawa ashed chèvre, Milawa gold, Cathedral chèvre, Mungabareena, merino gold, Wattle Valley brie; centre — Gippsland blue.

1 You will need 2 steaks weighing about 450–500 g in total. Cook and cool the salmon as directed, retaining poaching liquid. Remove skin and bones and place salmon in food processor bowl.
2 Cook onion and chilli in the butter until onion is soft. Add to salmon with lemon juice and process until smooth, adding some of the poaching liquid if necessary to facilitate processing. Turn mixture into a bowl.
3 Put the ¼ cup strained poaching liquid in a small bowl, stir in gelatine and stand in a pan of simmering water; stir until dissolved. Cool, add to salmon mixture with tomato paste and stir well. Fold in whipped cream and mayonnaise and season to taste with salt and pepper.
4 Beat egg white until stiff and fold in with a metal spoon or spatula. Turn into an oiled mould (a loaf pan or fish-shaped mould), or into individual oiled moulds. Cover with plastic film and refrigerate until set. To unmould, dip mould briefly into hot water, invert onto platter and shake until mousse is released. Serve as indicated in introduction. If serving as a main course, accompany with yoghurt mixed with chopped cucumber and a tossed salad.

Simply Salmon

How wonderful to be able to enjoy fresh Atlantic salmon Down Under! Further Down Under, in Tasmania, salmon farming is off and running — a success story if ever there was one. The beauty of this fish is that it can be prepared and served in the simplest of ways for ultimate enjoyment. You can also use this method to cook salmon as a substitute for canned red salmon.

Serves 4

4 Atlantic salmon steaks or fillets
salt
60 g butter, melted
2 tablespoons lemon or lime juice

1 If using fillets, choose fillets of even thickness and ask for skin to be removed. Lightly salt salmon and place in a single layer on a large dinner plate which will fit into a frying pan with lid to fit. You can use an electric frypan if necessary.

2 Place a round cake rack in the frying pan and add enough water to just come under the rack. Bring water to the boil with lid on pan.
3 When boiling, place plate of salmon onto rack, leaving plate itself uncovered. Put lid on pan and let salmon cook in the steam for 6 minutes for fillets, 10 minutes for steaks.
4 Meanwhile melt the butter in a small pan and beat in lemon or lime juice. Keep warm but do not let it burn.
5 Test salmon with the point of a knife — flesh should flake but still be moist. Remove salmon from pan, drain off any liquid from plate and carefully remove skin. Lift onto hot dinner plates.
6 Spoon some hot butter mixture over each serve and serve immediately. Keep accompaniments simple, such as boiled, small, whole potatoes tossed with a little butter and snipped chives and lightly cooked asparagus and/or snow peas.

Note: Sea-run trout may be cooked in the same way.

Smoked Salmon Appetiser

We now have a choice between imported smoked salmon and home-grown. As with fresh salmon, smoked salmon should be served very simply. This is a very refreshing starter reminiscent of Carpaccio, an Italian dish of paper-thin raw fillet steak; in larger serves, it makes a light summer meal.

Serves 4

12–16 slices smoked salmon, depending on size
2 medium-sized red onions
2–3 teaspoons Pickled Nasturtium Pods, page 175, or capers
Australian extra virgin olive oil
  OR Salad Oil, page 80
lemon wedges

1 Arrange salmon on four individual plates.
2 Slice onion fairly thinly and separate into rings. Discard solid inner sections on rings. Strew onion rings over salmon.
3 Sprinkle a few drained, pickled nasturtium pods (or use locally packed capers) onto each serve.
4 Put oil in an attractive oil bottle and place on table with bowl of lemon wedges and a pepper mill. Oil, lemon juice and pepper are added to individual taste.

Australian Smoked Salmon

With our own farmed Atlantic (or should that be Tasmanian) salmon, we can now enjoy locally processed smoked salmon. Not so many years ago we had to rely entirely on imports of this delicacy. There are a number of brands of smoked salmon on the market; processing is done in Tasmania as well as mainland cities. Each processor has his own secret recipe; in Tasmania, processors such as Tassal and Aquatas make use of local hardwoods to give a special aroma in the cold-smoking process; in Sydney, Mohr's uses herbs and spices in the brining process to add special flavours before smoking with aromatic woods. Try to buy the local product, even if it costs a little more than subsidised imports; its quality and 'Australian' flavour are reward enough.

Serve with warm, crusty bread rolls for mopping up the juices.

Fish Cakes

This is an alternative to fish fingers; although it is not as convenient, it helps towards reducing imports of frozen fish. You can use canned Australian salmon, tuna or poached fresh fish.

Serves 4–6

3 medium-sized potatoes
450-g can Australian salmon or tuna
  OR 1½ cups flaked, poached fish
2 tablespoons finely chopped spring onions
1 tablespoon finely chopped parsley
1 teaspoon mustard powder
1 tablespoon lemon juice
2 eggs
salt
freshly ground black pepper
flour
dried breadcrumbs
sunola oil for shallow frying

1 Peel potatoes and boil or microwave, drain and mash until smooth.
2 Drain salmon if used, remove bones and skin and flake the fish; tuna only needs to be drained. Remove bones and skin from poached fish before flaking.
3 Add to potatoes with spring onions and parsley. Mix mustard with lemon juice and add with 1 egg and salt and pepper to taste. Mix thoroughly.
4 With moistened hands, shape mixture into twelve thick patties. Coat with flour. Beat remaining egg with a little water. Dip patties, one at a time, into egg wash, then coat with breadcrumbs and place on a tray. Patties may be covered and stored in the refrigerator until required up to one day ahead.
5 Add oil to a frying pan to a depth of 5 mm. Heat and shallow fry patties for 3 minutes each side. Drain on paper towels and serve hot with lemon wedges or tartare sauce. Parsley Sauce (page 68) is also good served on the patties.

Fish Florentine

Fish Florentine is one of the popular frozen fish meals found in the supermarket freezer cabinet. Being low in fat, it is a favourite with those restricting fat intake. This version is also low in fat, but uses local fish, not imported.

Oven temperature: 180°C (350°F)

Serves 4

750 g snapper, ling or bream fillets, poached, page 88
1½ cups cooked, chopped leaf spinach
¼ teaspoon grated nutmeg
2 tablespoons lemon juice
salt
freshly ground black pepper
1 quantity Mornay Sauce, page 68
2 teaspoons grated Parmesan cheese
sprinkling of paprika

1 Poach fish as directed and cool to lukewarm in poaching liquid. Lift fish onto a plate and remove skin and bones from fish. Flake flesh into large pieces.
2 Mix the well-drained, chopped spinach with the nutmeg, lemon juice and salt and pepper to taste. Spread in the base of a shallow oven dish.
3 Place flaked fish on top of spinach. Make Mornay Sauce according to directions, using low-fat cheddar cheese, and pour over fish. Sprinkle with Parmesan cheese and dust lightly with paprika.
4 Bake in preheated oven for 20–25 minutes until heated through and top is lightly browned. Alternatively, heat in microwave oven on MEDIUM HIGH until hot, about 6–8 minutes, then brown under a hot grill. Serve hot with boiled jacket potatoes tossed with snipped chives.

TARAMOSALATA

Prepared taramosalata is a very popular dip, available at delicatessens and supermarkets. However, it is made from imported, salt-cured cod's roe, called tarama. While our tarama is imported from Greece, its tarama producers import the cod's roe from Iceland, and process it for local use and export. The genuine Greek taramosalata is made with roe from the grey mullet, but over-fishing and pollution in the Mediterranean has changed all that.
This is not so in Australia. Mullet is our second-largest fish catch after tuna, and at spawning time, the mullet roe is keenly sought by fish smokers and exporters, as it is very popular in Japan and Taiwan. Fortunately enough is brine-cured and smoked for local use — you will find the flat

sausage-shaped, amber coloured roes, sold as smoked fish roe, at better fishmongers. It is delicious to eat as it is, thinly sliced on buttered bread with a squeeze of lemon.

To make the taramosalata, remove the fine membrane from 100 g of smoked fish roe and slice thinly. Place in food processor bowl with 100 g stale, crustless white bread, previously soaked in cold water and squeezed dry. Add ½ small onion, 1 chopped clove garlic, some freshly ground pepper and 2 tablespoons lemon juice. Break in an egg and process to a smooth paste. With motor running, pour in ½ cup Salad Oil (page 80). when thick and creamy, transfer to a bowl, cover and chill. Serve with savoury biscuits, crusty bread or crisp vegetable pieces.

Grilled Fish with Fresh Mango Relish

Choose a moist, white-fleshed fish available in your area: barramundi, dhu fish, blue-eye cod or trevally, flathead and snapper are some. Fish fillets can look pale and uninteresting when cooked under the domestic griller; the light flour coating and paprika help to give the fish colour. Most of the butter drains off after grilling, but it is necessary for browning.

Serves 4

4 thick fish fillets
2 tablespoons flour
½ teaspoon salt
freshly ground black pepper
½ teaspoon paprika
3 tablespoons melted butter

Fresh Mango Relish
2 mangoes
½ teaspoon chopped fresh chilli or to taste
1 tablespoon finely chopped spring onion
1 teaspoon finely chopped fresh ginger
1 tablespoon finely chopped fresh coriander
grated rind of 1 lime or ½ lemon
1 tablespoon lime or lemon juice

1 Remove skin from fillets if necessary. Mix flour, salt, pepper and paprika in a dish and coat fillets with flour, shaking off excess.
2 Brush a baking tray with butter, add fish with flat side of fillet facing upwards, and brush with the melted butter. Cook under a very hot grill for 2 minutes, turn fish carefully, brush again with butter and grill for further 3–5 minutes until golden brown and cooked through — test with the point of a knife.
3 Lift onto warm plates and serve with mango relish on the side, lime or lemon wedges and vegetables of choice.

Fresh Mango Relish: Peel and slice mangoes and dice flesh. Place in a bowl, add remaining ingredients and toss lightly to mix. Stand for 20 minutes to blend flavours. Serve as above or with any pan-fried, grilled or barbecued fish.

Using Australian Seafoods

Microwave Fish Fillets with Avocado Sauce

Serves 4

4 thick white fish fillets, about 750 g in total
lime or lemon juice
Mexican-style chilli powder
1 tablespoon canola or peanut oil
1 quantity Avocado Sauce, page 148

1 Select fillets of fish available in your area, such as snapper, bream, ling, silver warehou, dhu fish or barramundi. Wipe dry with paper towels and place in a greased microsafe dish, with thicker section towards outside edge of dish. If fillets have a thin 'tail', tuck this underneath.
2 Sprinkle with lime or lemon juice and a light dusting of chilli powder (the mixture of spices used for Chilli Con Carne, not hot chilli powder).
3 Drizzle on oil, cover dish with plastic wrap and cook on MEDIUM HIGH for 6–8 minutes until just cooked. Test at thickest part — flesh should flake with a little resistance. Stand 2 minutes then remove to warm plates.
4 Serve hot with some of the Avocado Sauce spooned on top of each fillet, with remainder served in a sauce boat. Accompany with vegetables or salad of choice.

Sardines with Tomato Sauce

This is a little like the imported canned sardines in tomato sauce, but tastier. Make the tomato sauce or use a commercial pasta sauce.

Serves 6 as an entree, 4 as a meal

750 g fresh sardines
salt
freshly ground black pepper
3 tablespoons Salad Oil, page 80
1½ cups Tomato Pasta Sauce, page 136
1 cup coarse, soft breadcrumbs

1 Rub fine scales from sardines with fingers and rinse under running water. Slit from body cavity to tail and remove guts with fingers. Snip or pinch backbone away from tail, pull towards head and snip off. Rinse and close up fish.
2 Place on oiled grill tray, season with salt and pepper and brush with some of the oil blend. Cook under a hot grill for about 3 minutes each side until lightly browned and crisp — fish is oily and grills easily.

SEAFOOD STORAGE

Good storage depends on proper handling from the time the seafood is obtained, either what you have caught yourself, or what you have purchased. Have a portable insulated container with ice or frozen 'bricks' on hand for storing your 'catch' for the trip home, particularly if the weather is hot. Thick newspaper wrapping is a good, short-term measure for keeping the seafood cool.
Live crustaceans (e.g. lobster, crab, Balmain or Moreton Bay bugs and yabbies), and shellfish should be placed in a damp hessian bag, or in a sealed bucket of seawater or fresh water, depending on source of catch.

Fish Storage
Only very fresh fish should be stored. Scale,

gut, remove gills, rinse well and dry with paper towels. Leave whole, fillet or slice into cutlets. Place on a plate and cover completely with plastic wrap, securing wrap underneath plate, or store in a sealed container. Refrigerate for up to three days.

For freezer storage, leave scales on whole fish for added protection, or remove before storage to save time when fish is required for cooking. Snip off sharp dorsal fins to prevent puncturing wrap. Wrap whole fish, fillets or cutlets individually in plastic film, place in freezer bag and press out excess air. Seal and label. Store oily fish for no more than three months, other fish for up to six months.

3 Spread tomato sauce in the base of a shallow oven dish and place sardines on top. Toss breadcrumbs with remaining oil and sprinkle on top of sardines. Cook in preheated moderately hot oven for 15 minutes until crumbs are lightly browned and sauce begins to bubble. Serve hot as an entree or light meal.

Blue-Eye Cod Steaks with Orange Butter

Blue-eye cod is known as trevally in Tasmania. It is a fabulous fish: white, sweet and moist.

Serves 6

6 blue-eye cod cutlets
canola oil
salt
freshly ground black pepper
4–5 fresh sprigs rosemary, rinsed

Orange Butter
250 g butter
2 cloves garlic, chopped
1 tablespoon fresh rosemary leaves
thinly peeled strip of orange rind
¼ cup fresh orange juice
1 tablespoon cider vinegar
freshly ground black pepper

1 Dry cod cutlets with paper towels. Brush each side with oil and season with salt and pepper.
2 Before placing cutlets on barbecue, put damp rosemary sprigs on coals, or lava rock if using gas barbecue.
3 When sprigs begin to give off smoke, place fish on grid and cook over glowing coals for 3–4 minutes each side until fish is just firm and turns white. Brush with oil during cooking and take care when turning. Serve immediately with a portion of Orange Butter placed on each cutlet.

Orange Butter: Put butter, garlic, rosemary leaves and orange rind in food processor and process until creamy, with garlic, rosemary and orange rind very finely chopped. With motor running, add orange juice, vinegar and a grinding of pepper. Turn into a butter crock, smooth top, cover and chill until required.

Note: Other fish cutlets or thick fillets may be cooked and served in the same way; try barramundi, ling, snapper or dhu fish.

Using Australian Seafoods • 95

Barbecued Honey Prawn Skewers

Serves 6

1.5 kg large green prawns
2 teaspoons grated fresh ginger
2 cloves garlic, crushed
2 tablespoons honey
½ teaspoon grated lemon rind
¼ cup soy sauce
¼ cup lemon juice
2 tablespoons peanut oil
freshly ground black pepper

1 Shell prawns, leaving tail intact. Devein, rinse and drain well. Thread onto 6 bamboo skewers.
2 Mix remaining ingredients in a square or rectangular plastic container which will take length of skewers. Add prawn skewers and turn in marinade. Seal container and marinate in refrigerator for 3–4 hours or overnight, shaking container occasionally to distribute marinade.
3 When required for cooking, drain marinade in a small pan and put on to heat on side of barbecue. Barbecue the prawns over glowing coals for about 3 minutes until prawns turn pink. Turn during cooking and baste with marinade. Serve hot with any remaining, well-heated marinade poured over the prawns.

Note: Prawns may be grilled; heat marinade on stove and bring any remaining marinade to the boil before pouring over prawns.

Curried Prawns

Serves 4–5

1 kg small whole prawns
3 tablespoons butter
1 medium-sized onion, chopped
½ cup chopped celery
½ cup thinly sliced carrot
1 tablespoon curry powder or to taste
4 tablespoons flour
2½ cups chicken stock
salt
1 tablespoon lemon juice
¼ cup cream

1 Shell prawns and devein if necessary. Keep aside.
2 Melt butter in a saucepan and add onion, celery and carrot. Cook gently, stirring occasionally, until onion is soft. Stir in curry powder, cook for 1 minute, then stir in flour.

STORING CRUSTACEANS

Green (uncooked) crustaceans (lobster, crab, bugs, yabbies) should be live when you take delivery of them; once dead, their flesh deteriorates very quickly. Keep in a damp hessian bag in a cool place for up to two days, as this allows more oxygen than storing in a bucket of water. Store cooked crustaceans in a covered container in refrigerator for up to three days, or in freezer, suitably wrapped, for up to three months. Unshelled green prawns are seldom purchased live; place in a bowl of iced water, cover and store in the refrigerator for up to three days; put shelled green prawns in a bowl, cover, refrigerate and use within two days. Cooked prawns are also better stored in the shell; even if shelled, store in a covered container in refrigerator for up to three days. For freezer storage, whether green or cooked, leave prawns in the shell, place in a freezer container and cover with iced water, leaving headspace. Seal and store in freezer for up to three months.

STORING MUSSELS AND OYSTERS

If still in the shell, these should not be stored in the refrigerator as the cold will kill them. Store as follows.

Mussels: store in damp hessian bag, in bucket of fresh water, salted water or seawater, or in a bowl covered with a wet cloth. Leave in a cool place for up to three days.

Oysters: store unopened oysters in a damp hessian bag in a cool place for up to one week.

Cover oysters on half shell with greaseproof paper and top with a wet cloth; store in refrigerator for up to two days, replacing wet cloth when necessary. Bottled oysters in their liquor will keep for seven to ten days in refrigerator.

3 Increase heat, pour in stock and stir constantly until thickened and bubbling. Add salt to taste.

4 Reduce heat, cover and simmer gently for 5 minutes until vegetables are tender. Stir occasionally to prevent sauce sticking to base of pan.

5 Add prawns, lemon juice and cream and cook gently until prawns are heated. Do not allow curry to boil or prawns could toughen. Serve hot with boiled rice.

Preparing Fresh Squid

To be certain your squid is locally caught, purchase it whole and prepare it. Choose squid with medium-sized hoods, not too large and not too small, if you require them for preparing rings. You can tell by looking at them just how large the finished rings will be. The following will help you to prepare squid for use in recipes from other cookbooks, as well as those in this book.

1 Pull off head and attached tentacles; the gut should also come away from the body (hood). Discard gut.

2 Cut off section of head containing eyes and beak and discard. You will be left with the hood and the tentacles joined together with a section of the head.

3 Pull out quill-shaped bone from the hood cavity and pull off fine purple skin to expose the white body. Skin may be rubbed off the tentacles if desired — use a cloth dipped in salt.

4 Rinse in cold water and drain.

For **stuffing:** Leave hood intact with flaps attached.

For **squid rings:** Remove flaps and slice hood into 6-mm thick rings.

For **strips:** Slice hood and flaps into strips according to recipes.

Tentacles: Chop tentacles or leave intact as required — intact tentacles from small squid make an interesting garnish as they curl up into rosettes during cooking.

If you are left with bits and pieces of edible squid after preparation, pack in a freezer bag and freeze for later use.

Using Australian Seafoods • 97

Fried Calamari

How tastes have changed! There was a day when squid was only used as bait; now we import to keep up with demand. This recipe does not require exact quantities; fry as many or as few as you need, but remember that squid can toughen into something resembling elastic bands if overcooked. This is a dish that should be cooked and served immediately — don't reheat it.

squid rings, page 97
canola or sunflower oil for shallow frying
flour
salt
lemon wedges for serving

1 Prepare squid rings as directed. Dry with paper towels.
2 Heat vegetable oil in a large frying pan until very hot. Only add oil to a depth of about 7 mm.
3 Put about 2 tablespoons flour in a plastic bag and add a handful of squid rings (enough to cover base of frying pan). Shake well and tip into a sieve set over paper. Shake off excess flour.
4 Tip squid into hot oil and spread over base of pan. Fry for a minute or so, then toss in the hot oil and fry until lightly browned — no more than 3 minutes. Lift out and drain on paper towels. Repeat with more squid, flouring just before frying.
5 Pile onto a hot serving dish, season with salt and squeeze on lemon juice. Serve immediately.

Mango Seafood Salad

Mango and seafood were made for each other, but then mango marries well with so many foods.

Serves 4

125 g small squid rings, see page 97
125 g shelled scallops
12 large cooked prawns
2 ripe mangoes
coriander sprigs and lemon or lime slices to garnish

Coconut Cream Dressing
½ cup coconut cream
½ cup sour cream
½ teaspoon grated lemon or lime rind
1 tablespoon lemon or lime juice
2 teaspoons finely chopped fresh coriander
salt to taste

STORING SCALLOPS, ETC.

Scallops, cockles and pipis can stay alive in the refrigerator if carefully stored. Scallops are also available already shelled; check that they have not been frozen if you plan to store them in the freezer.
Chilled storage: place the live shellfish in a colander and put this in a larger bowl. Cover top of shellfish with a wet cloth and store in refrigerator for up to two days, replacing wet cloth when necessary. Put fresh scallop meat in an airtight container, seal and store in refrigerator for up to three days.
Freezer storage: all should be removed from their shells for freezer storage. Place in freezer containers in meal-size portions, seal, label and store for up to three months.

Storing Smoked Fish

Any smoked fish should not be stored covered or wrapped in plastic as it sweats and deteriorates. Wrap in greaseproof paper, then overwrap in foil. This allows a certain amount of oxygen into the package, but gives sufficient protection to prevent drying. Store in refrigerator for up to ten days. If fish is vacuum-packed in plastic, leave unopened and go by the use-by date for length of storage.

1 Prepare squid rings as directed. Remove dark veins from scallops, retain coral. Rinse and drain.

2 Bring about 2 cups water to the boil, drop in squid rings and scallops and simmer gently for 1½ minutes — do not boil.

3 Drain in a colander, run cold water briefly over seafood, drain well and place in a bowl. Cover and chill.

4 Shell prawns, leaving tails in place, and devein. Rinse and dry with kitchen paper. Cover and chill until needed.

5 To serve salad, wipe mango skins with a damp cloth. Cut a thick slice from each side of the seed, as close to the seed as possible. Score flesh into 2-cm squares, cutting to, but not through, the skin. Press from the underside to open out mango.

6 Combine chilled seafoods in a bowl, add Coconut Cream Dressing and toss lightly. Divide onto 4 plates, place mango on one side and garnish with coriander and lemon or lime slices.

Coconut Cream Dressing: Open can of coconut milk, cover with plastic and leave in refrigerator for 2–3 hours undisturbed. Carefully spoon off ½ cup of the thicker milk which should have risen to the top on standing (freeze remainder to use in curries). Mix with remaining dressing ingredients.

Meat and Poultry

These are the foods that help us to eat within our means. Australia is an efficient producer of meats and poultry for local use and export. The cost of these items and the food value they contribute to the Australian diet make them essential to lowering our food import costs. It is all very well to recommend pulses as meat substitutes, which they are, but we are not yet self-sufficient in these foods. The same goes for including more fish in the diet — import figures for seafoods clearly show we must cut down on these imports and rely more on local products, even if it means reducing consumption.

In spite of being efficient meat and poultry producers, we still manage to import some $32 million worth of meat and poultry, a third of this in pork imports, the remainder mostly in processed products.

Because of recent developments in the marketing of all meats, with suppliers value-adding so that meats and poultry can simply be cooked with no extra preparation, even the busy cook can prepare meat and poultry dishes quickly and easily. However, the consumer pays a premium for such convenience. Many of the recipes given can help you put meat and poultry on the table with a minimum of fuss. Others are part of our heritage and should be retained rather than discarded.

More importantly, the beef, lamb and pork producers have answered the call to change their products, making them leaner and healthier by breeding leaner animals. Butchering has also changed to provide meat cuts trimmed of fat. There is little excuse for removing meats, particularly red meats, from the Australian diet.

Buyer's Guide
CHOOSING AUSTRALIAN MEAT AND POULTRY

Product	Australian-produced	Imported	What we can do
BEEF AND VEAL Fresh and frozen	Yes, fresh beef in abundance; veal supplies adequate for needs	Yes, some $8 million worth fresh and frozen; some used in manufacturing	Difficult for consumer to tell if beef is local or imported, but amount imported is small compared to total beef sales.
Processed — corned fresh and canned, brawns, smallgoods	Yes, ample for needs and any type required	Yes, some $5 million worth	Check labels of canned corned meats and other meat products.
LAMB AND MUTTON Fresh and frozen	Yes, fresh in abundance	Yes, very little frozen	Use more lamb in our diet; trim lamb excellent for low-fat and easy-to-cook meals.
PORK Fresh and frozen	Yes, fresh in abundance; new-fashioned pork excellent	Yes, see next item	Use more pork in our diet. See next item re processed pork.
Processed — ham, fresh or canned; bacon; other processed pork products; smallgoods	Yes, abundant supply of cured pork meats and smallgoods	Yes, some $11 million worth, mostly frozen, for processing	Check labels on packs and cans. Difficult to tell if ham or bacon made from local or imported meat. Buy from butcher or supermarkets promoting Australian products.
POULTRY Fresh and frozen	Yes, abundant supply	No	Improved poultry retailing has made chicken easier to prepare and cook.
Processed — poultry and livers, etc. in cans, jars, etc.	Yes, in abundance in fresh form, not canned	Yes, some $2 million worth	Buy fresh pâtés, terrines and smallgoods; avoid imported products.

Recipes
USING AUSTRALIAN MEATS AND POULTRY

Roast Lamb Dinner
This still ranks as Australia's favourite dish. However, this version is for today's cook — it contains less fat than the norm, but is full of flavour.

Oven temperature: 180°C (350°F)

Serves 6

1 leg lamb, about 2 kg
juice of ½ lemon
salt
freshly ground pepper
water
potatoes, pumpkin, carrots, parsnips for baking
1 tablespoon oil
green peas, beans or Brussels sprouts
1 chicken stock cube
1½ tablespoons plain flour
mint sauce or jelly for serving

1 Wipe lamb with paper towels, place in roasting dish, rub all over with lemon juice, salt and pepper. Add one cup water to dish. Cook in a moderate oven for 2 hours, turning leg occasionally. When water evaporates and juices brown, add a little more water to dish to prevent scorching.
2 Meanwhile, prepare 2 or 3 of the vegetables for baking, cutting them in even-sized pieces. Place in a bowl, pour on oil and toss to coat. Place on a rack set in another baking dish. After lamb has cooked for 1 hour, put vegetables in oven on shelf above lamb; turn during cooking to brown evenly. Vegetables and lamb should complete cooking together.
3 When cooked, remove lamb to a platter, cover with foil and leave in a warm place for 15 minutes. Keep vegetables hot in oven. Put green vegetable on to cook.
4 Drain off fat from roasting dish, add 1 cup hot water and stock cube. Stir well to dissolve juices and strain into a small saucepan placed over medium heat.
5 Put about ⅓ cup water in a jar, add flour and shake well to make a smooth paste. Stir gradually into pan contents and keep stirring until thickened and bubbling.

Simmer 2 minutes and strain into gravy boat. Carve lamb and serve on hot plates with vegetables, gravy and mint sauce or jelly.

Note: Other lamb roasting joints may be cooked in the same way; boned, rolled leg, loin, shoulder or forequarter with or without stuffing. Allow about 30 minutes cooking per 500 g.

Honey-glazed Lamb Racks
Oven temperature: 190°C (375°F)

Serves 6

3 lamb racks, each with 6 ribs
¼ cup honey
¼ cup lemon juice
¼ cup dry white wine
freshly ground pepper
1 tablespoon fresh rosemary leaves
additional ½ cup dry white wine
½ cup light stock

1 Trim fat from racks, leaving a thin covering. Cut each rack in half to give individual racks of 3 ribs. Score fat into diamonds.
2 Mix honey with lemon juice and wine in a plastic container. Add racks, seal container and shake well to coat with marinade. Refrigerate for at least 2 hours or overnight, shaking container occasionally.
3 Remove racks from marinade, place fat side up in a roasting dish and sprinkle lamb with pepper and rosemary. Pour additional wine and stock into dish and cook lamb in a moderately hot oven for 45 minutes, basting occasionally with honey marinade. Remove lamb to a warm platter, cover and keep warm.
4 Skim fat from dish juices and add any remaining marinade. Place over heat and stir well to lift browned sediment. Bring to the boil and thicken if desired with a cornflour-and-water paste. Adjust seasoning and strain into sauce boat. Serve the racks with the sauce and vegetables of choice.

Keep Meat and Poultry Cool

On a warm or hot day, don't leave meat or poultry purchases in the car while you make a few more calls at other shops. Either take along a portable cooler with frozen 'bricks' and place purchases in this, or make your purchases just before completing your shopping trip. Decide what meat or poultry you will need for the next two to three days and store in the meat drawer of the refrigerator. Package remainder and store in the freezer. Packaged meat and poultry from the supermarket can be left in its tray packaging, placed in a freezer bag and frozen.

Lamb with Orange and Mint Jelly

Here is another quick-to-put-together meat dish. Use the cheaper lamb cuts for economy.

Oven temperature: 160–180°C (325–350°F)

Serves 4

1 kg lamb shoulder, forequarter or best neck chops
2 tablespoons seasoned flour
grated rind of 1 orange
juice of 2 oranges
½ cup chicken stock
2 tablespoons mint jelly
1 teaspoon prepared English mustard

1 Trim fat from chops and coat meat with seasoned flour. Place in a casserole dish.
2 Mix remaining ingredients and pour over chops. Cover and cook in a moderate oven for 1½ hours until tender.
3 When lamb is cooked, skim off any fat and serve with jacket-baked potatoes and a green vegetable.

Curry Crumbed Cutlets

Serves 4–5

8–10 lamb cutlets
2 tablespoons flour
salt
2 teaspoons curry powder
grated rind of 1 lemon
1 egg
2 tablespoons milk
dried breadcrumbs
oil for shallow frying
lemon wedges and fruit chutney for serving

1 Trim cutlets and flatten if necessary. Mix flour with salt to taste, curry powder and lemon rind. Beat egg with milk in a shallow dish.
2 Coat cutlets with seasoned flour mixture, dip into beaten egg, then coat with breadcrumbs, pressing them on firmly. Place on a tray and chill for 15 minutes or so.
3 Heat about ¼ cup oil in a large frying pan and shallow fry cutlets for 3 minutes each side until golden brown and crisp. Drain on absorbent paper. Serve garnished with lemon wedges and provide a bowl of fruit chutney.

IRON FOR GOOD HEALTH

One of the most important minerals in a balanced diet is iron. Unfortunately the human body is not very efficient at absorbing iron, particularly from plant sources such as green vegetables, cereals and pulses. For continued good health and well-being, we need to maintain an adequate intake of iron. Women of child-bearing age, particularly, need to look at their intake of iron-containing foods, as there is an increase of the incidence of anemia amongst this group.
If following a vegetarian diet, eat pulses and plenty of green, leafy vegetables, and include a source of vitamin C, such as tomato, green or red pepper or citrus, in a meal containing any of those foods.
Vitamin C helps the body absorb more of the iron contained in the food. If, at the same meal, a very small piece of red meat is eaten, the body absorbs even more iron from the plant sources.
Iron from animal sources (haem iron) is more easily

absorbed by the body; it is unfortunate that the bad press given to red meat (based on American findings at a time when their beef was very high in saturated fats), still affects our attitudes to this valuable food.

The only drawback was red meat's saturated fat content; this has been considerably reduced in Australian meat in recent years. In fact, lean beef, lamb, veal and pork have similar fat and cholesterol levels to skinless chicken; the advantage of red meat is that it contains much more iron, particularly lean beef. For example, 100 grams of lean, grilled rump steak has 3.9 milligrams of iron, whereas a similar amount of grilled skinless chicken has .9 milligrams. For vegetarians, 100 grams of cooked (canned) red kidney beans contains 2.1 milligrams of iron, but it is not absorbed as well. From mid-teens to the age of 54, women need a daily intake of 12–16 milligrams of iron. Are you getting enough?

Lamb and Spinach Pie

Oven temperature: 190°C (375°F)

Serves 6

1 tablespoon oil
1 white onion, finely chopped
500 g minced lamb
¾ cup ricotta or cottage cheese
1 cup peeled, chopped tomatoes
1½ cups cooked, well-drained chopped spinach
2 tablespoons chopped parsley
¼ teaspoon ground nutmeg
salt
freshly ground pepper
2 eggs
8 sheets fillo pastry, page 17
2–3 tablespoons melted butter

1 Heat oil in a heavy frying pan, add onion and cook gently until soft.
2 Increase heat, add lamb and cook on high heat, stirring often to break up lumps. When juices evaporate and lamb is browned, remove to a bowl with a draining spoon and discard excess fat.
3 If using ricotta cheese, mash with a fork; add cheese to lamb with tomatoes, spinach, parsley, nutmeg, salt and pepper to taste. Beat eggs and mix in.
4 Lightly grease a lamington pan or oven dish of similar size. Line with 2 sheets fillo pastry and brush top with melted butter. Top with another 2 sheets fillo, brush with butter and spread filling in dish.
5 Top with remaining 4 sheets of fillo, brushing each second sheet with butter. Trim edges of fillo level with top of dish.
6 Brush top with butter and score lightly into 6 squares with a sharp knife. Sprinkle top with water to prevent pastry curling and bake in preheated oven 35–40 minutes or until puffed and golden. Cut into squares and serve hot with a tossed salad.

Middle Eastern Kebabs

Serves 6

750g boneless lamb from leg
½ cup lemon juice
1 tablespoon chopped fresh oregano
1 tablespoon finely chopped parsley
2 crumbled bay leaves
1 chopped onion
¼ cup olive oil
freshly ground pepper

For serving
pita breads
cos lettuce leaves
Tabouli (page 168)
Yoghurt and Cucumber Sauce (page 70), optional

1 Trim lamb and cut into 2-cm cubes. Place in a bowl with lemon juice, herbs, onion, oil and pepper to taste. Stir well, cover and marinate in refrigerator for 2 hours at least or overnight, stirring occasionally.
2 Thread lamb onto 6 skewers and grill or barbecue, basting frequently with marinade. Cook to pink stage — meat should feel fairly springy when pressed; if preferred well done, do not overcook or lamb will toughen. Slide lamb cubes off skewers on to a warm dish.
3 Place cos lettuce leaves and Tabouli on warmed pita breads and top with lamb cubes. Add some Yoghurt and Cucumber Sauce if desired, and roll up for eating.

Roast Stuffed Topside

Oven temperature: 180°C (350°F)

Serves 6

1 topside roast, about 1.5 kg
salt
freshly ground black pepper
oil
1 cup water or stock

Herb Stuffing
1 small onion, finely chopped
1 tablespoon butter
1 cup soft breadcrumbs
1 tablespoon chopped parsley
1 teaspoon chopped fresh thyme leaves
1 teaspoon chopped fresh marjoram
salt
freshly ground black pepper
beaten egg to bind

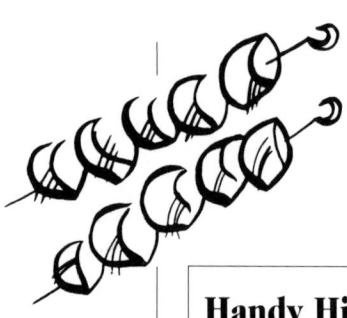

Handy Hint

When coating meat or chicken with flour, seasoned or otherwise, don't hold bag in one hand and shake up and down. Some plastic bags can easily burst from the weight. Hold neck of bag closed with one hand and bounce bag back and forth between hands. Chops with sharp bones are best coated in flour placed in a dish as the bones could tear the bag.

1 Have butcher cut a pocket in the topside, or cut one yourself in the following way. Cut a thin slice at the narrow meaty end of the topside, but do not cut all the way down — this flap must be attached at the base. Cut a deep pocket into the meat. The flap is used later to hold in the stuffing.

2 Prepare stuffing and insert into pocket. Lift flap over the opening and fasten end to top of roast with a poultry skewer. Season roast with salt and pepper and brush with a little oil. Place roast on a rack in a roasting dish and cook in a moderate oven for 1¼ hours for medium beef.

3 Remove to carving platter, cover with foil and leave in a warm place for 15 minutes. Drain fat from dish and dissolve juices with stock. Boil, thicken if desired, and serve with the sliced beef. Baked vegetables (see Roast Lamb Dinner, page 102) and a green vegetable are traditional accompaniments.

Herb Stuffing: Cook onion in butter until soft. Add to breadcrumbs with herbs, and season to taste with salt and pepper. Add enough beaten egg to bind stuffing, mixing it in lightly.

Steak Diane

This has been a favourite with Australian restaurant diners for decades. We tend to forget these old-timers, but this one is well worth remembering.

Serves 2

2 fillet steaks about 3 cm thick
freshly ground pepper
2 tablespoons butter
2 teaspoons Worcestershire sauce
2 cloves garlic, finely chopped
2 tablespoons chopped parsley

1 Flatten each steak between two pieces plastic film until very thin. Season steaks with pepper. Have remaining ingredients prepared and on hand.

2 Heat butter in a large frying pan and when foam subsides add Worcestershire sauce, then add steaks. Cook on high heat for 1 minute, sprinkle garlic and parsley over the steaks, then turn them and cook for another minute.

3 Remove steaks to two warm plates and pour butter and garlic mixture from pan over steaks. Serve immediately with steamed asparagus or zucchini, glazed carrot straws and boiled new potatoes tossed with chives.

Beef and Onion Skewers
Serves 6

1 kg thickly sliced rump steak
2 medium-sized onions

Red Wine Marinade:
2 sprigs fresh rosemary
½ cup red wine
2 bay leaves, broken in pieces
2 tablespoons canola or sunflower oil
freshly ground black pepper

1 Trim steak and cut in 3-cm cubes. Cut onions into quarters, remove roots and separate into leaves. Thread beef cubes alternately with onion leaves on previously soaked bamboo skewers.

2 In a plastic container long enough to take skewers, add filled skewers and marinade. Seal container and shake well to distribute marinade. Leave at room temperature for 1 hour, shaking container occasionally, or refrigerate for several hours, giving the container an occasional shake.

3 Barbecue over glowing coals, turning and brushing occasionally with marinade. Serve hot with salads.

Red Wine Marinade: Bruise rosemary sprigs by beating gently with a rolling pin or the side of a meat mallet. Add to remaining ingredients and pour over beef.

Quick Beef Casserole

This is quick to put together, but slow to cook, which gives it a delicious, beefy flavour. It is a recipe for the person with a second job outside the home, who needs to save time on meal preparation. As it is a casserole, cook it at night or over the weekend, store in the refrigerator and reheat when required. You can ring all sorts of changes to present it differently.

Oven temperature: 160°C (325°F)

Serves 5–6 for two meals

2 kg chuck or boneless blade steak, cubed
½ cup seasoned flour
2 large onions, chopped
1 tablespoon oil
2 carrots, cut in chunks

Preparing Meat with Care

Have a chopping board of a non-porous, man-made material (not wood), especially for preparing fresh meat and chicken (and fish for that matter). Immediately after use, the board, as well as knives, should be washed separately in hot suds. Or wash in the dishwasher where the temperature of the water is sufficiently high to destroy bacteria. Be particularly careful when preparing pet's meat as this can contain a high level of micro-organisms potentially harmful to humans.

Storing Stews and Casseroles

....

Stews and casseroles cooked a day or two before required should be cooled for no more than an hour before storing in a sealed container or casserole dish in the refrigerator. If you can't wait that long, place the hot food in the refrigerator — modern units can cope quite well with the heat. Just make sure that the hot food is not close to dairy foods or seafoods. For longer storage of stews and casseroles, package in containers, leaving headroom for expansion, seal and freeze.

3 tablespoons chopped parsley
3 beef stock cubes, crumbled
1 teaspoon sugar
1 teaspoon Parisian essence
1 tablespoon Worcestershire sauce
1½ cups water

1 Have butcher chop the meat into cubes to save time, asking him to first trim off any fat. Or buy cubed stewing steak from the supermarket meat section.
2 Coat meat in seasoned flour and place in a large casserole dish.
3 In a frying pan, cook onion gently in oil until soft to enhance the flavour of the onion. Add to meat with carrots and parsley. Toss with a wooden spoon to mix ingredients. Stir stock cubes, sugar, Parisian essence and Worcestershire sauce into the water and pour over casserole contents.
4 Cover and cook in a moderately slow oven for 2 hours until meat is tender. Serve up half the casserole with creamy mashed potatoes and a green vegetable, and refrigerate remainder. Or cool and store in refrigerator for up to 4 days. Remove fat from top before reheating.

Variations

Beef Pie

Use half quantity of the cooked casserole and place in a deep pie dish. Place a pastry funnel or inverted china egg cup in the centre. Top with shortcrust or puff pastry and brush with milk. Cut a vent in the centre of the pastry. Bake in a hot oven, 210°C (425°F) for 10 minutes, reduce to moderate and cook for further 25 minutes until meat filling shows signs of bubbling.

Beef Stroganoff

If you are planning to use this recipe when reheating leftover casserole, serve all the carrots the first time round. Melt 1 tablespoon butter in a saucepan, add 1½ cups sliced mushrooms and cook gently until limp, stirring often. Add leftover casserole, stir and heat gently until bubbling. Stir in ½ cup light sour cream and serve with boiled noodles or rice and a green vegetable.

Using Australian Meat and Poultry

Beef in Red Wine

This is a quick way to make the popular Boeuf Bourguignonne (Beef in Burgundy). Use a claret or other full-bodied Australian red wine. This takes about 10 minutes to put together; the oven or slow cooker does the rest while you get on with more interesting things. The amount is generous as this dish is very good for entertaining.

Oven temperature: 150–160°C (300–325°F)

Serves 6–8

1.5 kg chuck steak or shin (gravy) beef, cubed
1/3 cup seasoned flour
4 medium-sized onions, quartered
3 bacon rashers, chopped
125 g small mushrooms, trimmed
bunch of flavouring herbs, page 167
1 teaspoon sugar
1 tablespoon tomato paste
1 1/4 cups claret or other full-bodied red wine

1 To save time, ask butcher to trim and cube the meat for you. Put seasoned flour into a plastic bag, add beef and shake well to coat.
2 Tip meat into a colander, shake off excess flour over sink, then turn meat into an 8-cup casserole dish or crockpot.
3 Add quartered onions, bacon and mushrooms, mix lightly to distribute ingredients. Push bouquet of herbs into the centre of the contents.
4 Mix remaining ingredients and pour into dish. Cover and cook in a moderately slow oven for 2 1/2–3 hours, depending on meat used. For crockpot, cook on LOW for 7–8 hours.
5 Remove bunch of herbs, wipe edge of dish and sprinkle with chopped parsley. Serve with jacket-baked or boiled potatoes and cooked green beans or broccoli.

Variation

Chicken in Red Wine

Replace beef with 2 kg chicken casserole pieces. Prepare as above, using a little more seasoned flour if necessary. Add an extra 1/4 cup red wine and cook for 1 1/2 hours in oven or 7–8 hours in crockpot.

Sharp Steak

This is an old stand-by recipe, used by Australian cooks for many years. It takes minutes to put together; it might take a while to cook, but you can do lots of other jobs in the meantime, or simply relax.

Cut 1 kg boneless blade steak into serving portions and coat with seasoned flour. In a casserole dish, mix together 1 tablespoon each brown sugar, malt vinegar, tomato sauce and Worcestershire sauce and stir in 3/4 cup water. Add floured steak, spoon liquid over to moisten, cover and cook in a moderately slow oven, 160°C (325°F), for 1 1/2 hours or until tender. Serve with jacket-baked potatoes cooked alongside the casserole, and other vegetables of choice.

Storing Smallgoods

....

Ham, corned beef, sliced sausage meats, salamis, bacon and so on are often stored in plastic film. This causes the meats to sweat and spoil. For longer and safer storage, wrap in greaseproof paper and overwrap with foil. Most meats keep well for five to six days in the refrigerator; bacon can be stored for up to two weeks.

By the way, when purchasing vacuum-packed smallgoods, check package and make sure that the plastic clings tightly to the food. If it is loose, air has entered and the food could be spoiled. Once food is removed from vacuum packaging, any left over should be stored as above.

Corned Beef Dinner

Old-fashioned it might be, but hot corned beef with parsley sauce is one of those comfort foods we remember in moments of nostalgia. Leftover meat, in the time-honoured tradition, is served with salad or in sandwiches.

Serves 6 with meat left over

1 piece corned silverside, about 2 kg
1 onion, quartered
½ teaspoon whole peppercorns
1 carrot, quartered
1 stick celery, cut in pieces
1 bay leaf
6 small whole carrots
6 small whole onions
6–8 medium potatoes
6–8 cabbage wedges
Parsley Sauce, page 68

1 Rinse beef in cold water and place in a large saucepan with onion, peppercorns, carrot, celery and bay leaf. Cover with warm water. Bring slowly to the boil, skimming when necessary. Cover and simmer for 1½ hours.

2 Add whole carrots and onions, with root end of onions cross cut to prevent centres popping. Cover and simmer for 15 minutes, add potatoes and cook for further 20 minutes.

3 Prepare cabbage so that each wedge has some core attached. Place on top of pan contents, cover and cook 10 minutes longer or until vegetables are tender. Remove vegetables to a platter and keep hot. Leave beef in water for 10 minutes before carving. Serve beef and vegetables with Parsley Sauce.

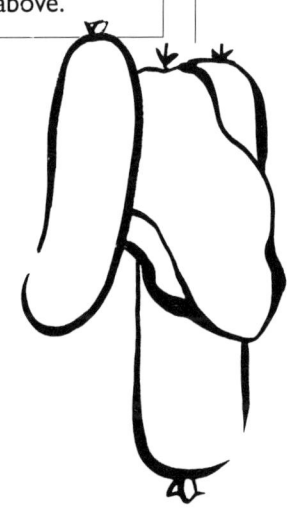

Using Australian Meat and Poultry

Italian Meat Sauce

Makes about 5 cups

1 large onion, finely chopped
2 cloves garlic, crushed
2 tablespoons canola or sunflower oil
1 cup chopped fresh mushrooms (optional)
750 g minced lean beef
2 x 425-g cans tomatoes, crushed
½ cup tomato paste
½ cup red wine
½ cup water
1 tablespoon chopped fresh basil or ½ teaspoon dried
2 tablespoons chopped parsley
2 teaspoons sugar
1 teaspoon salt
freshly ground black pepper

1 In a large frying pan with a lid to fit, cook onion and garlic gently in oil until onion is soft. Add mushrooms if used and cook for further 3–4 minutes.
2 Increase heat, add minced beef and cook, stirring often to break up lumps. When meat loses red colour, add remaining ingredients.
3 Cover and simmer gently for 20–25 minutes until thick. Serve over boiled spaghetti with grated Parmesan cheese, or use as directed in recipes. Leftover sauce may be stored in a sealed container in refrigerator for 4–5 days, or frozen.

Lasagne

This is another of those recipes that has become naturalised in the Australian kitchen. Remember when you tried to make it years ago in the traditional way? Big pot of boiling water, cooking lasagne sheets two or three at a time, having the sheets stick together even though you were ever so careful? Thankfully our pasta makers came to the rescue; we now have instant lasagne!

Oven temperature: 180°C (350°F)

Serves 6

1 quantity Italian Meat Sauce, above
½ cup water
250-g packet instant lasagne sheets
250 g ricotta cheese
1 cup shredded mozzarella cheese
double quantity hot Easy White Sauce, page 67

TENDER HAMBURGERS

If beef or hamburger mince is used on its own, hamburgers can be dry and chewy. I like to mix breadcrumbs into the meat; this makes the hamburgers tender and juicy.

In a bowl place ½ cup dried breadcrumbs and add 1 small, grated onion, 1 egg, 1 tablespoon each chopped parsley and tomato sauce, about ½ teaspoon salt and freshly ground pepper. Beat with a fork and stand 5 minutes. Mix in 500 g fine beef or hamburger mince. With moistened hands, shape into six thick patties. Cook in a greased pan or on barbecue hotplate and serve in toasted buns with additions as desired.

¼ teaspoon ground nutmeg
1 egg
2 tablespoons grated Parmesan cheese

1 Mix meat sauce with ½ cup water. Grease a 28- x 18-cm oven dish and spread a quarter of the sauce in the base of the dish. Cover with 4–5 sheets lasagne and spread another quarter of the sauce on top. Dot with half the ricotta cheese, sprinkle on half the mozzarella cheese and cover with 4–5 sheets lasagne.

2 Repeat layers until dish is full, finishing with a layer of meat sauce.

3 Beat nutmeg and egg into white sauce and pour over meat. Sprinkle with Parmesan cheese.

4 Bake in preheated moderate oven for 40–45 minutes until top is golden brown. Insert a fine knife blade into the lasagne to check that pasta is tender. Stand 5 minutes before cutting into squares to serve.

Beef and Feta Patties

Use Australian feta cheese for these delicious patties. They are excellent cooked on the barbecue hot plate, or cook them in a frying pan on the stove.

Serves 6

3 slices stale white bread, crusts removed, soaked and squeezed
750 g finely minced beef
1 small onion, grated
2 tablespoons chopped parsley
1 tablespoon chopped fresh basil
1 egg
juice of ½ lemon
½ teaspoon salt
freshly ground black pepper to taste
6 thin slices feta cheese
flour for coating
oil for frying

1 Trim crusts from bread, soak in water and squeeze dry. Place in a bowl and add beef, onion, herbs, egg, lemon, salt and pepper. Mix well, using hands.

2 Divide into twelve and shape each into a flat pattie. Place a slice of feta on six of the patties, keeping feta away from edges. Top with remaining patties and press edges well to seal.

3 Coat with flour and shallow fry in hot oil until browned, or put some oil on barbecue hot-plate and

Using Australian Meat and Poultry • 113

cook patties on this; there is no need to flour them if cooking on barbecue. Patties take about 3 minutes each side to cook. Serve with salad.

Frypan Moussaka

Moussaka, while well known in Australia, is not cooked often because of the effort involved. However, this version, using potatoes and zucchini in place of the traditional eggplant, is quick to prepare and just as delicious.

Serves 6

1 large onion, chopped
1 tablespoon oil
1 clove garlic, crushed
750 g finely minced lean beef
⅓ cup red wine
4 tablespoons tomato paste
¼ teaspoon ground cinnamon
1 teaspoon sugar
2 tablespoons chopped parsley
salt and pepper to taste
4 medium-sized potatoes, peeled
4 zucchinis
5 slices processed cheddar cheese
1 tablespoon grated Parmesan cheese

1 In a 23–25-cm frying pan with lid to fit, cook onion in oil until soft. Add garlic, increase heat and add mince. Stir over high heat to break up mince and cook until colour changes.
2 Reduce heat to medium low and add wine, tomato paste, cinnamon, sugar, parsley and season to taste. Cover and simmer for 20 minutes, adding a little water if mixture looks dry.
3 Meanwhile peel and cut potatoes in 5-mm slices; trim zucchini and cut lengthwise in slices.
4 When meat is cooked, remove to a bowl. In same pan, pour in enough water to just cover base, layer half the potatoes in the base, top with half the mince and spread zucchini over this. Spread remaining mince on top and cover with remaining potatoes.
5 Cover and cook on low heat for 20 minutes until potato is tender. Place cheese slices on top and sprinkle with Parmesan cheese. Cover and cook for 2–3 minutes until cheese melts. Stand 5 minutes, then cut into wedges and serve with a tossed salad.

POPULAR SCHNITZELS

There are many simple meat and poultry dishes we can prepare without a recipe as such. Schnitzels are one of these.
Veal, of course, is the traditional meat, but it is rather expensive. Schnitzels can also be made with pork, lamb and chicken breasts. Pork and lamb schnitzels are available already trimmed and flattened; chicken breasts need to be flattened between sheets of plastic film — beat gently with a mallet and halve if very large.
Simply coat the meat or poultry with seasoned flour, dip in egg beaten with a little milk, then coat with dried breadcrumbs. Place on a baking tray and chill for 20 minutes or so. Shallow fry in hot oil until golden brown on each side. Keep heat moderate so that meat or chicken can cook through before the crumb coating burns. Drain on crumpled kitchen paper.

Citrus Rack of Veal
Oven temperature: 180°C (350°F)

Serves 5–6

1 rack of veal with 5–6 ribs
freshly ground black pepper
1 tablespoon melted butter
grated rind of 1 orange
juice of 2 oranges
juice of 1 lemon
¼ cup honey
1 cup chicken stock
2 teaspoons cornflour

1 Tie veal rack between rib bones with white string and season with pepper. Place upright in a baking dish and brush with melted butter. Cook in a moderate oven for 20 minutes.
2 Mix grated orange rind and citrus juices with honey and pour over veal. Cook, basting occasionally with dish juices, for a further hour or until veal juices run clear when meat is pierced. If dish juices scorch during cooking, add a little water to dish. Remove veal to a platter, cover with foil and keep warm.
3 Add stock to baking dish and stir to dissolve juices. Bring to the boil and thicken with cornflour mixed with a little cold water. Adjust seasoning and strain into sauce boat.
4 Carve the veal into chops and serve with the sauce and vegetables of choice.

Roast Pork with Prunes and Apples
Oven temperature: 180°C (350°F)

Serves 6–8

1 pork neck, about 1.5 kg, tied in a roll
salt
freshly ground black pepper
1 tablespoon canola oil
1 cup prunes
2 Granny Smith apples
1 cup red wine
2 small pieces cassia bark
2 tablespoons redcurrant, quince or apple jelly
¼ cup cream

1 Ask butcher to tie pork into a neat roll if this is not already done.

Using Australian Meat and Poultry • 115

2 Season pork with salt and pepper and brush with oil. Place in a baking dish and cook in oven for 20 minutes.
3 Meanwhile, pit prunes and leave whole. Peel, halve and core apples and cut each half into 3–4 thick wedges.
4 Turn pork over, place fruit around pork and add wine and cassia bark to dish. Return to oven and cook for further 1¼ hours, turning pork occasionally.
5 Remove pork to carving dish, cover with foil and stand in a warm place for 15 minutes.
6 Place baking dish over direct heat, add fruit jelly and stir until jelly is dissolved. Remove cassia bark. Stir in cream and bring to the boil, adding a little water to the dish if necessary.
7 Transfer prunes, apples and sauce to a deep bowl. Carve pork and serve with the fruit sauce. Serve with vegetables of choice.

Note: You may use a small piece of cinnamon bark in place of the cassia if necessary.

Pork and Apricot Skewers
Serves 6

18 small dried apricot halves
1 cup boiling water
1 kg cubed pork from loin or fillet
canola or peanut oil

Apricot Baste
¼ cup sieved apricot jam
2 tablespoons chilli sauce
1 tablespoon canola or peanut oil
1 tablespoon soy sauce
1 tablespoon cider vinegar
¼ teaspoon ground allspice

1 Put apricots in a bowl and cover with boiling water. Stand for 15 minutes until plump. Soak 6 bamboo skewers in water for 15 minutes.
2 Thread pork cubes onto skewers, alternating with apricot halves. Brush with oil. Place on barbecue grid over glowing coals and cook for about 2 minutes each side.
3 Brush with Apricot Baste and continue to cook on cooler section of barbecue for 10 minutes, turning and brushing with baste occasionally. Serve hot with Fruit and Nut Pilaf (page 24) and salad.

Apricot Baste: Mix ingredients together in a small saucepan. Heat on side of barbecue and brush onto pork skewers.

Sausage Rolls

Oven temperature: 230°C (450°F), reducing to 180°C (350°F)

Makes 40

1 kg sausage mince
1 cup soft breadcrumbs
1 onion, grated
1 tablespoon finely chopped parsley
2 tablespoons tomato sauce
4 sheets puff pastry
1 egg, beaten

1 Mix sausage mince with breadcrumbs, onion, parsley and sauce until combined. Divide into 8 even portions and shape each into a roll the length of a pastry sheet. Dust work surface and hands with flour to shape the mince.

2 Cut each pastry sheet in half. Place a roll of sausage mince along one edge of one strip, moistening opposite edge with water. Turn pastry over filling and tuck moistened edge underneath, pressing lightly to seal join. Cut roll into five even portions and place on lightly greased baking sheet. Shape remaining rolls.

3 Glaze tops with beaten egg and cut 2–3 small diagonal slits on top of each roll. Bake in preheated hot oven for 15 minutes, reduce to moderate and cook for further 10–15 minutes.

Note: Sausage rolls may be prepared and frozen. Place on oiled baking sheets, do not glaze. Cover with foil and freeze until firm, lift off and pack into foil containers, separating layers with plastic film. Seal, label and return to freezer. Store for up to 2 months. When required, place frozen rolls on baking sheets, thaw and complete as above.

Using Australian Meat and Poultry

Bacon and Egg Pie

This is an old-fashioned pie that still has appeal. It carries well for picnic fare, or serve it when dining *al fresco*. It is also delicious served hot.

Oven temperature: 200°C (400°F)

Serves 6

1 quantity Shortcrust Pastry, page 15
375 g bacon rashers
6 spring onions, chopped
6 eggs
salt
freshly ground black pepper
2 tablespoons chopped parsley
beaten egg for glazing

1 Divide pastry so that one piece is slightly larger than the other. Roll out larger piece on a floured board. Grease a 28- x 18-cm lamington pan and line with pastry.
2 Remove rind and most of fat from bacon and cut bacon into small pieces. Mix with spring onions and sprinkle over pastry in pan. Make 6 indentations in the bacon-onion mixture.
3 Break an egg into each indentation. Season lightly with salt, grind pepper over pan contents and sprinkle on parsley.
4 Roll out remaining pastry. Moisten edges of pastry in pan, place second sheet on top and press edges to seal. Trim edges neatly and crimp with fingers or press with a fork.
5 Glaze top with beaten egg and bake in preheated oven for 30–35 minutes until golden brown. Serve hot, cut in squares. If required for a picnic, cool in pan, cover and chill. Serve with a tossed salad.

Mango and Ginger Chicken

Serves 6

6 chicken breast fillets
2 tablespoons seasoned flour
1 tablespoon canola oil
1 tablespoon butter
1 cup water
1 chicken stock cube
2 tablespoons thinly sliced preserved ginger
2 tablespoons syrup from ginger
2 tablespoons lemon juice
2 mangoes, peeled and sliced

CHICKEN WITH CARE

Chicken is one of those foods which can harbour harmful micro-organisms. While all due care is taken in processing, transport, and storage at the retail outlet, most problems occur once it has been purchased. Golden rules to follow, particularly with regard to whole chicken, are:
- Carry chicken home in an insulated container or wrapped in newspaper. Refrigerate immediately.
- After roasting, serve immediately; if a barbecued chicken is purchased, eat immediately once you reach home, or refrigerate and reheat in oven or microwave oven.
- Left-over roast chicken should be covered and refrigerated after meal has been served; do not leave at room temperature.
- If making chicken sandwiches, serve immediately they are made; if to be carried in packed lunches, add a frozen container of fruit juice to the lunch box to keep the sandwiches chilled.

1 Dry chicken with paper towels. Coat lightly with seasoned flour, dusting off excess. Reserve leftover flour.
2 Heat oil and butter in a large frying pan, add chicken and fry gently for 25–30 minutes, turning often, until browned and cooked through. Remove to a plate and keep aside.
3 Make up reserved flour to 1 tablespoon and sprinkle into fat in pan. Stir well and cook for 2–3 minutes until lightly browned.
4 Stir in water and keep stirring with a fork until thickened and bubbling, scraping up browned sediment as you stir. Add crumbled stock cube, ginger, syrup and lemon juice and simmer for 2–3 minutes, then add mango slices and chicken and heat through gently. Serve hot with vegetables of choice.

Variations

Herb and Lemon Chicken
Omit ginger, syrup and mangoes. Use ½ cup water and ½ cup dry white wine in Step 4, and to thickened sauce add the stock cube, lemon juice, 1 teaspoon grainy mustard and 2 tablespoons chopped fresh mixed herbs (choose from parsley, chives, tarragon, thyme, chervil). Stir in ¼ cup cream, return chicken to pan and heat through gently.

Chicken Cacciatore
Omit all ingredients except for chicken, flour, oil and butter. When chicken is cooked, pour 1½ cups Tomato Pasta Sauce (page 136) over chicken and heat gently. Do not allow chicken to boil in the sauce as it could become stringy. Sprinkle with ¼ cup drained black olives, if desired, and serve with boiled pasta and a tossed green salad. You can use 1.5 kg chicken legs, thighs or Marylands in place of the breast fillets if desired; if you do so, cover and simmer gently in the sauce for 20 minutes until chicken is tender.

Roast Chicken with Fruit Stuffing

Oven temperature: 180°C (350°F)

Serves 4–5

1 chicken, about 1.5 kg
juice of 1 lemon
1 quantity Fruit Stuffing, below
salt
freshly ground black pepper
½ cup chicken stock
½ cup dry white wine
2 tablespoons butter
3 teaspoons cornflour
¼ cup water

1 Check body cavity of chicken and clean if necessary. Rinse and dry inside and out with paper towels. Squeeze some lemon juice into the cavity. Make stuffing according to directions and pack loosely with stuffing.

2 Truss chicken and rub all over with remaining lemon juice. Season with salt and pepper and place in roasting dish. Add stock and wine to dish. Spread top of chicken with butter.

3 Roast in a moderate oven for 2 hours, basting occasionally with dish juices. Add water to dish if juices begin to scorch.

4 Check if cooked by pushing leg forward — if it moves easily, chicken is cooked. Remove to serving platter, cover with foil and leave in a warm place for 10 minutes.

5 Spoon fat from dish juices. Add a little more stock or water to dish if necessary so that there is about 1 cup liquid in dish. Place over direct heat and bring to the boil, stirring and scraping browned juices to dissolve them.

6 Mix cornflour with water and add to dish juices, stirring constantly until thickened and bubbling. Adjust seasoning and strain into gravy boat. Joint or carve chicken and serve with the gravy, baked vegetables and a green vegetable. (See Roast Lamb Dinner, page 102, for baking vegetables the low-fat way.)

Fruit Stuffing

½ cup chopped dried apricots
¼ cup chopped pitted prunes
2 tablespoons butter
¼ cup slivered almonds
1 small onion, finely chopped

Smoked Salmon Appetiser (page 90), Mango Seafood Salad (page 98)

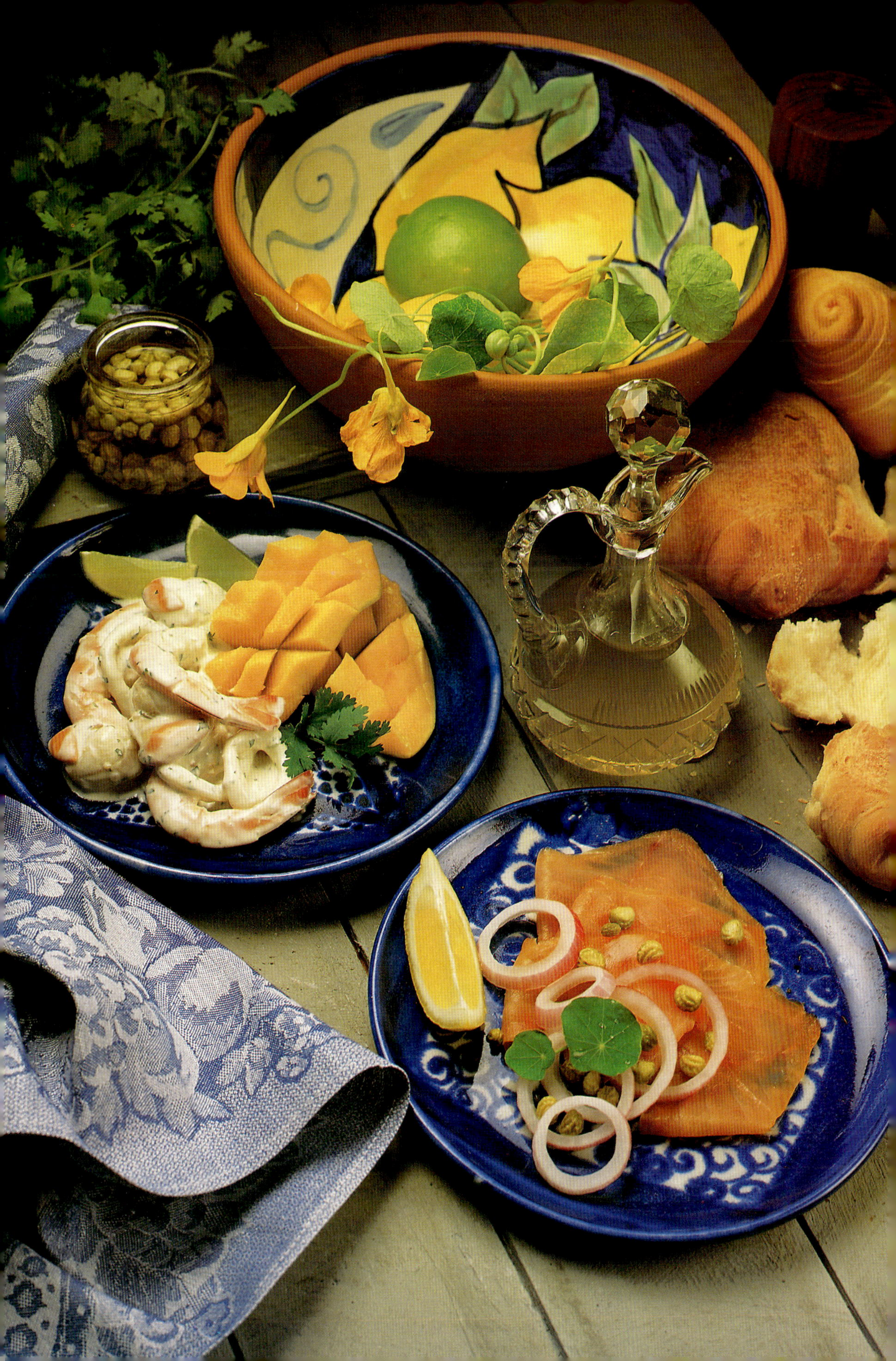

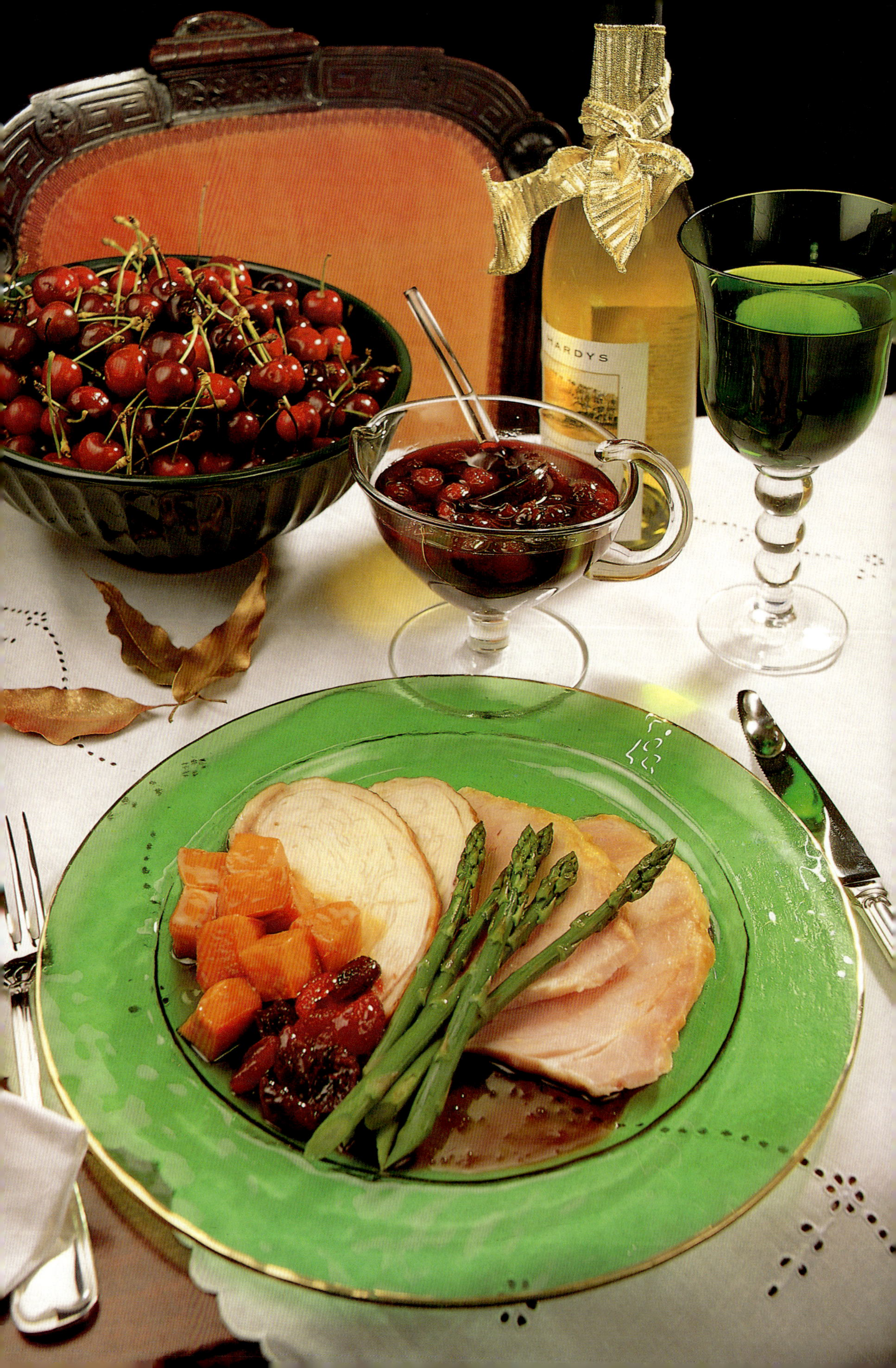
HARDYS

2 cups soft white breadcrumbs
grated rind of 1 lemon
1 tablespoon lemon juice
salt
freshly ground black pepper
1 small egg, beaten

1 Put chopped apricots in a bowl and cover with boiling water. Leave for 20 minutes then drain. Add prunes (these do not need soaking).
2 Heat butter in a frying pan, add almonds and fry gently until a light golden brown, add onion and cook gently until soft.
3 Add to fruit with breadcrumbs, lemon rind and juice and salt and pepper to taste. Add enough egg to bind mixture, mixing it lightly. Use to stuff poultry, lamb or pork for roasting. For turkey, triple ingredients, but only use grated rind of 2 lemons and 2 eggs.

Chilli Chicken Wings
Serves 5–6

1.5 kg chicken wings

Chilli Marinade:
1/3 cup mild or hot chilli sauce
1 tablespoon oil
2 tablespoons tomato sauce
2 tablespoons soy sauce
2 cloves garlic, crushed

1 Cut off wing tips and store in freezer for making stock later. Put wings in bowl and pour on marinade. Turn to coat, cover and marinate in refrigerator for 2–3 hours or overnight, turning wings occasionally.
2 Drain marinade into a small pan and place on side of barbecue to heat. Place chicken wings on barbecue grid and cook, turning and basting often with marinade. Cook for about 25–30 minutes until juices run clear when pierced at thickest point. Serve hot with a rice dish and salads.

Chilli Marinade: Mix ingredients together and pour over chicken.

Variations

Chilli Chicken Drumsticks
Use 1 kg chicken drumsticks in place of chicken wings. Marinate and place drumsticks and marinade in a baking

Roast Lamb Dinner (page 102)

dish. Cook in a moderate oven for 1 hour, turning often. Serve with jacket-baked potatoes and a salad.

Glazed Honey and Ginger Chicken Wings
In place of Chilli Marinade, mix 3 tablespoons honey with 2 teaspoons finely shredded fresh ginger, 1 crushed clove garlic, 2 tablespoons each lemon juice, soy sauce and sherry. Marinate chicken wings and barbecue, basting with marinade.

Chicken Parcels

With the ever-growing trend to value-added meats and poultry, that is the raw products prepared by the butcher or poultry supplier so that all you have to do is cook them, it is obvious that we want to spend less time in the kitchen, but still yearn for something different. With chicken breast and thigh fillets so readily available, it is very easy to make up these popular, fillo-wrapped parcels, store them in the freezer and have them on hand for those days when you haven't time to cook from scratch.

Swiss Chicken in Fillo
Oven temperature: 180–190°C (350–375°F)

Serves 8

8 chicken breast fillets
8 small slices double-smoked ham
340-g can asparagus spears, drained
8 small slices Swiss cheese
2 tablespoons seasoned flour
16 sheets fillo pastry
melted butter
paprika

1 Slit each breast fillet. Insert a slice of ham, 2 asparagus spears and a slice of cheese in each breast and close up, pressing cut edges together (no need to secure). Coat chicken lightly with seasoned flour.
2 Follow instructions for Fillo Parcels on page 18. Place on a greased baking tray, brush tops with butter and sprinkle lightly with paprika.
3 Bake in a preheated moderately hot oven for 25 minutes until juices begin to ooze out of parcel and

THAWING FROZEN CHICKEN

With better chicken marketing, frozen chicken is not as widely used as in the past. However, it is always handy to have one in the freezer for emergencies. To thaw it safely, the chicken should be placed in a dish and left in the refrigerator. As this can take at least 24 hours, there are a couple of safe methods which take less time.
Thaw in the microwave oven, following manual instructions if oven has an automatic defrosting programme. If oven doesn't have this facility, remove wrapping and place chicken on a plate.

sizzle on baking tray. Serve hot with vegetables of choice or salad.

To Freeze: Place chicken parcels on a baking tray lined with waxed paper. Put into freezer and, when frozen, repack carefully in a rigid freezer container. To cook from frozen state, use a moderate oven (lower temperature given above), and cook for 35–40 minutes or until juices begin to sizzle.

Variations:

Apricot Chicken in Fillo

In place of ham, asparagus and cheese, use the following: Heat 16 dried apricots in $1/3$ cup fresh orange juice until boiling. Leave until cool. Have on hand $1/4$ cup toasted almond slivers or chopped macadamia nuts. Insert 2 apricot halves and about $1 1/2$ teaspoons nuts into each slit breast. Coat with seasoned flour and proceed from Step 2.

Chicken Thighs in Fillo

Use 16 thigh fillets in place of chicken breasts. Make Fruit Stuffing, page 120, to use in place of ham, asparagus and cheese. Open out thighs and spread with stuffing. Fold over to enclose filling and coat with seasoned flour. Use 2 stuffed thighs for each fillo wrap. Proceed from Step 2.

Roast Turkey

Oven temperature: 180°C (350°F)

Serves 10–12

1 turkey, about 5 kg
Bacon and Herb Stuffing, page 125
  OR Chestnut Stuffing, page 124
1 lemon
salt
freshly ground black pepper
125 g butter, melted
1 cup water

Giblet Gravy
giblets and neck from turkey
3 cups chicken stock
1/2 small onion
1 small carrot, sliced
1/4 teaspoon whole peppercorns
3 tablespoons flour

Defrost for 3 minutes on HIGH for microwaves to penetrate ice, turning chicken over half-way through. Complete defrosting on 30 per cent power or LOW. Turn chicken occasionally, and check for warm spots, covering these with pieces of foil. When thawed, drain well, dry with paper towels and cook immediately.
Alternatively, leave chicken in its sealed wrapping and place in a deep pan of tap water. As the water becomes cold, change it. It takes about 1 1/2 hours to thaw an average-sized bird.

1 Remove giblets and neck from turkey. Clean turkey cavities, rinse and dry with paper towels. Insert selected stuffing in body cavity and crop. Secure neck skin over crop stuffing with poultry skewer. Sew up body cavity with thick thread. Truss turkey.
2 Place in large roasting dish and squeeze lemon juice over turkey, rubbing it into flesh. Season with salt and pepper. Brush butter over turkey and add water to dish. Tent turkey with foil and cook in moderate oven for $3^1/_2$–4 hours, until juices run clear when the breast is pierced. Baste turkey occasionally with dish juices and butter mixture, and remove foil during last 45 minutes of cooking to brown.
3 Remove turkey to serving platter. Make gravy as directed below and serve turkey with gravy, stuffing, Cherry Sauce (page 181) and vegetables of choice.

Giblet Gravy: Clean and rinse giblets and neck and place in a saucepan with chicken stock, onion, carrot and peppercorns. Simmer gently, covered, for 1 hour, then strain into a jug. Transfer 3 tablespoons fat from roasting dish to a saucepan. Drain off remaining fat and pour hot giblet stock into dish. Stir and scrape to dissolve browned juices and strain liquid back into jug. Stir flour into fat in saucepan and heat for 3–4 minutes until lightly coloured. Remove pan from heat and pour in stock, stirring constantly. Return to heat and stir until lightly thickened and bubbling. Simmer on low heat for 5 minutes or so, adjust seasoning and strain into gravy boat.

Chestnut Stuffing

If you have prepared chestnuts in autumn and frozen them, then you can make this stuffing for the festive turkey, unless you do the Christmas-in-July bit.

4 cups stale white bread cubes
125 g butter
1 large onion, chopped
½ cup finely chopped celery
2 teaspoons chopped fresh thyme
1 teaspoon chopped fresh sage
3 tablespoons chopped parsley
2 tablespoons lemon juice
3 cups shelled, skinned and boiled chestnuts, page 56
salt
freshly ground black pepper

1 Cut bread into 1-cm cubes. Spread onto baking trays and bake in a moderate oven for 10 minutes until lightly toasted. You can do this a few days ahead and store the cubes in a sealed container.
2 Melt butter in a frying pan, add onion and celery and cook gently until onion is soft. Tip into a large bowl.
3 Add toasted bread cubes and herbs. Break up chestnuts into smallish pieces and add to bread mixture with salt and pepper to taste. Mix lightly to combine. Use to stuff turkey cavities.

Bacon and Herb Stuffing (for turkey)

4 bacon rashers, chopped
60 g butter
1 large onion, finely chopped
½ cup finely chopped celery
1 cup chopped pecan nuts
1 teaspoon grated lemon rind
2 tablespoons lemon juice
2 tablespoons chopped parsley
2 teaspoons chopped fresh thyme
6 cups soft white breadcrumbs
2 eggs, beaten
salt
freshly ground black pepper

1 Leave a little fat on the bacon when preparing. Place in a heated pan and cook until lightly browned.
2 Add butter, onion and celery and cook gently until onion is soft. Turn into a bowl.
3 Stir in remaining ingredients, adding enough beaten egg to bind. Mix lightly. Season to taste with salt and pepper. Use to stuff body cavity and crop of turkey.

Note: Do not stuff turkey until just before cooking; if stuffed too far ahead, juices in the cavity soak into the stuffing. During cooking, the centre of the stuffing does not reach the high temperature required to kill off any potentially harmful micro-organisms in these juices. You can prepare stuffing a day or two beforehand; store in a covered bowl in the refrigerator.

Vegetables

There is hardly a vegetable that isn't grown in our vast land. With our varied climatic zones, not only can we grow a great variety, but most of them are available for most of the year. Yet imports of fresh, frozen and canned vegetables amount to more than $150 million; with the amount of dehydrated vegetables and extracts used in food manufacturing, you can add another $20 million at least. Some $12 million is spent on fresh produce, and just over 40 per cent of this for one vegetable — garlic! That certainly says something for the changing flavour of Australian cooking!

It isn't necessary to go through every vegetable available in Australia, but only those where a change in our buying habits could make a difference. (Pickled vegetables are covered in the chapter on Vinegars, Pickles, Sauces and Condiments.)

Besides the fresh vegetables listed in the Buyer's Guide, we import fresh chicory, witloof (Belgian endive), celeriac, eggplants and small quantities of other vegetables, to make up shortfalls in supply or when the local produce is out of season. The amounts of these vegetables imported are not great, but they do add up.

Mushrooms

Because of the high cost of imports of mushrooms, special mention should be made of these so that the Australian industry can be better supported. We also import truffles, but too few to be concerned. Australian production of cultivated mushrooms is capable of fulfilling our requirements, but imports of canned and dried mushrooms do affect the mushroom industry, so check labels on cans. It pays not to be a purist when cooking Asian recipes which call for dried Chinese (shiitake) mushrooms; sliced fresh cultivated mushrooms can do almost as well. However, fresh shiitake mushrooms are now available in some Australian cities, along with fresh oyster mushrooms, Swiss brown and enoki (also known as golden or winter) mushrooms, now cultivated by a few dedicated growers for the restaurant trade and retail. Morels, imported in dried form, do grow in the wild in mountainous regions of Victoria and New South Wales. The locations are a closely guarded secret by those who gather them for select restaurants.

Choosing Australian Vegetables

Buyer's Guide
CHOOSING AUSTRALIAN VEGETABLES

Product	Australian-produced	Imported	What we can do
Artichokes, globe — fresh, canned and jar-packed	Yes, fresh only	Yes, canned and in jars; amount not known	Use fresh artichokes in season, from May for 4 months. Avoid using preserved artichokes.
Asparagus — fresh, canned and jar-packed	Yes, fresh and canned	Yes, some $18 million worth of fresh and preserved	Buy fresh asparagus when in season — spring to mid-summer. Check labels on cans and jars.
Beans, green — fresh, canned and frozen	Yes, fresh, canned and frozen	Yes, some $3 million worth, mostly canned and frozen	Buy fresh beans to be certain of local product. Check labels on canned and frozen products.
Garlic — fresh, wet minced, jar-packed; granules and powdered	Yes, fresh; wet minced jar-packed and powdered, processed locally from imported garlic products	Yes, some $6 million worth (80% of our needs); fresh and processed	No way of telling if fresh garlic is local; garlic processed locally usually from imported product, but at least buy local garlic products. Substitute garlic chives in recipes where possible.
Mushrooms — fresh, canned, jar-packed and dried	Yes, fresh and canned, sliced mushrooms in various sauces. Brine-packed sliced and champignons only in catering packs	Yes, some $20 million worth, mostly preserved (especially champignons), some fresh and dried	Use fresh mushrooms in place of dried and canned (see page 126 for more detail). Check labels on canned mushrooms. Avoid canned champignons; use fresh instead.
Onions — fresh, frozen chopped; dried flakes and powdered	Yes, fresh and frozen; powdered and granules processed, often from imported dried onions	Yes, some $6 million worth, mostly dried with some fresh	Use fresh or frozen chopped onion in preference to dried. Many processed foods contain imported product.
Peas, green and snow — fresh; green peas canned and frozen	Yes, fresh green and snow peas; canned and frozen green peas	Yes, some $8 million worth, mostly frozen, some fresh and canned	Use fresh green and snow peas; some snow peas imported. Check labels on canned and frozen green peas.
Potatoes — fresh, canned, frozen and dried	Yes, fresh, canned, frozen fried potatoes, and dried for convenience potato products	Yes, over $8 million* worth, canned, frozen (fried wedges, chips) and dried	Use fresh as much as possible. Check labels on canned potatoes, frozen fried potato products and dried potato products.
Spinach — leaf, fresh, frozen, canned and jar-packed	Yes, fresh	Yes, over $2 million worth frozen, canned and jar-packed	Use fresh English spinach — it is readily available and easy to prepare (see page 135).

128

Choosing Australian Vegetables • 128

Product	Australian-produced	Imported	What we can do
Sweet corn — fresh, canned and frozen	Yes, fresh, canned and frozen	Yes, over $9 million worth, canned and frozen, including baby corn cobs	Use fresh sweet corn and check labels on canned and frozen sweet corn. Avoid canned baby corn cobs.
Tomatoes — fresh, canned, dried, purée, paste	Yes, fresh, canned, dried, purée, paste, and capable of fulfilling needs	Yes, some $20 million worth, canned, dried and preserved for further processing	Use fresh tomatoes as much as possible. Check labels for local canned tomatoes, purée, paste. Sun-dried tomatoes now made in Australia; avoid imports.
Vegetables, mixed — canned, frozen and dried	Yes, canned and frozen	Yes, some $25 million worth of frozen and canned; dried used for food manufacture	Prepare from fresh vegetables. Check labels on canned and frozen products, stir-fry mixes; limit use of processed foods such as packet soups, rice mixes, etc.

* The actual figure for 1992–93 was $19 million. An unusual occurrence caused the extra expenditure, one which is not likely to recur.

Recipes
USING AUSTRALIAN VEGETABLES

Chilled Potato and Leek Soup
Serves 6

4 leeks, washed and sliced
1 large onion, chopped
2 tablespoons butter
3 medium-sized pontiac potatoes
5 cups chicken stock
salt
freshly ground white pepper
½ cup milk
½ cup cream
snipped chives to garnish

1 Put leeks, onion and butter in a large saucepan and cook gently, stirring often, until leeks and onions are soft.
2 Peel and chop potatoes and add to pan with chicken stock, salt and pepper to taste. Cover and simmer for 30 minutes until potatoes are very soft.
3 Stir in milk, return to the boil, then stand until cool. Purée in food processor or blender or rub through a sieve. Pour into a bowl, stir in cream, cover and chill. Serve chilled, sprinkled with snipped chives.

Note: Soup may be served hot; purée, return to pan, then add milk and cream and reheat until almost boiling. Serve with croutons if desired, page 25.

Cream of Pumpkin Soup
Serves 5–6

1 medium-sized onion, chopped
2 tablespoons butter
1 clove garlic, crushed
750 g pumpkin, peeled and chopped
3 sprigs parsley
5 cups chicken stock
salt
freshly ground black pepper
½ cup cream
extra cream for serving
chopped parsley or snipped chives to garnish

1 Cook onion gently in butter in a large saucepan. When soft, add garlic, cook a few seconds, then add pumpkin, parsley, stock and salt and pepper to taste.
2 Cover and simmer gently for 20 minutes until pumpkin is soft. Purée in food processor or blender or rub through a sieve.
3 Return to saucepan and stir in cream. Reheat almost to boiling point and serve with a little cream swirled in the centre of each serving, topped with a light sprinkling of chopped parsley or snipped chives, or serve with croutons, page 25.

Variations

Cream of Carrot Soup
Replace pumpkin with 600 g carrots, scraped and sliced. Cook and finish as above.

Cream of Broccoli Soup
Add 2 washed and sliced leeks to the onion and cook until soft. Replace pumpkin with 500 g washed, trimmed and chopped broccoli and 1 large peeled and chopped potato. Cook and finish as above, adding ¼ teaspoon grated nutmeg with the cream.

Glazed Kumara
Serves 6

2 kumara (orange sweet potato), about 750 g
3 tablespoons butter
3 tablespoons brown sugar
2 tablespoons dry sherry

1 Peel kumara and cut into 2-cm cubes. Cook in boiling, lightly salted water until just tender. Drain.
2 In a frying pan, melt butter and stir in brown sugar. Heat gently until sugar melts. Stir in sherry.
3 Add drained kumara and simmer on medium–low heat for 6–7 minutes, turning kumara in the glaze with the aid of a wide metal spatula. Serve hot with roast turkey, chicken or pork, or glazed ham.

Variations

Glazed Carrots
Peel and thickly slice 500 g carrots. Boil, drain and finish as above. The grated rind and juice of 1 orange may be added to the glaze in place of the sherry.

Imported Soups and Broths

Because statistics do not indicate type, it is difficult to place these in a particular category. Imports amount to over $8 million worth, most of these in dried form. They could be meat- or poultry-based or vegetable-based. Many of the dried preparations come from Asian countries, and would include Asian-style soup and stock bases. Other packaged dried soups and canned soups would be of types also manufactured in Australia, so check labels on packs and cans and, if imported, look for a local substitute.

Glazed Pumpkin

Choose a firm pumpkin such as jap or jarrahdale. Peel and seed 750 g pumpkin, boil until just tender, drain and finish as above.

Stir-fried Vegetables

This is a good way to cook vegetables to retain nutrients and preserve flavours. You can use a variety of vegetables, or only one. Firm vegetables such as carrot take a while to soften, but can be used if you slice them very thinly.

Serves 4–6

Flavouring base
1 tablespoon canola or sunflower oil
1 clove garlic, finely chopped
1 teaspoon finely shredded fresh ginger
1 tablespoon soy sauce
1 tablespoon sweet sherry
½ cup walnut pieces (optional)

Vegetables
1 cup broccoli florets
6 spring onions, cut diagonally in 3-cm pieces
1 cup mixed green and red pepper pieces
1½ cups trimmed snow peas

1 In a deep-sided frying pan or wok, add oil, garlic and ginger and stir-fry for 1 minute until garlic is lightly browned.
2 Add broccoli, spring onions and pepper pieces and stir-fry for 4–5 minutes, sprinkling with water occasionally to create steam to help cook vegetables. Add snow peas and stir-fry for 1–2 minutes longer.
3 Sprinkle with soy sauce and sherry, add walnuts and toss over heat for a few seconds. Serve immediately as part of a Chinese meal or as an accompaniment to grilled meats and chicken.

Variations: Individual vegetables may be prepared in the same way.

Stir-fried Asparagus

Wash 2 bunches green asparagus, snap off woody ends and cut spears diagonally in 2–3 pieces. Add in Step 2, in place of the mixed vegetables, cook for 3–4 minutes, sprinkling with water. Complete as above, omitting walnuts if desired.

FREEZING ASPARAGUS

It is unfortunate that less Australian asparagus is being canned. If you cannot find local asparagus, at least choose one from New Zealand. As an alternative, you can freeze Australian-grown fresh asparagus when it is in season (spring); usually it is reasonably priced at this time.

To prepare the asparagus, snap off woody end of each spear. There is no need to remove the 'scales' as you are often told to do. Leave spears whole, or cut in pieces, keeping tips aside. Bring a large pan of water to the boil, place asparagus in a wire basket and immerse in the boiling water. Return to the boil and boil for 2 minutes; if tips have been separated, add these during last minute of boiling. Lift out and plunge into a bowl of iced water. Drain and spread out on kitchen paper. Pack in rigid containers in meal-sized portions, seal, label and freeze. Use within ten months.

> **Handy Hint**
>
> When canned, chopped tomatoes are required, open can and drain off some of the liquid into a cup or into dish being prepared. Chop tomatoes in the can with a medium-sized, sharp knife. If you have a hand-held food processor, put this in the can and chop the tomatoes.

> **Money Saver**
>
> If you use tomato paste frequently, it is more economical to buy a large jar rather than single or meal-sized portions. When using, scrape down the paste from the side of the jar as this is the portion which usually gets mouldy. Store in the refrigerator. You can add a thin layer of oil on top, but this is only necessary if you use tomato paste infrequently, in which case meal-sized packs would be better.

Stir-fried Broccoli

Prepare 2–3 cups broccoli florets, halving florets with thick stems. Use in place of asparagus, extending cooking time if necessary.

Mediterranean-style Vegetables

When you tire of plain vegetables, this basic recipe will hold you in good stead. If you have cooked too much, store leftovers in the refrigerator and reheat when needed — they keep for 3–4 days.

Serves 4–6

3 tablespoons Salad Oil, page 80
1 large onion, sliced
2 cloves garlic, crushed
½ cup chopped celery
425-g can tomatoes, chopped
2 tablespoons tomato paste
½ cup white wine or water
2 tablespoons chopped parsley
2 tablespoons chopped fresh basil
 OR 1 teaspoon dried basil
2 teaspoons chopped fresh marjoram (optional)
1 teaspoon sugar
salt
freshly ground black pepper
prepared vegetable (see below)

1 Put oil and onion in a large saucepan and cook gently until onion is soft. Add garlic, cook a few seconds, then add remaining ingredients except vegetable to be used. Cover and simmer gently for 10 minutes.
2 Add prepared vegetable (or combination of vegetables), stir gently, cover and simmer gently for further 20–30 minutes until tender. Depending on vegetable, it might be necessary to add a little more water to pan during cooking. Serve with roast or grilled meats and chicken.

Choose from the following vegetables:
- 500 g green beans, topped, tailed and slit
- 750 g zucchini, trimmed and sliced thickly
- 4–6 chokoes, peeled, seeded and cut into thick wedges
- 750 g potatoes, peeled and quartered

Vegetable combinations:
- 250 g prepared green beans with 250 g prepared zucchini

- 2 prepared chokoes with 250 g prepared green beans
- 500 g prepared potatoes with 1½ cups frozen green peas
- 250 g each prepared green beans and zucchini with 1 red and 1 green pepper, seeded and cut in chunks.

Fried Potato Wedges *(cold-start method)*

This is my favourite method for frying potato chips. The advantages are that you don't have oily fumes filling the kitchen when the cold chips meet the hot oil, and there is less danger of the oil overheating and catching alight because you forgot you put it on to heat. The potatoes do not absorb any more oil than in traditional deep frying, unless you use a potato which is not right for chip-making.

For this variation on traditional chips, I only recommend using pontiac, bison or désirée potatoes as the skins are left on, and these reddish-skinned potatoes take little or no scrubbing. (Fried potato skins are an 'in' food, but why stop at the skins?)

Serves 4–5

750 g pontiac, bison or désirée potatoes
sunola oil for frying

1 Choose medium-sized potatoes. Rinse and cut in half lengthwise, then cut each half into 3–4 thick wedges, as evenly sized as possible. Dry potatoes with a clean cloth.
2 Put oil into deep fryer. Place potatoes into basket and immerse in oil. If oil does not cover potatoes, add a little more. Turn heat onto highest setting.
3 Give the basket a shake now and then as the oil heats, to separate wedges. When oil is bubbling well, shake basket occasionally. When potatoes begin to float and are tender, with a crust formed (test with the point of a knife), lift basket from the oil.
4 Allow oil to heat until bubbles cease to rise — these are bubbles of moisture from the potatoes. Immerse potatoes back in the oil and fry until lightly browned and crisp. Remove, shake basket over the fryer to remove some of the oil, then turn potatoes out onto crumpled paper towels to drain. Serve immediately.

Note: To prevent oil boiling over, deep-fryer should only be one-third filled when potatoes are added to the

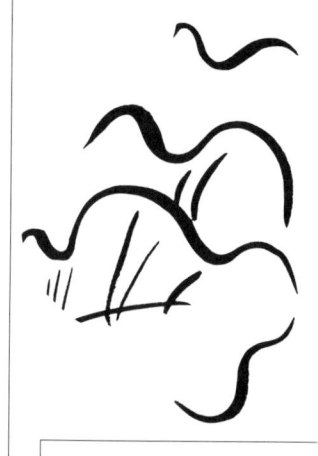

Silverbeet isn't Spinach

This large-leafed vegetable is very often labelled as spinach, when it is no relation at all to leaf spinach. Of course it can be used in place of spinach in recipes, but the flavour is completely different. It grows well in the garden, and is usually reasonably priced in the marketplace, hence its popularity. If using in place of spinach, cut out the white rib and remove the white stems, using the leaves only. The stems may be cooked as a separate vegetable, dressed with white sauce.

PREPARING SPINACH

While frozen packaged spinach may be sold under well-known Australian brands, it's all imported. It is worthwhile preparing your own and freezing it, so that it may be used in the same way as the convenient frozen product. In fact, it is better, as frozen chopped spinach, in my opinion, is chopped far too finely. Trim roots from a bunch of leaf spinach; leave stems on as these are very tender. Remove any decayed or damaged leaves. Drain, and taking handfuls of the leaves, place on a board and chop roughly. Place in a large stainless steel or enamelled saucepan, cover and cook on medium heat for 2–3 minutes, shaking pan occasionally. When leaves show signs of wilting, remove from heat and toss spinach with a fork. Cover and spinach will complete cooking in the stored heat. Drain in a colander, pressing with the back of a wooden spoon to extract moisture. Turn onto a board and chop to desired degree. Pack in 1-cup portions in freezer bags, seal and store in freezer until required.

oil. Also, do not use this cold-start method for other fried foods.

Cauliflower with Cheese Sauce

Cauliflower needs a sauce or dressing of some kind to make it more palatable; it's a good-for-you vegetable which should be served frequently. If you are in a hurry, simply serve with a squeeze of lemon juice and pour on a little oil, like the Salad Oil (page 80), or make this popular version.

Oven temperature: 180°C (350°F)

Serves 6

1 medium-sized cauliflower
water
salt
small piece celery
1 quantity Mornay Sauce, page 68
1 tablespoon grated Parmesan cheese
dusting of paprika

1 Divide cauliflower into large florets and cut slits into thicker stems.
2 Bring enough water to the boil to cover cauliflower, add salt and celery (the celery prevents cauliflower from developing a strong odour). Add cauliflower, cover and boil until just tender. Drain immediately.
3 Place in a greased oven dish and cover with the Mornay Sauce. Sprinkle with Parmesan and dust with paprika. Cook in a moderate oven for 15 minutes until top is lightly browned. Serve hot as an accompaniment to meat and poultry meals.

Variations

Broccoli with Cheese Sauce

Prepare 500–600 g broccoli, leaving a good portion of stems on sprigs. Boil until just tender and finish as above.

Chokoes with Cheese Sauce

Peel and seed 6 medium-sized chokoes and cut into wedges. Boil in lightly salted water until tender and

Using Australian Vegetables

Eggplant Parmigiana

Normally the eggplant is fried for this dish. As it soaks up a lot of oil, and in the interests of healthy eating, grill the eggplant instead for fewer calories but no loss of flavour.

Oven temperature: 180°C (350°F)

Serves 5–6

3 large eggplants
salt
Salad Oil, page 80
1 medium-sized onion, chopped
1 clove garlic, chopped
500 g ripe tomatoes, peeled and chopped
2 tablespoons Tomato Paste (page 137)
1 tablespoon chopped fresh basil
1 teaspoon sugar
freshly ground black pepper
3 tablespoons grated Parmesan cheese
1 cup shredded mozzarella cheese

1 Remove stems from eggplants and cut in 1-cm slices. Sprinkle with salt and leave for 30 minutes. Rinse, drain and press slices in a cloth to remove excess moisture.

2 Brush a baking tray with oil, place eggplant on tray and brush with oil. Cook under a very hot grill until browned on each side. Do in 2–3 lots if necessary.

3 In a saucepan, cook onion gently in 1 tablespoon oil until soft, add garlic, cook a few seconds, then add tomatoes, tomato paste, basil, sugar, salt and pepper to taste. Cover and simmer for 30 minutes. When sauce is thick, rub through a sieve or food mill to remove seeds.

4 Place a layer of eggplant in a rectangular baking dish. Spoon some of the sauce on top and sprinkle with 1 tablespoon Parmesan cheese. Repeat layers, finishing with sauce.

5 Cover sauce with shredded mozzarella cheese. Sprinkle with remaining Parmesan and cook in preheated moderate oven for 30 minutes until cheese is golden brown. Serve hot as a starter or as an accompaniment to grilled or roast meats or poultry.

Tomato Pasta Sauce

To be really sure your tomato pasta sauce is all-Australian, you have to make it yourself. Use Australian canned tomatoes and paste for convenience; there's a recipe for Tomato Paste opposite.

Spring Onions

Much confusion exists about these onions. In some States they are known as shallots, which is incorrect. Spring onions can be the long, slender green onion, white just above the root, with the white and most of the green part used. Or they can be the small, round onions, in which case use only the bulbous white part. Spring onions used in recipes are the long variety, unless otherwise specified.

Onions without Tears

Onions should be stored in a cool, dark place, not in the refrigerator. However, if you shed tears every time you chop an onion, make it a habit to always have one or two onions in the vegetable crisper. If the onion is chilled, the irritant remains in the onion as you chop — no more tears!

Peeling Small Onions

If you need a number of small onions for a dish, or have decided to make pickled onions, cut off the top and root of each onion and place in a bowl. Pour on boiling water, leave for 2 minutes and drain. The skins will slip off easily.
If using whole onions for a stew or casserole, cut a cross in the root end — this prevents the centres popping.

Makes about 6 cups

2 x 810-g cans tomatoes
3 tablespoons Salad Oil, page 80
2 large onions, finely chopped
4 cloves garlic, chopped
½ cup tomato paste
½ cup white wine
3 tablespoons chopped fresh basil
3 tablespoons chopped parsley
3 teaspoons chopped fresh marjoram or oregano
2 bay leaves
3 teaspoons salt
1 teaspoon freshly ground black pepper
1 tablespoon sugar

1 Press tomatoes and their liquid through a sieve or pass through a food mill to remove seeds. Keep resulting purée aside.
2 Put oil in a large saucepan and add onion. Cook gently for 10 minutes until soft, add garlic and cook for a few seconds.
3 Add prepared purée with remaining ingredients, cover and simmer for 30 minutes. Remove lid and cook for further 20 minutes until thick. Remove bay leaves and discard.
4 Pour hot sauce into hot, sterilised jars, seal when cold and store in refrigerator. Heat amount required and serve on hot pasta with Parmesan cheese, or use as directed in recipes.

Tomato Paste

One for the home gardener, or make it if you can buy plum tomatoes cheaply. At least you can be sure it is all-Australian! This makes a thicker, more concentrated paste than the one you buy, so use less of it in recipes. Also take care when adding salt to the recipe as this paste contains salt to help preserve it.

Oven temperature: 100°C (200°F)

Makes about 1.5 kg paste

6 kg plum tomatoes
2 tablespoons salt

1 Tomatoes must be ripe with no signs of decay. Wash well, cut out stem ends and chop tomatoes.
2 Place in a large boiler, cover and simmer gently until soft.

3 Rub through a sieve over a large bowl or use a food mill, to separate seeds and skins.
4 Pour pulped tomatoes back into boiler and boil gently until reduced to half original volume.
5 Turn purée into 2 large enamelled or teflon-coated baking dishes and place in a cool oven for 4–6 hours, stirring now and then. When reduced to a paste consistency, combine the dishes of paste and stir in salt.
6 Transfer to hot, sterilised jars, packing it in well with the minimum of air bubbles. Wipe round tops of jars with a clean, damp cloth and leave until cool. Pour a layer of oil on top of each. Seal and store in a cool, dark place or in refrigerator. Once a jar is opened, it must be stored in refrigerator.

'Sun-dried' Tomatoes

When sun-dried tomatoes hit the marketplace in the late eighties, they began to appear so often that they almost went out of fashion because of over-use. They have a unique flavour and are now firmly entrenched in the Australian kitchen.

While sun-dried tomatoes are still imported, local processors are giving the imports a lot of competition, producing them packed in oil or dry so that you can finish them off. You can also make them with little effort, but I recommend oven-drying because the sun cannot be relied on to shine uninterrupted for a number of days. The result is the same anyway. It is unnecessary to give quantities in this recipe.

Oven temperature: 100–125°C (200–250°F)

cherry, plum or small ripe tomatoes
salt
sugar
a few sprigs fresh oregano
garlic cloves
Salad Oil, page 80
black peppercorns (optional)

1 Wash tomatoes. Cut cherry tomatoes in half crosswise, other tomatoes lengthwise. Place directly on lightly oiled baking trays, cut side up, and sprinkle lightly with salt and sugar. Put oregano sprigs and halved garlic cloves amongst the tomatoes.
2 Place in a cool oven. If fan-forced, have oven closed and use the lower temperature; if not fan-forced, use higher temperature and leave door slightly ajar with the

HOME-GROWN TOMATOES

Of course the tomato is a fruit, but as it is used as a vegetable, it is included in this chapter. Growing your own tomatoes can be very rewarding, particularly if you would like to dry them or make tomato paste. The effort is worthwhile if you haven't needed to buy them. The varieties suggested are a cross-section of tomato types available, from the cherry tomato to the traditional. However, the novice gardener might find growing tomatoes a frustrating experience. Seed packets give good information, or read up on them in a reliable book on vegetable growing.

Grosse Lisse: A very popular tomato with home gardeners because of its excellent flavour. It is high-yielding, fruits mid-season, and must be staked and pruned. However, it is not as disease-resistant as other varieties, and as the skin is thin, could be more prone to fruit fly infestation.

Improved Apollo: Reintroduced in spring of 1994, this is disease-resistant and also resistant to nematodes. Sets fruit at lower temperatures.

Quick Pick: A plum (egg) tomato with bushy growth, it doesn't need staking. Very quick to fruit and high-yielding. Good for sauces, drying and making tomato paste as it is fleshy with few seeds. Also good to eat fresh. Its thick skin makes it more resistant to fruit fly.

Summer Taste: A traditional tomato with good disease-resistance. It fruits mid-season and grows well in tropical areas. Good flavour.

Sweetie: A cherry tomato, bushy and rambling in growth. Fruits prolifically in bunches.

Tiny Tim: A small tomato, somewhat like a large cherry tomato. It is a small, bushy plant, excellent for growing in pots as well as in the garden. A tomato of excellent flavour.

aid of a wad of foil. Leave for 5–7 hours until shrivelled and darkened.

3 Pack into cold, sterilised jars, adding 2 **garlic** pieces to each jar, a sprig of the dried oregano and peppercorns if desired. Cover with oil.

4 Store for a week or so before using; however they will keep for months if stored in the refrigerator. The dried cherry tomatoes look very good tossed through a salad of mixed greens; dress with Italian Dressing, page 81.

Note: If you have a fruit and vegetable dehydrator, this is much more efficient; follow the instructions in the manual.

Preparing dry sun-dried tomatoes: If you have purchased dried tomatoes — that is, not packed in oil — or if the tomatoes you have prepared have become too dehydrated and leathery, boil some water, drop in number of tomatoes required for immediate use and leave for 20 seconds. Drain well, spread out between paper towels and press to remove excess moisture. Pack into sterilised jars, add a halved garlic clove and a few peppercorns. Cover with Salad Oil, seal and store in refrigerator until required.

Preparing dry sun-dried capsicum: This is a new item found in greengrocers alongside the dry sun-dried tomatoes. Prepare as for dry sun-dried tomatoes above.

Tomato and Basil Salad
Serves 6

5 medium-sized firm ripe tomatoes
4–5 pieces oil-packed sun-dried tomatoes
3 tablespoons shredded fresh basil leaves
salt
freshly ground black pepper
2–3 tablespoons Salad Oil, page 80
fresh basil sprigs to garnish

1 Wash and dry tomatoes and slice onto a platter, overlapping slices.

2 Cut sun-dried tomatoes into thin strips and strew over tomatoes. Sprinkle with shredded basil and a little salt and pepper to taste. Drizzle with oil just before serving. Garnish with fresh basil sprigs. Serve at room temperature to enhance the flavour of the tomatoes.

Using Australian Vegetables

Variations

Tomato and Basil Salad with Mozzarella
Top salad with thin slices of mozzarella cheese or, if obtainable, thin slices of chilled bocconcini (fresh mozzarella).

Tossed Tomato and Basil Salad
Put some crisp, mixed salad greens into a bowl. Cut 4 fresh tomatoes into wedges, add with remaining ingredients and toss lightly. A little white wine vinegar may be splashed onto the salad before adding the oil.

Pasta and Tomato Salad
Cook 250 g green and white tagliatelle pasta until *al dente*. Drain and run cold water through it. Drain well and turn into a bowl. Toss with 1 tablespoon of the oil, cover and chill long enough to cool it. Use 1 punnet cherry tomatoes cut in halves in place of the 5 tomatoes, add to pasta with remaining ingredients. Toss lightly and serve.

Green Salad with Macadamia Dressing

It is good to see mixed salad greens readily available at many greengrocers. To make up your own salad mix requires buying whole lettuces and bunches of salad greens and herbs, unless you have a vegetable garden in your backyard. Salad mixes vary according to the supplier; they can contain leaves of mignonette, oak leaf, coral and butter lettuce, young English spinach leaves, radicchio, lamb's lettuce (corn salad), rocket, watercress and sorrel, sometimes with marigold or rose petals added. The mixture will keep for up to 3 days in the refrigerator in a plastic bag.

Serves 6

250 g mixed salad greens
1 ripe avocado
lemon juice
¼ cup Australian Nut-flavoured Dressing, page 82
¼ cup chopped, toasted macadamia nuts

1 Lightly rinse salad greens if necessary, shake well and dry in a salad spinner or roll loosely in a tea towel to remove excess moisture.
2 Pile into salad bowl, cover with plastic film and chill until required — this crisps the salad.

Storing Crisphead Lettuce

Remove outer leaves and rinse off any dirt visible on outside of head so that lettuce is ready for use. Leave until dry, then place in a plastic container or bag and seal well. Store in refrigerator or crisper. Lettuce must be well protected as it can go brown from the ethanyl gas given off by any fruit stored in the refrigerator.

3 Just before serving the salad, slice avocado and sprinkle with lemon juice. Add to salad and sprinkle macadamia nuts on top.
4 Pour on dressing, toss lightly and serve.

Potato Salad with Sun-dried Tomato Dressing
Serves 6–8

1.5 kg small white-skinned potatoes
1 medium-sized red onion
1 yellow pepper (green if yellow not available)
1 red pepper

Sun-dried Tomato Dressing
½ cup drained sun-dried tomatoes
1 clove garlic, chopped
2 tablespoons cider vinegar
½ cup Salad Oil, page 80

1 Wash potatoes and boil in lightly salted water until just tender. Cool, cut in half and place in salad bowl.
2 Halve onion and cut out root. Slice into slender wedges and separate leaves. Wash and halve peppers, remove stems, seeds and white ribs. Cut into 2-cm squares. Add onion and peppers to potatoes and toss lightly to mix.
3 Make dressing and dribble over the salad so that the various colours of the salad are still visible for effect. Toss just before serving.

Sun-dried Tomato Dressing: Put all ingredients in food processor or blender, adding pepper to taste. Process to a coarse purée.

Storing Broccoli and Cauliflower

Do not wash before storage. Remove outer leaves from cauliflower. Chill either vegetable, uncovered, in refrigerator, then place in plastic bag and tuck end of bag loosely underneath. Store in crisper. The initial chilling prevents moisture forming in bag, which can cause decay on the flower heads. This initial chilling is a good idea for any leafy vegetables, or for soft-skinned vegetables such as zucchini and Lebanese cucumbers, which can be affected by condensation.

Using Australian Vegetables

Potato Salad with Pesto Dressing
Serves 6–8

1.5 kg small pontiac potatoes
½ cup chopped spring onions
1 tablespoon grated Parmesan cheese

Pesto Dressing
¾ cup Almond Pesto, page 53
½ cup ricotta cheese
¼ cup dry white wine
freshly ground black pepper

1 Wash potatoes and boil in their skins until just tender — do not allow to break up. Drain, cool and cut in 2-cm slices.
2 Arrange in a shallow dish with slices slightly overlapping. Sprinkle on chopped spring onions.
3 Make dressing and spoon over the potatoes, without covering them completely. Sprinkle Parmesan cheese on top. Cover and chill until required and bring to room temperature for serving.

Pesto Dressing: Mix dressing ingredients in food processor or blender until combined, adding pepper to taste.

Carrot and Beetroot Salad
Serves 6

500 g young carrots
3 medium-sized raw beetroots
1 red onion
mignonette or coral lettuce leaves

Mustard Dressing
1 tablespoon grainy mustard
2 tablespoons cider vinegar
2 teaspoons honey
4 tablespoons canola or sunflower oil
salt and freshly ground black pepper

1 Peel carrots and shred, holding carrots diagonally against shredder so that shreds are as long as possible. Wash and peel beetroot and shred. Cut onion in half, remove root and slice in slender wedges; separate leaves.
2 Wash and crisp lettuce leaves and arrange in a shallow bowl. Toss carrot, beetroot, onion and dressing lightly together and pile onto lettuce. Serve immediately to retain separate colours.

NO ADDED SALT

In this health-conscious age, many consumers look for products so labelled. However, when you look at the nutritional information on such products, sodium could be listed; for example, canned tomatoes with no added salt. Sodium occurs naturally, in small quantities, in many foods, and this should not deter you from buying canned or packaged products proclaiming 'no added salt'.

Mustard Dressing: Beat ingredients together, adding salt and pepper to taste.

Marinated Eggplant
Serves 4–6

4 medium-sized eggplants
salt
2/3 cup Salad Oil, page 80
2 cloves garlic, crushed
2 tablespoons finely chopped flat-leaf parsley
freshly ground black pepper

1 Remove stems from eggplants and cut into 6-mm slices. Spread out on baking trays and sprinkle with salt. Leave for 30 minutes.
2 Rinse eggplant and press slices dry in a clean cloth.
3 Oil a baking tray, add a layer of eggplant and brush with oil. Cook under a very hot grill, turning to brown evenly. Remove to a shallow dish and cook remaining eggplant.
4 Mix remaining oil with garlic, parsley and pepper to taste. Pour over eggplant slices and leave to marinate for 2–3 hours. Serve at room temperature as a starter with crusty bread, as an accompaniment to barbecue meals, or use as directed in recipes.

Marinated Roasted Peppers
In place of eggplants, use 6 large red peppers. Wash and place one at a time on the end of a cooking fork and hold over a gas flame until skin blackens and blisters. As each is roasted, place in a paper bag. Alternatively, roast the peppers under a very hot grill, turning frequently until skins blacken and blister. Place in a large paper bag, close and leave for 10 minutes. Remove skins and rinse off any black specks. Halve, remove cores and seeds and cut each half into quarters. Place prepared peppers in a shallow dish, mix and pour on oil dressing as above. Green peppers may be included with the red to give colour, but the flavour of the red is superior.

Note: The roasted red peppers, simply marinated in oil, may be used in recipes calling for canned or bottled pimento, which is imported.

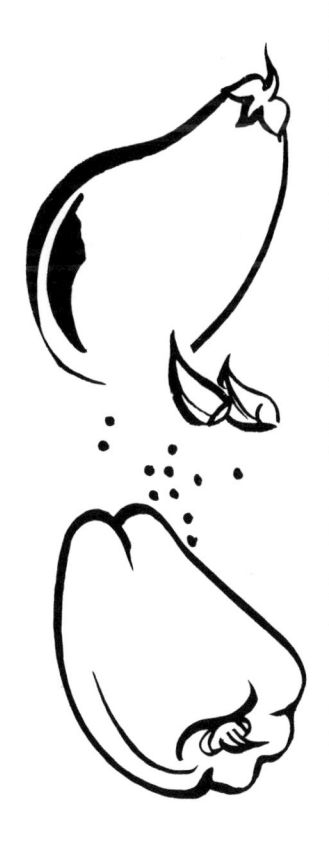

Using Australian Vegetables

Fruit

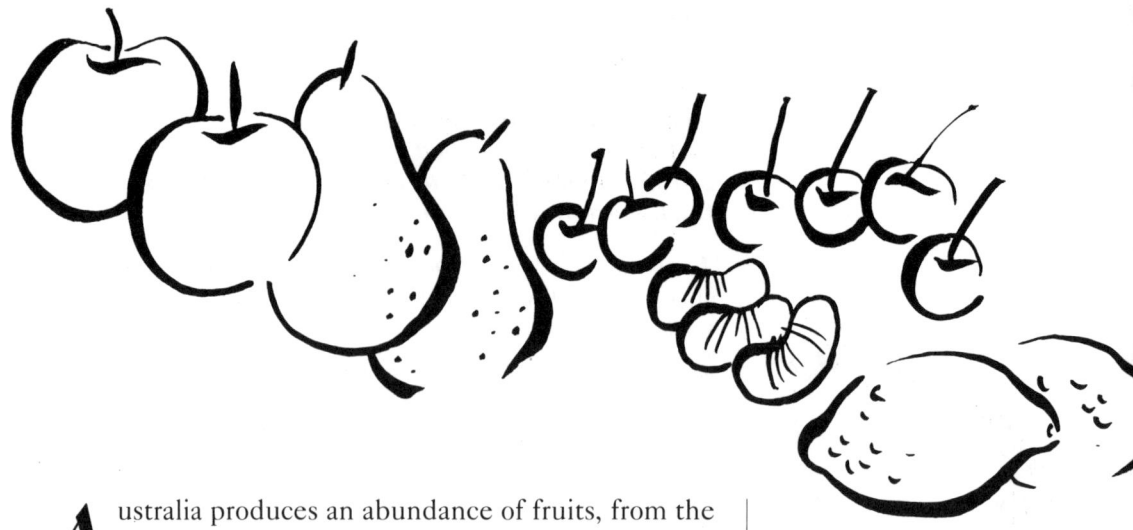

Australia produces an abundance of fruits, from the exotic tropical to the popular cold-climate varieties, which should be sufficient for our needs but apparently is not. Over $110 million a year is spent on fresh, dried, canned and frozen imported fruits. Surely we consumers can turn this around by judicious buying.

Fresh Fruit

Fresh fruit accounts for some $40 million worth of imports, about half of which come from New Zealand. That makes it difficult to say don't buy when we are party to ANZCERTA (Australia–New Zealand Closer Economic Relations Trade Agreement).

Dried Fruit

Dried fruit presents another problem not easily resolved. We do produce excellent dried fruits and could be self-sufficient but for the competitively priced imports of some $30 million, about a third of our total consumption of dried fruits. Our local industry, particularly in dried vine fruits, is moving towards total mechanisation, which will improve production, make local products more competitive in price, and further increase the already high standard of hygiene.

Of the tree fruits, apples, apricots, bananas, citrus peels, mangoes, peaches, pears and plums (prunes) are dried in Australia. A more recent addition is dried pineapple, which was all imported until recently. Check packs carefully, as almost all locally produced dried fruit has to compete with imports.

Dried fruits are widely used in prepared foods such as cereal mixes, breads, cake mixes and confectionery; with support, the dried fruit industry can continue to fulfil our needs. It is good to see responsible cereal and bread manufacturers making a point of including Australian dried fruit in their products and indicating this on packaging; however, many of these products do contain imports.

Canned Fruit

The canned fruit industry has also received a battering from imports. Imports of canned and other preserved and pulped fruit, many for further processing in Australia, are worth about $19 million a year.

Frozen Fruits

Australia does not do much in the way of fruit freezing. Some small processors do freeze a few of our exotic fruits, such as mango 'cheeks' (peeled slices taken from each side of the fruit). Berry fruits are imported frozen for general sale, and some stone fruits are available in bulk from selected retail outlets. Strawberries, raspberries and blueberries are the most widely available of the packaged berry fruits. Altogether we import some $19 million worth of frozen fruits, but a proportion is used in jam manufacture and the preparation of glacé cherries.

The following Buyer's Guide only lists the fruits for which consumer preferences and choices can make a difference.

Choosing Australian Fruit • 145

Buyer's Guide
CHOOSING AUSTRALIAN FRUIT

Product	Australian-produced	Imported	What we can do
Apples — fresh, canned and dried	Yes, fresh, canned and dried	Yes, $2.5 million worth of dried	Check labels of dried apples; imports could be used in some muesli mixes.
Apricots — fresh, canned, dried, glacé	Yes, fresh, canned, dried and glacé	Yes, some $7 million worth of dried, $1 million worth of canned	Use fresh when in season, canned and dried local product when out of season.
Avocados — fresh	Yes, in abundance	Yes, almost $4 million worth from NZ	Select local product; imports are sometimes identified.
Bananas — fresh and dried	Yes, both fresh and dried	Yes, a small quantity	Check labels on packs of dried bananas.
Blueberries — fresh, canned and frozen	Yes, fresh only	Yes, some $2 million, mostly canned and frozen	Local product is excellent; avoid canned and frozen.
Cherries — fresh, canned, bottled (sweet and sour varieties), glacé	Yes, seasonal, some local used for glacé; sour cherries not grown in Australia	Yes, some $11 million worth, canned, bottled and for further processing	Use fresh product when in season; less of canned and bottled cherries; be aware that glacé cherries could contain imports.
Currants, red, white, black — fresh and frozen	Yes, red and black fresh, some white	Yes, some $5 million worth, mostly fresh	Use local product when in season (summer); frozen currants imported — check labels.
Dates — fresh and dried	Yes, fresh only in NT around Alice Springs, and only available there	Yes, over $7 million worth, fresh and dried	Use fewer dates; try local product if visiting Alice Springs.
Figs — fresh and dried	Yes, fresh	Yes, over $2 million worth, mostly dried	Enjoy fresh figs in season (late summer). Use fewer dried figs.
Kiwi fruit — fresh	Yes, industry expanding	Yes, over $8 million worth	Try to obtain local product.
Lemons — fresh	Yes, for most of year	Yes, some $1.5 million worth, including limes	When in season, juice and freeze for summer use. Local limes fruit in summer and are cheap then; use in place of imported lemons.
Mandarins — fresh and canned	Yes, fresh only	Yes, over $1 million worth, mostly canned	Use fresh when in season; avoid canned mandarins.
Mangoes — fresh, canned, dried and frozen	Yes, fresh, canned, dried and small quantity of frozen, including pulp	Yes, some $2 million worth, fresh, canned and dried	When in season, peel, slice and freeze for later use. Check labels on canned and dried mangoes. Use frozen pulp for icecream, mousses.

Product	Australian-produced	Imported	What we can do
Oranges — fresh and candied peel (including other citrus peel)	Yes, fresh and candied peel	Yes, over $5.5 million, mostly fresh, navel oranges in summer; peel used in food manufacture	Do not reject local oranges in summer; the green tinge is caused by the sun. Fruit is still sweet and juicy.
Peaches — fresh, canned, dried, glacé	Yes, fresh, canned, dried, glacé	Yes, over $3 million worth, mostly fresh, some canned and dried	Use fresh when in season; check labels on cans and packs of dried peaches.
Pineapple — fresh, canned, dried and glacé	Yes, fresh, canned, dried and glacé	Yes, over $10 million worth, mostly canned, some dried	Use fresh, available year-round. Check labels on cans (especially house brands) and on dried.
Prunes — dried	Yes	Yes, over $2 million worth	Check labels on packs for local product; all pitted prunes are imported and packed locally.
Raspberries — fresh and frozen	Yes, fresh only	Yes, some $2 million worth, mostly frozen	Use fresh when in season; avoid canned and frozen.
Strawberries — fresh, frozen, canned	Yes, fresh only; available year round, with competition when not in peak season	Yes, over $6.5 million worth, some fresh and canned, mostly frozen	Enjoy during peak season (spring); check for origin on punnets when not at peak. Avoid canned and frozen.
Vine fruits — dried sultanas, raisins, currants and muscatels	Yes, in abundance — sultanas, raisins, currants and muscatels	Yes, some $7 million worth, mostly sultanas	Check labels for local product, also check labels on cereals, fruit loaves, cake mixes and confectionery.

Choosing Australian Fruit

Recipes
USING AUSTRALIAN FRUIT

Avocado Dip or Sauce

This flavoursome dip, the guacamole of Mexican origin, is firmly entrenched in our cooking repetoire. Besides being served in the traditional way with corn chips, it is also good with crisp vegetable pieces or hot or cold seafoods.

Makes about 2 cups

1 small white onion, finely chopped
1 tablespoon lemon juice
2 firm, ripe tomatoes
2 large ripe avocados
1 teaspoon finely chopped red chilli
2 teaspoons finely chopped fresh coriander (optional)
2 teaspoons finely chopped parsley
salt

1 Mix onion with lemon juice and leave to stand until remaining ingredients are prepared.
2 Peel tomatoes, halve and scoop out seeds. Cut flesh into small dice. Halve avocados, remove seeds, reserving one of the seeds. Scoop flesh from skin and mash well on a plate. Purée should be a little coarse to give texture.
3 In a bowl, combine avocado with tomato, marinated onion, chilli, coriander (if available), parsley and salt to taste. Mix well, place avocado seed into mixture, cover and chill. The seed prevents the avocado from discolouring.
4 To serve, remove avocado seed and turn into serving bowl. Serve as a dip with corn chips and/or crisp vegetable sticks, or as directed in recipes.

Note: If fresh chilli is not available, use ¼–½ teaspoon dried chilli flakes to taste.

Ripe Avocados

Avocados should be purchased ripe if needed within 2–3 days. Store in the refrigerator until needed to prevent them over-ripening. If, however, you have firm avocados and need them in 1–2 days, place in a paper bag with 1–2 apples or bananas, even banana skins, close bag and leave at room temperature. These give off ethanyl gas which will ripen the avocados.

Poached Fruit

While canned Australian fruit is of excellent quality, it is worthwhile cooking your own when fruit are in season and reasonably priced. Some fruit, such as quinces, are not available canned, and are definitely worth the effort. To poach, fruit is cooked gently in a sugar syrup. Stewed fruit is simply fruit cooked in a small amount of water with sugar added when fruit is tender.

Basic Poaching Directions

Dissolve 1½ cups sugar in 3 cups water in a wide pan. Stir over heat until sugar is dissolved. Add flavouring ingredients as indicated for each fruit and bring to the boil. Boil for 2–3 minutes. Add prepared fruit, cover and simmer gently until tender, turning large fruit pieces in syrup to cook evenly. Test if fruit is cooked with a fine skewer. Remove fruit to a bowl with a slotted spoon, return syrup to heat and boil for 10 minutes to reduce by half. Cool and strain syrup over fruit, cover and chill until required. Syrup quantity is sufficient for about 1 kg fruit; most fruits take 10–15 minutes to cook.

Apples: Use new-season apples for best results, such as Granny Smith, Jonathan or Delicious. Peel, remove stems, halve and core. Cut into quarters or thick slices. Use 4 whole cloves to flavour syrup. Poach as in basic directions.

Apricots: Select firm, slightly under-ripe apricots. Wash, halve and remove stones. Poach as in basic directions, adding 2–3 drops almond essence at end of cooking.

Peaches: Select firm, just-ripe, free-stone peaches. Wash peaches and place in a bowl. Cover with boiling water, leave for 2–3 minutes, drain and gently remove skins. Halve, remove stones and brush with lemon juice to prevent discolouration. Leave in halves, quarter or slice just before poaching. Use thinly peeled lemon rind in the syrup as flavouring.

Pears: Select pears that are almost ripe. Peel, halve and remove stems. Remove core with melon baller or teaspoon. Place fruit in a bowl of water with lemon juice added to prevent it discolouring. Poach as in basic

Dried Apricots

Australian dried apricots are of excellent quality. They have a superb flavour and good colour. Because of improved packaging, apricots do not require the lengthy soaking often recommended in cookbooks. Recipes give details on soaking where necessary. Apricots are also imported from Turkey. These are usually whole with stone removed, and are softer than the Australian apricot (dried in halves). However their colour is pale, and flavour is not as intense as the local product.

Using Australian Fruit • 149

directions and, when cooked, add 1 teaspoon vanilla essence. Thinly peeled lemon rind, a piece of cinnamon stick or a small knob of bruised fresh ginger may be used in place of vanilla to flavour syrup, added at beginning of cooking.

Quinces: Wash fuzz from quinces, peel, halve, then cut into quarters or sixths, depending on size. Remove cores with a small knife. Don't be concerned if quinces discolour, as this does not affect final appearance. Add 1–2 washed rose geranium leaves or 2 strips lemon peel to syrup and, when boiling, add quinces. Cover and simmer gently for 1$\frac{1}{2}$ hours or until tender — some types of quinces cook in much less than this time, so check after 30 minutes. When cooked, quinces should have a rosy hue. Finish as in basic directions.

Serving suggestions:
- Serve chilled fruit with Custard Cream (page 71) or whipped, slightly sweetened cream, or use as directed in recipes.
- **Peach Melba**: Put 2 scoops vanilla icecream in each dessert dish and top each scoop with a drained peach half, rounded side up. Pour on some raspberry purée (see Berry Fruit Purées, below). Top with a little whipped cream and toasted slivered almonds.

Fruit Purées

• •

A fruit purée, or to use the popular French term, coulis, can be used as a sweet sauce for a dessert or mixed with custard and cream for Fruit Fool. Purées can also be served on icecream, mixed into home-made icecream or added to thick natural yoghurt.

To purée fruit: Use a blender, food processor or hand-held food processor, or press through a sieve.

Apricot: Cook dried apricots in water to cover, adding sugar to taste. When soft and liquid is considerably reduced, purée the fruit. Add 2–3 drops of almond essence if using for Fool. Drained, canned apricots may be used for convenience.

Peaches in Champagne

Peel number of peaches required as described on page 149 (Basic Poaching Directions). Halve, remove stones and brush lightly with lemon juice. Just before serving, place a peach half in each of required number of stemmed dessert glasses (champagne saucers are ideal). Pour on chilled Australian dry, champagne-style wine. Serve with a dessert spoon and fork for attacking the peach after the wine is drunk, or vice versa.

Berry fruit purées: Fresh strawberries, raspberries, mulberries, boysenberries or a mixture of berries, may be used. Hull strawberries, remove stems from mulberries. Rinse fruit, drain well and purée. Stir in caster sugar to taste. If the fruit is very seedy, such as raspberries or boysenberries, purée may be passed through a sieve unless sieve was used to make purée.

To use in Fool or to mix into icecream, cook gently to reduce by one-third in volume or until fairly thick. Add sugar to taste, then cool and chill.

Gooseberry purée: Top and tail the gooseberries and rinse well. Place in a pan with a little water ($1/4$ cup water to 2 cups fruit), and cook gently until soft. Press through a sieve to purée, then add sugar to taste.

Rhubarb purée: Cook washed and chopped rhubarb in a covered dish in the microwave oven without any water — it takes about 6–8 minutes per 500 g. Add sugar to taste while hot, then purée. This makes an excellent Fool, and it is also good with yoghurt.

Refreshing Fruit Desserts

With the abundance of fruits available, summer desserts can be prepared with little fuss. Select fruit with flavour and colour contrast, and peel and slice as required. On individual plates, spread some fresh fruit purée such as raspberry or strawberry, or a mixture; see page 150. Arrange fruit attractively on purée. Whipped, slightly sweetened cream or mascarpone cheese may be offered in a bowl to be added to individual taste.

Fruit Fools

The Fruit Fools of England are simple yet inspired. A thick fruit purée is combined with custard and whipped cream for a delicious dessert. Serve with sponge fingers — Australian-made, of course. You can make your own stirred custard (use custard powder and milk and make according to package directions, make Stirred Custard recipe, page 70) or use ready-made custard from a carton for convenience.

Using Australian Fruit • 151

Serves 6

2 cups thick Fruit Purée, page 150
1 cup vanilla custard
1 cup whipped cream
caster sugar to taste
additional whipped cream for serving
sponge fingers for serving

1 Make purée of choice and chill in a covered bowl; apricot, mixed berry fruits, gooseberry or rhubarb are recommended.
2 Fold custard and cream into purée, taste and add a little sugar if necessary. Pour into dessert glasses, cover and chill until required. Decorate tops with swirls of whipped cream if desired. Serve with sponge fingers.

Almond Fruit Tarts

Almond tarts with fruit toppings are featured in many of our local French patisseries. They make excellent desserts, or can be served as a cake, and are easy to make and an excellent means of using Australian-grown produce.

Oven temperature: 180°C (350°F)

Serves 6–8 for large tart, makes 6 x 12-cm small tarts

½ or 1 quantity Sweet Shortcrust Pastry, page 15

Almond Filling
90 g soft butter
⅓ cup caster sugar
2 large eggs
1 cup ground almonds
2 tablespoons plain flour
¼ teaspoon almond essence

Fruit for Topping
pears, apples, quinces, blueberries, mulberries or cherries

Glaze
apricot jam, redcurrant, apple or quince jelly

1 Use a half quantity of pastry for large tart, full quantity for the small tarts. Roll out and line a greased 23-cm flan tin or 6 x 12-cm small flan tins. Chill until required.
2 Using a bowl and balloon whisk, beat butter, sugar and eggs until light and fluffy. Stir in almonds, flour and almond essence. Pour into pastry-lined flan tin(s) and level top.

Roast Turkey (page 123)
Glazed Kumara (page 131), Cherry Sauce (page 181)

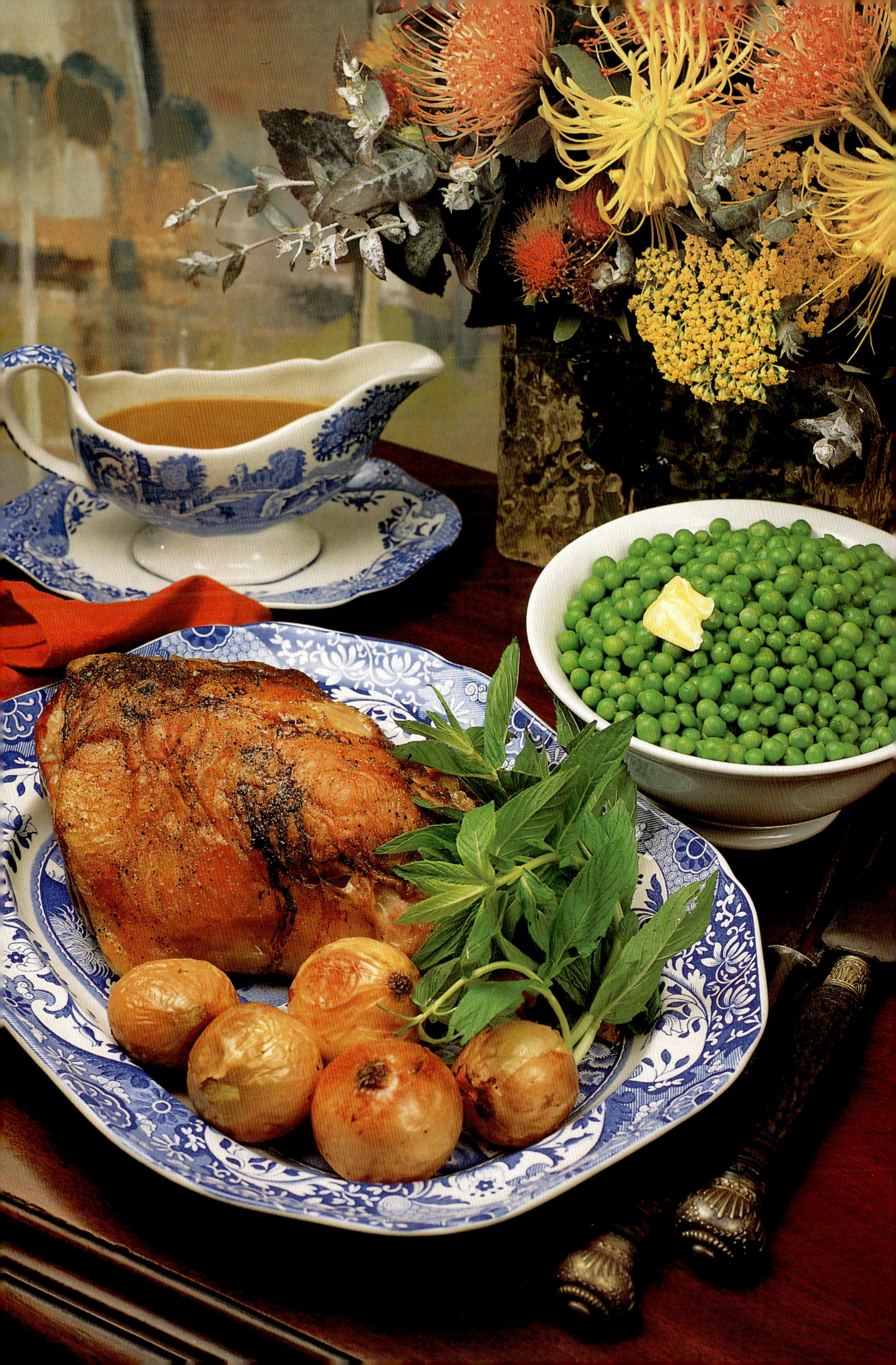

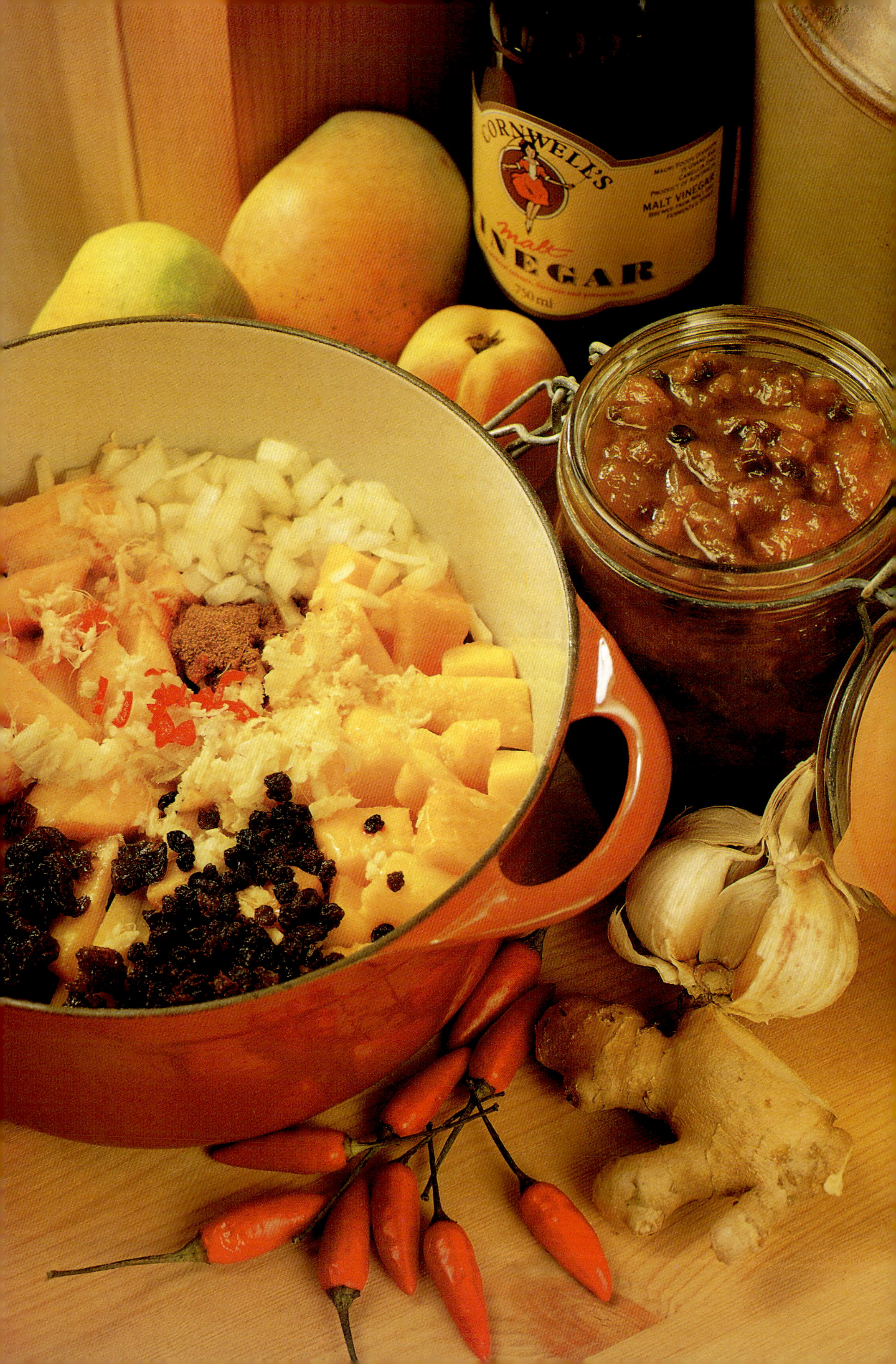
CORNWELL'S
MALT VINEGAR
malt
750 ml

AUSTRALIAN APPLES

Apples are at their best soon after harvest. Some are available year-round as they are held in controlled atmosphere storage for release when the varieties are out of season. Always store apples in a closed plastic bag in the refrigerator to maintain crispness — they should keep for 2 weeks.

Besides the familiar varieties such as Granny Smith, Red and Golden Delicious, Jonathan, Democrat and Bonza, new varieties are well worth trying — Pink Lady, Lady Williams, Red Fuji, Royal Gala and Sundowner. These new varieties have superb flavour, good colour and stay crisp under refrigeration longer. If you like to make fruit salad, Granny Smith apples are the best to use as they do not turn brown; other apples should be sprinkled with lemon juice to prevent browning, or stir a teaspoon of glycerine into the fruit salad.

As far as cooking is concerned, use the apple variety you have on hand. However, Granny Smith is regarded as one of the best apples for cooking, and Golden Delicious runs a close second.

Mango and Peach Chutney (page 179)

3 Arrange fruit decoratively on top (directions on fruit preparation below), and bake in a preheated moderate oven for 35–40 minutes for both large and small flans. Centre should be springy when cooked.

4 If using apricot jam to glaze, press about ¼ cup through a sieve. Heat jam or jelly just enough to make liquid and brush over top of hot tart(s), particularly onto fruit. Cool and remove from tin(s). Serve plain or with whipped cream.

Fruit for topping:

- Canned or poached pear halves: drain well and cut each half in halves. With a sharp knife, slice each quarter along its length and press out to a compact fan. Lift onto tart with narrow point of fan pointing towards centre. Space fans a little apart and place one in the centre. Use one fan for each small tart.
- Canned dessert apples or poached apple quarters: dessert apples are usually quartered. Prepare and arrange as for pear halves.
- Poached quinces: prepare quinces in quarters or sixths for poaching. Slice and arrange as for pear halves.
- Blueberries, mulberries or cherries: use fresh fruit only — the canned ones are usually imported. Blueberries need no preparation; remove stems from mulberries; pit cherries with a cherry stoner and leave whole. Strew a generous ¾ cup of fruit over top of large tart or a heaped tablespoonful over each small tart.

Fruit Crumble

This is an old-fashioned hot pudding that has been rediscovered in recent years, probably because it is easy to make. Our cooks of yesteryear didn't differ from today's cook in the save-time stakes!

Oven temperature: 180°C (350°F)

Serves 6–8

Fruit Base
Choose from the following —
800-g can unsweetened pie apple
2 x 410-g cans pie apricots
825-g can sliced peaches in natural juice, drained
410-g can unsweetened pie apple mixed with 1 cup chopped, pitted prunes

¼–½ cup sugar, depending on sweetness of fruit
1 teaspoon cinnamon

Using Australian Fruit

Crumble Topping
½ cup quick-cooking rolled oats
½ cup plain flour
¼ cup desiccated coconut
½ cup packed brown sugar
¼ teaspoon cinnamon
90 g soft butter
¼ cup chopped almonds or pecans

1 Mix your choice of fruit with sugar to taste and the cinnamon. Place in a 6-cup oven dish and spread evenly.
2 To make Crumble Topping, mix all dry ingredients except for nuts in a bowl, add soft butter and rub in with fingertips or cut in with two knives until mixture is crumbly. Stir in the nuts.
3 Sprinkle Crumble Topping evenly over fruit and bake in preheated moderate oven for 30–35 minutes until topping is golden brown. Serve hot with custard or warm with lightly whipped cream.

Passionfruit Sauce Pudding

Oven temperature: 180°C (350°F)

Serves 6

1 cup self-raising flour
¾ cup caster sugar
grated rind of 1 lemon
pulp of 1 passionfruit
1 egg
¼ cup milk
60 g butter, melted

Sauce mixture
pulp of 3 passionfruit
2 tablespoons lemon juice
water
¼ cup sugar
30 g butter

1 Put flour in a bowl with sugar and mix well. Add lemon rind, passionfruit, egg, milk and warm, melted butter. Mix with a wooden spoon until smooth.
2 Spread on the base of a 6-cup ovenproof dish. Place passionfruit pulp and lemon juice in a 2-cup measure and make up to 1½ cups with water. Pour into a saucepan, add remaining sauce ingredients and heat until just beginning to boil, stirring to dissolve sugar.
3 Pour while hot over the back of a spoon onto the batter. Bake in preheated moderate oven for 30 minutes

---

Giant Limes

A recent arrival in our markets is the giant lime from Queensland. The size of a lemon, it is just as flavourful and juicy as the small lime. If you have recipes which call for the grated rind and zest of 1 lime, this would be the amount of rind removed from a small lime — about ½ teaspoon — so measure your rind and substitute accordingly. Juice amount also varies; as a general rule, a small lime yields about 2 tablespoons juice, while a large lime yields twice as much.

or until cake topping shrinks from sides of dish and sauce is bubbling. Serve warm with cream or icecream.

Fruit and Nut Ring

This chunky fruit and nut cake has become a festive favourite, although I often think it is a cake more suited to baking after Christmas, to use up all those glacé fruits and nuts we don't seem to get through on the big day. The usual recipe contains dates and Brazil nuts, both imported foods. To keep it Australian, prunes and macadamia nuts are used as substitutes, with delicious results. You can vary the quantities of the individual nuts and fruits according to what is on hand — altogether, 1 kg is required.

Oven temperature: 150°C (300°F)

1 cup blanched almonds
1 cup pecan nut halves
1 cup unsalted macadamia nuts
¾ cup pitted prunes
1 cup raisins
3 rings glacé pineapple, cut in chunks
3 whole glacé apricots, cut in chunks
½ cup glacé cherries
3 eggs
½ cup firmly packed brown sugar
1 tablespoon golden syrup
90 g very soft butter
1 teaspoon baking powder
½ cup plain flour
½ cup ground almonds
2 tablespoons brandy
extra nuts and glacé fruits to decorate (optional)

1 Prepare a 20-cm plain ring cake pan. Cut a piece of greaseproof paper to fit into base. Grease pan very well with melted butter, place paper in base and grease paper. Chill, then dust pan with a little flour, shaking out excess. Leave in refrigerator until required.
2 Put nuts and fruit in a large bowl, separating raisins so that they do not clump together. Toss well to mix.
3 Beat eggs with brown sugar and golden syrup until frothy, beat in butter and baking powder. Fold in flour and ground almonds and add half the brandy.
4 Mix fruit and nuts into batter. Spoon into prepared pan, then knock base of pan sharply onto bench to settle mixture.

5 Bake in preheated slow oven for 1½ hours until cake is cooked (test with a skewer). Pour remaining brandy evenly over hot cake, stand for 5 minutes, then turn out onto cake rack and turn right side up onto another rack. Cover loosely with a clean tea towel and cool. Store for up to 1 month in a sealed container, although cake can be used 3–4 days after baking.

6 If desired, when presenting cake for serving, arrange chunks of glacé fruits, pecan nut halves and toasted almonds and macadamia nuts on top in a wreath. Serve cut in thin slices.

Boiled Carrot Fruit Cake

This recipe is easy enough for baking through the year, and delicious enough for Christmas. Being a boiled fruit cake, it may be made even a week before Christmas without the need for the cake to be left to develop flavour. Use Australian rum or brandy, and Australian dried fruits, of course!

Oven temperature: 150–160°C (300–325°F)

1½ cups raisins, chopped
1½ cups sultanas
1 cup currants
1 cup pitted prunes, chopped
½ cup chopped dried apricots
1½ cups grated carrot
1 teaspoon grated orange rind
½ cup fresh orange juice
1 tablespoon golden syrup
185 g butter
1 cup firmly packed brown sugar
2 teaspoons mixed spice
1 teaspoon bicarbonate of soda
3 eggs, beaten
½ cup chopped blanched almonds (optional)
1½ cups plain flour
1 cup self-raising flour
¼ cup rum or brandy
blanched almonds or pecan halves to decorate (optional)

1 Line base and sides of a deep, round 23-cm or a deep, square 20-cm cake pan with greaseproof paper.

2 Place prepared fruits in a large saucepan with carrot, orange rind and juice, golden syrup, butter, sugar and mixed spice. Bring to the boil, stirring occasionally, until butter is melted. Simmer, uncovered, for 5 minutes,

'GREEN' ORANGES

Local oranges are available year-round. Valencias have a long season lasting through spring and summer. In the hot summer months they develop a greenish tinge on sections of skin exposed to strong sunlight while on the tree; this does not indicate that the fruit is unripe. They are sweet and juicy, and you should buy them in preference to the navel oranges imported during summer. The local oranges are cheaper too.

HANDY HINT

Rich fruit cakes should cook slowly for maximum development of flavour. This is usually done by lining pan with 2 layers of brown paper and one of greaseproof paper. The following alternative method is an old-fashioned one, much easier to do and very modern with today's recycling trends!
Line base and sides of cake pan with greaseproof paper, grease it and add cake mixture. Make an even pad of newspaper about 6 layers thick and place on a baking tray. Put cake pan on this, then wrap a wide band of newspaper around outside of pan, again about 6 layers thick — band should extend about 5 cm above rim of pan. Secure with tape, then tie string around pan to keep paper in place. With the low-temperature cooking of fruit cakes, there is no danger of burning the paper.

stirring occasionally. Remove from heat, stir in soda and leave until cool.

3 Stir in eggs, almonds if used, sifted flours and rum or brandy. Place mixture in prepared cake pan, knock base of pan sharply on bench to settle mixture, and even the top with a spatula. Arrange almonds or pecan halves on top if desired.

4 To insulate pan so that cake cooks slowly, follow directions in Handy Hint (opposite). Bake cake in pre-heated oven. Cook for 2$1/2$ hours, or until cooked when tested with a fine skewer.

5 Remove newspaper and trim greaseproof paper so that it is level with rim of pan. Place a round of greaseproof paper on top of cake and wrap in two thick towels so that it cools slowly.

6 Remove cake from pan, leaving paper in place. Store in a sealed container at room temperature until required. If made more than 2 weeks before cake is needed, store in refrigerator.

Last-minute Christmas Pudding

It's a couple of days before Christmas and you decide to make a pudding. So what if it doesn't have time to mature as the books say, it still tastes great. By boiling the fruit mixture as you would a boiled fruit cake, flavour is developed more quickly. My second short-cut is in the crumbs used — the dried breadcrumbs found in most pantries are much more convenient than having to crumb stale bread.

Serves 10–12

5 cups mixed dried fruit (see Note *below*)
1 cup chopped, pitted prunes
$1/2$ cup mixed peel (optional)
1 cup firmly packed brown sugar
$1/2$ teaspoon salt
$11/2$ teaspoons mixed spice
$1/4$ teaspoon grated nutmeg
1 cup water
125 g butter
$1/2$ cup dried breadcrumbs
1 teaspoon bicarbonate of soda
$1/2$ cup chopped or slivered almonds
4 eggs, beaten
1 cup plain flour
1 cup self-raising flour
$1/4$ cup brandy
Brandied Custard Cream for serving, page 71

Using Australian Fruit • 157

1 Put dried fruit in a large saucepan with prunes, mixed peel if using, brown sugar, salt and spices. Add water and butter. Bring to the boil, stirring occasionally. Boil gently, uncovered, for 5 minutes, stirring occasionally to prevent fruit sticking to pan.

2 Remove from heat and stir in breadcrumbs and bicarbonate of soda. Leave to cool, or stand pan in cold water to cool more quickly.

3 Stir in almonds and beaten eggs. Sift flours, fold into fruit mixture, then stir in brandy.

4 Grease a 10-cup pudding steamer with butter and place a round of greased greaseproof paper in the base. Dust steamer with flour, tipping out excess. Turn pudding mixture into steamer, level top and rap base on bench to settle mixture.

5 Cover top of steamer with greased greaseproof paper, then with a sheet of foil. Clip on lid and press foil around rim as an extra seal. Tie string through clips and around knob to secure lid.

6 Half fill a large boiler with water and bring to the boil. Place a round cake rack or upturned plate in base. Put pudding into boiler, cover and boil for 4 hours, adding more boiling water to pan as necessary during cooking.

7 When pudding is cooked, remove lid, foil and paper and leave until cold. Replace paper, foil and lid, tie again and pudding is ready for steaming on day of serving. If making further ahead than 2–3 days, store pudding in refrigerator.

8 To reheat for serving, steam in boiling water for 2 hours. Turn out and serve hot with Brandied Custard Cream.

Note: About 750 g mixed fruit is required. I prefer to mix up my own so that I am sure all ingredients are Australian. Besides, I prefer the pudding without cherries. I use 2 cups chopped raisins, 2 cups sultanas and 1 cup currants. Use the ½ cup mixed peel if you haven't used packaged mixed fruit.

Handy Hint

If your pudding steamer is aluminium and you wish to store the pudding for more than 2–3 days, it is advisable to remove the pudding from steamer when cooled as the fruit can have a corrosive effect on the aluminium. Turn cooled pudding out onto a plate and cover base and sides with pastic film. Return to the steamer, cover with paper, foil and lid. Remember to remove plastic before reheating.

Money Saver

Is sultana bran a popular breakfast cereal with your family? It is cheaper to mix your own at the breakfast table — buy plain bran flakes and have a jar of Australian sultanas on hand. This way you can save money — almost half the cost of a packet of sultana bran — and know it is all-Australian.

Passionfruit Meringue Pie

Oven temperature: 200°C (400°F), reducing to 160°C (325°F)

Serves 6–8

1/2 quantity Sweet Shortcrust Pastry, page 15
4 tablespoons cornflour
2/3 cup sugar
1 1/4 cups water
pulp of 5 passionfruit (5 tablespoons pulp)
1/2 teaspoon grated lemon rind
1 tablespoon lemon juice
pinch of salt
3 tablespoons butter
2 eggs, separated
1 egg white
1/3 cup caster sugar
extra 1 teaspoon cornflour

1 Roll out pastry on lightly floured board and line a greased 23-cm pie plate. Prick pastry well with a fork. Bake blind (see page 16) until fully cooked. Leave until cool.
2 Put cornflour in a heavy-based saucepan and stir in sugar. Add water, passionfruit, lemon rind and juice, salt, butter and egg yolks and stir well with a balloon whisk to mix thoroughly.
3 Place pan over moderate heat and stir constantly until thickened and bubbling. Use a wooden spoon, but if mixture is not thickening evenly, use balloon whisk to stir out any lumps. Reduce heat and leave to simmer for 1 minute. Cool a little, then pour into cooled pie case.
4 Put the 3 egg whites in small bowl of electric mixer and beat until stiff. Gradually add caster sugar and extra cornflour and beat well until stiff and glossy. Pile onto cooled filling and spread meringue so that it touches the pastry. Swirl meringue with the back of a spoon.
5 Cook in preheated moderately slow oven for 25 minutes until meringue is golden brown and set. Serve warm or cold with lightly whipped cream.

Variation

Lemon Meringue Pie

Omit passionfruit in above recipe. Increase lemon rind to 2 teaspoons and lemon juice to 1/2 cup.

Sticky Toffee Pudding

This popular dessert traditionally uses dates. As it is delicious, I tried it with prunes and it worked beautifully. Prunes suffer from an unjustified image problem; they are highly regarded in French cuisine for pâtisserie and desserts.

Oven temperature: 180°C (350°F)

Serves 8

1 cup chopped pitted prunes
1 cup water
1 teaspoon bicarbonate of soda
melted butter
125 g soft butter
¾ cup caster sugar
½ teaspoon vanilla essence
2 eggs
1½ cups self-raising flour

Toffee Sauce
90 g butter
1 cup brown sugar, packed
½ cup cream
½ teaspoon vanilla essence

1 Place prunes in a pan with the water, bring to the boil and simmer, uncovered, for 15 minutes. Remove from heat and stir in soda. Purée prunes in food processor and leave to cool.
2 Brush a 20-cm springform pan with some melted butter and place in refrigerator to chill. Dust with flour, shaking out excess.
3 Beat butter, sugar, vanilla and 1 egg until light and fluffy, then beat in remaining egg. Fold in flour alternately with puréed prunes.
4 Pour into prepared pan and bake in a moderate oven for 40 minutes until cooked when tested. Spoon 4 tablespoons of the Toffee Sauce over the cake and return to oven for a further 8–10 minutes until topping bubbles.
5 Remove from pan and serve hot, cut in slices, with remainder of sauce spooned onto slices. Serve with thick cream or vanilla ice cream on the side.

Toffee Sauce: Make sauce while cake is baking. Place sauce ingredients in a pan, stir over heat until butter melts, then bring to the boil. Boil gently for 3 minutes. Use as directed above.

Storing Bananas

In warm weather, bananas ripen very quickly and often end up being thrown out. While room temperature storage is usually recommended, they can be stored in the refrigerator. Wrap in plenty of newspaper and store in the crisper section or on an upper shelf. The skins usually turn black, but the flesh remains firm.

Herbs and Spices

The fresh herb market is is adequately supplied by Australian growers, but because of various problems associated with harvesting, dehydration, consistency of product and industry requirements, we are still a long way from producing enough dried herbs for the retail market and food industries. When you buy dried herbs, look for those processed and packaged locally.

The medicinal herb and herb tea industry is expanding, but a large proportion of these products are imported. Some are packaged with the source easily identified, and some are imported for repackaging and therefore their source is not so easily identified. Organically grown medicinal herbs and herb teas are mostly locally grown.

Spices are a world resource, produced by some countries for the benefit of all. Because of the intense labour required in the production of many spices, developing countries have certain advantages.

Imports of herbs and spices amount to some $20 million. While we have little choice in the matter of spices, wider use of fresh herbs could make at least a small difference. The most popular herbs and spices are covered in the Buyer's Guide. (Garlic and onion in dried form are covered in the chapter on Vegetables.)

Choosing Australian Herbs and Spices • 161

Buyer's Guide
CHOOSING AUSTRALIAN HERBS AND SPICES

Product	Australian-produced	Imported	What we can do
HERBS			
Anise — fresh	Yes, seeds can be harvested if you grow the plant	Yes, seeds only	Grow in garden; not easy to buy fresh. Harvest seeds and use as a spice.
Basil — fresh and dried	Yes, fresh	Yes, dried	Use fresh when in season. Dried basil cannot always be substituted for fresh.
Bay leaves — fresh and dried	Yes, in home gardens and markets (rarely)	Yes, dried	Bay tree can be grown in garden or pot; use leaves fresh or dried.
Chives — fresh (onion and garlic varieties); dried (onion)	Yes, fresh, both varieties	Yes, dried (onion variety)	Easy to buy and easy to grow in pot or garden. Use in preference to dried.
Chervil — fresh and dried	Yes, fresh	Yes, dried	Grow your own as fresh is not readily available. Dried has good flavour.
Coriander — fresh and minced fresh, jar-packed	Yes, fresh	Yes, minced fresh, jar-packed	Easy to buy and easy to grow. Avoid imported, minced, jar-packed coriander.
Dill — fresh and dried (dill weed)	Yes, fresh	Yes, dried dill weed	Readily available fresh. Dill weed has good flavour but fresh is preferable.
Fennel — fresh	Yes	No	Grows wild in many areas; can be used in place of dill in many recipes.
Herbs, medicinal/teas — large variety	Yes; organically grown mainly sourced locally, as are Penelope Sach's herbal teas	Yes, loose and packaged	Check labels for locally grown or packed products. Big range of local products at health food stores and gourmet food shops. Make your own from fresh herbs, see page 169.
Herbs, mixed — dried	No, but processed here	Yes	Blends from well-known herb processors are very good; cheaper blends can be overpowering — use these sparingly.
Horseradish — fresh and prepared	Yes, fresh and prepared	Yes, prepared	Check labels for local product.

162

Product	Australian-produced	Imported	What we can do
Lemon grass — fresh and dried	Yes, fresh and minced preparations	Yes, dried and minced preparations	Look for local, jar-packed preparations. Use lemon rind if you cannot obtain fresh lemon grass. Dried lacks the flavour of fresh.
Marjoram — fresh and dried	Yes, fresh	Yes, dried	Buy fresh or grow your own. Dried marjoram has a good flavour.
Mint — fresh and dried	Yes, fresh	Yes, dried	Easy to grow or buy fresh. Dried mint has good flavour. Various types available for growing in garden.
Oregano — fresh and dried	Yes, fresh	Yes, dried	Fresh has better flavour than dried. Use dried sparingly.
Parsley — fresh (curly and flat-leaf) and dried	Yes, fresh, both types	Yes, dried	Easy to grow, or buy fresh. Freeze chopped parsley in ice cube trays for convenience, pack into container.
Rosemary — fresh and dried	Yes, fresh	Yes, dried	Easy to grow or buy fresh. Dried has a slightly different flavour.
Sage — fresh and dried	Yes, fresh	Yes, dried	Easy to grow or buy fresh. Dried has a good flavour, but use cautiously.
Tarragon — fresh (French and Russian varieties) and dried	Yes, fresh, both types	Yes, dried	Only grow or buy fresh French tarragon; don't bother with the coarse Russian variety. Dried French tarragon has a good flavour.
Thyme, garden — fresh and dried; lemon — fresh	Yes, fresh, both types	Yes, dried	Easy to grow or buy both types fresh. Dried thyme has a good flavour.
SPICES Allspice/pimento — whole and ground	No, but further processed here	Yes	Excellent spice to have on hand — use in place of mixed spice in smaller amounts.
Cardamom — pods and ground	No, but further processed locally	Yes	Buy pods, remove seeds and pulverise them for better flavour.
Cassia — bark and ground	No, but further processed locally	Yes	Regarded as an inferior cinnamon, cassia nonetheless has a pleasant flavour. Use bark in place of cinnamon sticks.

Choosing Australian Herbs and Spices

Product	Australian-produced	Imported	What we can do
Chilli — whole dried, flakes and ground, also cayenne pepper	No, but fresh chillies and wet, jar-packed, chopped chillies produced locally, see page 172	Yes, wet, jar-packed and dried	Use fresh and local minced, jar-packed chillies. Buy dried chilli in form you use most.
Cinnamon — stick/quills and ground	No, but further processed locally	Yes	Buy sticks or ground in small quantities so that they are used in a short time.
Cloves — whole and ground	No, but further processed locally	Yes	Whole cloves keep well; ground cloves retain flavour well; use cautiously.
Coriander — seeds and ground	Yes, also exported	Yes, small quantity	Most coriander sold is local product; buy ground product for convenience.
Cumin — seeds and ground	No, but you can grow the plant and harvest the seeds	Yes	If you grow your own seeds, gather and pulverise them for convenience.
Curry powder — many blends	Yes, blended from local and imported ingredients	Yes	Look for local blended curry powders — known brands and boutique blends.
Fenugreek — seeds and ground	Yes, also seeds for sprouting	Yes	Buy local product, check label.
Garam masala — ground (Indian spice mix)	No, but blended locally	Yes, the various spices are imported	Buy locally blended product.
Ginger — ground	No	Yes	Use ground ginger mainly for baking.
Juniper berries	No	Yes	Buy whole and crush just before use.
Mace — blades and ground	No, but further processed locally	Yes	Blades are preferable for pickles as flavour is better; use ground in baking.
Mustard — white/yellow, brown and black, seeds	Yes, white and brown grown and processed locally	Yes	Buy local mustard seeds and powder. See page 172 for mixed mustards.
Nutmeg — whole and ground	No, but further processed locally	Yes	Buy whole and grate as needed for better flavour.
Paprika — ground	No	Yes, almost $2 million worth	Buy a reliable brand as quality can vary.
Pepper, black and white — whole and ground; green and pink — whole dried or brine-packed	Yes, by one grower in northern Queensland. Imported peppercorns processed locally	Yes, over $4 million worth — black, white, canned green and pink	The most-used spice. Buy whole and use a pepper mill; flavour more pungent and less is used, which should be our aim. Buy brined green in small cans if you only use them occasionally.

Product	Australian-produced	Imported	What we can do
Saffron — threads or ground	No	Yes	Very expensive spice — buy as you need it, preferably in threads.
Star anise — whole or ground	No	Yes	Buy either whole or ground. Whole star anise is good as a pickling spice.
Turmeric — ground	No	Yes	Use as a substitute for saffron when you want colour more than flavour, such as in spicy dishes.
Vanilla — whole bean and essence	No, but made into essence locally	Yes, mostly as beans, some essence	Buy locally made vanilla essence. Vanilla bean is excellent for custards, etc — rinse off, dry and re-use.

Choosing Australian Herbs and Spices

Recipes
USING AUSTRALIAN HERBS AND SPICES

Drying Herbs

Whether you grow or buy fresh herbs, you can dry them to ensure you are using a local product. You often buy a particular fresh herb and don't use the remainder of the bunch quickly enough. Make it a practice to dry or otherwise preserve such herbs 3–4 days after purchase if they are still languishing in the refrigerator.

Herbs suitable for drying: Basil, bay leaves, chervil, coriander, dill, fennel, marjoram, mint, oregano, parsley, rosemary, sage, savory, tarragon (French), thyme (garden and lemon)

1 If harvesting herbs, pick them on a dry day well before noon, while the aromatic essences are at their peak. If drying herbs bought from the market, cut tie and spread sprigs out on newspaper in the kitchen so that any moisture can evaporate.

2 Tie herbs in small bundles with string and hang in a shady, airy, dry place where they are unlikely to gather dust. Because basil has such fleshy stems, spread sprigs out on newspaper for drying. Leave herbs to dry until brittle.

3 Untie each bundle and check that there are no traces of mildew — discard if there are. Strip leaves from stems, crumble lightly if necessary and store in clean, dry, glass jars. Seal, label and store in a cool cupboard or in a herb and spice drawer, away from light.

Storing Fresh Herbs

For short-term storage chill the herbs, as listed for 'Herbs suitable for drying', and chives as well. Wrap in paper towels, place in a plastic bag and tuck end of bag loosely underneath to allow herbs to breathe. The pre-chilling prevents condensation in the bag. Return to refrigerator and store for up to 3–4 days, or 2 weeks or so for hardy herbs such as parsley.

Basil can turn black very easily. Place in a glass of water in the refrigerator and, when chilled, cover loosely with a plastic bag to prevent leaves from becoming limp.

Of course, other herbs may be stored in the same way, but it depends on space available.

Herbs can also be chopped and frozen in ice cube trays in some water, packing them in meal-size quantities. Unmould when frozen and place in freezer bags, suitably labelled. Basil is the exception for freezer storage as it turns black, and bay leaves should only be dried.

Mint Sauce
Makes about 2 cups

1 cup chopped fresh mint leaves, well packed
1 cup sugar
1½ cups malt vinegar

1 Half-fill small, sterilised jars with mint leaves, packing them in lightly.
2 Put sugar in a pan with vinegar and heat, stirring to dissolve sugar. Bring to the boil and pour over mint leaves, filling jars. Seal when cold and store in a cool, dark place.

Green Sauce
Makes about 1 cup

½ cup roughly chopped parsley
½ cup roughly chopped fresh basil
½ cup roughly chopped watercress
2 tablespoons chopped chives
¼ cup pickled cucumber slices, drained
1 clove garlic, chopped
3 slices stale white bread, crusts removed
¼ cup white wine vinegar
2 tablespoons Salad Oil, page 80
salt
freshly ground black pepper

1 Put all ingredients, except for oils, salt and pepper, into food processor and process to a thick paste.
2 Gradually add oils, then season to taste. Serve as a dressing on a mixed green salad, pasta or potato salad, or serve with prawns, lobster or Balmain/Moreton Bay bugs.

BUNCH OF FLAVOURING HERBS

This is generally known by the French term, 'bouquet garni'. Little bags of dried bouquets garnis are available and usually imported. Even if they are made here, the dried herbs are usually imported. However, fresh herbs give a far superior flavour, although you may have to use dried bay leaves if you do not have fresh leaves on hand.
For general cooking purposes, put together 2 large sprigs of parsley, the leafy top of a celery stalk, 2–3 sprigs of fresh thyme and 1 bay leaf. Double up the parsley stalks to make the bunch compact — don't cut them off, because the stalks have the best flavour. Tie with white string and place in the middle of the dish being prepared. Remove and discard at end of cooking.

Tabouli

When supermarkets and delis sell it in abundance, you know food of ethnic origin has found its niche in the Australian kitchen. Tabouli, because of its healthy image, is one of those foods and is here to stay. It may be served as an appetiser, as a salad, or as part of the filling in sandwiches, rolls and pitta breads. Australian-produced burghul does not require rinsing; however burghul must be moistened to soften and swell the grains.

Makes about 6 cups

3/4 cup burghul
2 bunches flat-leaf parsley
1/2 cup finely chopped spring onions
1/4 cup finely chopped fresh mint
1 1/2 teaspoons salt
freshly ground pepper to taste
1/8 teaspoon ground cinnamon (optional)
2–3 tablespoons lemon juice
2 large ripe, firm tomatoes
3 tablespoons virgin olive oil
2 tablespoons sunflower or maize oil

1 Place burghul in a large bowl, cover with cold water, then pour off water through a sieve, returning any burghul from sieve to bowl. Cover bowl with a cloth and leave for 20 minutes until burghul has swelled and softened. Stir occasionally.
2 Wash parsley and shake bunches to remove excess moisture. Cut off thick stems and chop leaves finely using a knife (do not chop in food processor as it could pulp the parsley). You will need about 4 cups chopped parsley.
3 Add spring onions to burghul and mix in with a wooden spoon, pressing down on the mixture so that the onion flavour can be released into the burghul. Stir in chopped parsley, mint, salt and pepper and cinnamon if used.
4 Add lemon juice to taste, cover and refrigerate at this stage if not required immediately. Keep until next day if necessary.
5 To complete salad for serving, peel tomatoes, halve crosswise and scoop out seeds. Cut tomatoes into fine dice. Add to salad with combined oils, toss and adjust seasoning if necessary. Serve as suggested above. Leftover salad may be stored in the refrigerator for 3–4 days.

HERBAL TEAS

Herbal teas in tea bags are imported. Health food stores carry a wide range of locally grown dried herbal teas, many organically grown, usually with advice as to their medicinal uses. Of course herb teas are mostly taken as a substitute for tea and coffee.
One particular local producer, Penelope Sach, who is qualified in herbal medicine, combines herbs with ingredients such as rose petals, rose hips, lavender, chamomile and calendula. She makes a range of six tea blends, with intriguing names such

Herbed Wine Marinade

½ cup white wine
1 tablespoon leatherwood or yellow box honey
2 tablespoons Salad Oil, page 80
2–3 sprigs fresh herbs (rosemary, thyme or marjoram)
1 clove garlic, sliced

1 Mix wine, honey and oil until honey is dissolved.
2 Finely chop selected herb and add to mixture with garlic.
3 Place meat to be marinated into a plastic container with lid to fit. Pour on marinade, seal and shake container to distribute marinade.
4 Refrigerate for 3 hours or longer, shaking container now and then. Grill or barbecue meat until cooked to taste, basting with marinade. Use any of the herbs for lamb, thyme or marjoram for pork or chicken.

Rosemary Red Wine Marinade

½ cup red wine
2 tablespoons canola oil
1 teaspoon cracked black peppercorns
1 clove garlic, sliced
2 sprigs rosemary, roughly chopped

1 Combine ingredients in a shallow glass dish. Add meat, turn to coat, cover and refrigerate for at least 3 hours.
2 Drain meat and grill or barbecue, basting with marinade. Use for beef, lamb or pork.

Fresh Herb Teas

Fresh herbs can be grown easily in the garden or in pots. Besides using in cooking, most may be brewed for refreshing herb teas.

Pick herbs early in the morning when flavour is at its peak; rinse sprigs and shake off excess moisture. Crush lightly in your hand to bruise the leaves, allowing maximum flavour in the brew. Place in a glass or china teapot, or even a jug. Pour on boiling water, leave to infuse for 5–10 minutes, then strain into a tea glass. If your brew is too strong, simply add boiling water. A large amount can be brewed early in the day, strained and refrigerated. You can reheat the tea, if necessary, in the microwave oven. Serve hot or cold with honey if desired; a slice of lemon or lime adds a refreshing tang.

as Petal, Après, Summer Delight, Lemon Tang, Triple-E and Berry. Her packaging is stylish, and the organically grown ingredients are mostly sourced in Australia. They are available at some gourmet food stores as well as at her shop in Woollahra, Sydney. A few of our large hotels serve her teas and she has begun exporting. Penelope recommends brewing her teas in a fine-mesh tea ball, glass pot with infuser, or coffee plunger pot. Several brews may be made with the one tea ball or pot infusion.

Using Australian Herbs and Spices • 169

Popular garden herbs for teas: Anise, balm/lemon balm, basil, bay leaf, borage, chervil, coriander, dill, fennel, lemon grass (use the leaves), lovage, marjoram, oregano, parsley, peppermint, rosemary, sage, salad burnet, spearmint and thyme.

These may be used on their own or in combination; for example, balm or lemon grass may be added to most other herbs for a tangy, lemon flavour. Peppermint and spearmint may be added to parsley, marjoram, chervil or thyme.

Note: For medicinal uses, consult a reliable publication such as *Herbs — Their Cultivation and Usage*, by John and Rosemary Hemphill (see Further Reading).

Australian Pepper

At Silkwood in far northern Queensland, Levis and Louis Campagnola have gone from sugar cane to pepper production. In the mid-1980s, after researching a possible crop to replace the cane, they planted their first pepper vines, trained onto posts for easier hand-picking. Currently they have 2500 vines, most producing peppercorns. From July to November they market punnet-packed spikes of fresh, green peppercorns, used in restaurants and also sold in some Sydney and Canberra Coles stores and produce markets in Sydney, Melbourne and Adelaide. They have a superb flavour — crush them and use in place of canned green peppercorns. The Campagnolas also dry the pepper and market whole black peppercorns and cracked, kibbled and ground pepper under the Aussie Pepper label. Such an industry deserves our support. (See Acknowledgements for supplier.)

Pickles, Sauces and Condiments

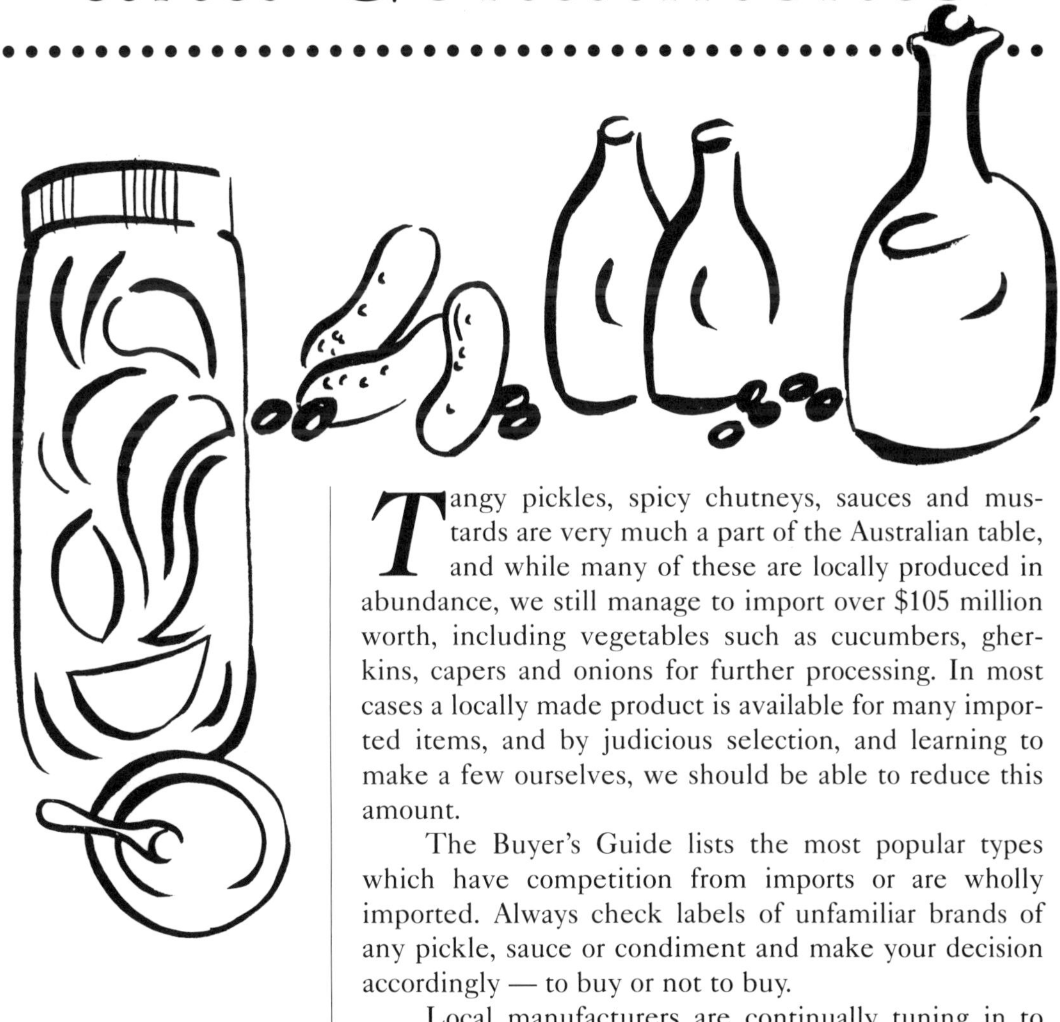

Tangy pickles, spicy chutneys, sauces and mustards are very much a part of the Australian table, and while many of these are locally produced in abundance, we still manage to import over $105 million worth, including vegetables such as cucumbers, gherkins, capers and onions for further processing. In most cases a locally made product is available for many imported items, and by judicious selection, and learning to make a few ourselves, we should be able to reduce this amount.

The Buyer's Guide lists the most popular types which have competition from imports or are wholly imported. Always check labels of unfamiliar brands of any pickle, sauce or condiment and make your decision accordingly — to buy or not to buy.

Local manufacturers are continually tuning in to consumer needs. For instance, Asian and Mexican style sauces, previously imported, are now being locally produced; a couple of well-known American companies producing Mexican-style foods, who export to Australia, have licensed local manufacturers to make certain products. Imported Italian pasta sauces now have to compete with an increasing range of local similar sauces. The range of sauces, condiments, marinades and dressings is continually expanding, and the decision to buy locally made products should be an easy one to make.

Choosing Australian Pickles, Sauces and Condiments

Buyer's Guide
CHOOSING AUSTRALIAN PICKLES, SAUCES AND CONDIMENTS

Product	Australian-produced	Imported	What we can do
Apple sauce	Yes	Yes	Buy local product or make it.
Capers	No, but some are processed locally	Yes	Use sparingly or substitute Pickled Nasturtium Pods, page 175.
Chilli, minced, jar-packed	Yes, minced jar-packed	Yes; for example, sambal ulek, harissa	Buy a local product — it can often substitute for imports, or use fresh chillies.
Chilli sauce — hot, mild; tabasco, taco, etc.	Yes, many of these now locally made	Yes, chilli sauces and tabasco	Check labels for local product; use tabasco sparingly.
Chutneys — some types such as mango	Yes, many types	Yes, quite a lot	Buy local product; easy to make your own. See Mango and Peach Chutney, page 179.
Cranberry sauce and jelly	No. Fresh cranberries can be used — imported from NZ	Yes	Use sparingly. Try turkey and ham with Cherry Sauce, page 181.
Cucumbers, pickled — whole and sliced	Yes, whole and sliced, from local and some imported cucumbers	Yes, almost $6 million worth, including gherkins	Check labels for local product. Source of cucumbers usually not given.
Curry pastes	Yes, with local and imported ingredients	Yes	Buy locally made curry pastes; check labels.
Fish sauces — anchovy, fish, oyster, shrimp, etc.	Only anchovy sauce made locally from imported ingredients	Yes	Use sparingly or avoid recipes using such sauces.
Gherkins, pickled	Yes, from local and imported gherkins	Yes, including gherkins for further processing	Check labels for local product, though source of gherkins might not be given.
Ginger — minced, jar-packed	Yes, from locally grown ginger	Yes	Check labels and buy local product or use fresh ginger; make your own, see page 179.
Mustards, prepared — English, French, Dijon, grainy, herbed, etc.	Yes, most types, plus some unique to our boutique preserve makers	Yes, amount not known	Buy local product; many special mustards made by boutique preserve makers.
Olives — black, green, stuffed, in brine or vinegar	Yes, small quantity but increasing slowly; plenty of fresh olives available May, June for home preserving	Yes, some $20 million worth	Try local product when you can get it; Kalamata olives from McLaren Vale are excellent. To cure fresh olives, see page 177.

Product	Australian-produced	Imported	What we can do
Onions, pickled	Yes, ample for our needs	Yes, small quantity	Check labels for local product.
Peppers, pickled — mild, medium and hot, in vinegar	Yes, mild, medium and hot	Yes	Check labels for local product, or make your own, see page 174.
Sauces — black bean, hoisin, plum (Chinese and spiced), satay, etc.	Yes, some types made with local and imported ingredients	Yes, over $34 million worth, including chilli and fish sauces	Check labels for local products; use less of imported sauces which have no local equivalent.
Soy sauce — light, dark, low-salt, etc.	Yes, light	Yes, over $9 million worth	Buy local product for standard uses; use less of imported sauce.
Tomato — sauce, ketchup, Italian pasta sauce	Yes, all types	Yes, some $7 million worth	Buy local products; plenty to choose from.
Vegetables, mixed — pickled in vinegar	Yes	Yes, some $8 million worth	Check labels for local product, or make your own.
Vinegars — cider, malt/brown, white; white and red wine, flavoured (fruit or herb), balsamic	Yes, cider, malt/brown, white; white and some red wine vinegar with more to come in the future; some flavoured vinegars	Yes, over $2 million worth, wine and flavoured vinegars, balsamic	Use local vinegars as much as possible; seek out local red wine vinegar (Coriole, Cornwell's gourmet, Yalumba), look for boutique flavoured vinegars.

Choosing Australian Pickles, Sauces and Condiments • 173

Recipes
USING AUSTRALIAN PICKLES, SAUCES AND CONDIMENTS

Pickled Peppers

The elongated banana or Hungarian peppers appear in the markets in summer. They can be green, yellow or red, and a mixture of colours gives a most attractive pickle. They are usually sweet, but smaller peppers can be mildly hot, yet not nearly as hot as the slender chillies. You can also pickle the ordinary, bell-shaped peppers, also called capsicums, in the same way.

1 kg long sweet peppers or ordinary peppers
3 red or green chillies
6 cups water
3 tablespoons cooking salt
double quantity Spiced Vinegar, page 175
3 cloves garlic, halved

1 Trim stems of peppers and chillies and wash well. If using ordinary peppers, have a mixture of red, green and yellow, if you can find them; wash, halve lengthwise and remove cores, seeds and white ribs. Cut each half into quarters.
2 Place peppers in a bowl, add water and salt. Stir occasionally with hand until salt dissolves. Leave for 24 hours.
3 Drain and rinse peppers. Drain thoroughly, then pack into 3 cold, sterilised jars, placing 1 chilli and 2 garlic halves in each jar.
4 Make vinegar according to directions. After steeping, strain, return vinegar to saucepan and bring to the boil. Pour boiling hot vinegar over peppers. Seal when cold and leave for 2 weeks before using.

Spiced Vinegar

Makes 2 cups

2 cups white, cider or brown vinegar
6 whole allspice berries
12 whole peppercorns
4 whole cloves
1 teaspoon white mustard seeds
1 tablespoon sugar

1 Choose vinegar to suit produce to be pickled — white or cider vinegar when you want the colour of the pickling item to show, brown when you want its mellow flavour, such as pickled onions.

2 Put vinegar in a stainless steel saucepan with spices and sugar. Bring to the boil, stirring to dissolve sugar. Boil gently for 5 minutes, remove from heat and stand for 1–2 hours. Strain into a just-emptied vinegar bottle or a clean, dry bottle. Seal and use as required.

Pickled Nasturtium Pods

Capers are not grown in Australia, but some are imported and prepared locally. Even if they were grown, it would be up to the home pickler to prepare them as costs of picking the caper buds would preclude their exploitation. But we have no substitute, except in nasturtium pods. These are often referred to as nasturtium seeds, which they are, but it is the pod with the seed enclosed that is pickled. Nasturtiums grow easily in our gardens, with many plants escaping the confines of the suburban plot to flourish on public embankments. Pick the green pods when they are nicely plump; they are usually clumped in threes — break them apart gently. If the flowers are prolific, you can also pick off the tiny buds and add them to your pods. After all, capers are the buds of the caper flower, and conversely, in countries where capers flourish, the seed pods are also pickled for home use.

Makes about 1 cup

1 cup nasturtium pods
1/2 teaspoon cooking salt
about 1 cup Spiced Vinegar, see above, using white vinegar

1 Remove any stems from pods. Separate the pod clumps by breaking them gently apart. Put them in a sieve and rinse under running water.
2 Spread pods onto a baking tray lined with paper towels and place in oven set onto lowest possible temperature. Leave for 3 hours until they have wilted a little — they should feel spongy when pressed. This process removes some of the moisture. Alternatively leave in hot sun for 8 hours or so.
3 Place pods in a sterilised jar. Dissolve salt in vinegar and bring to the boil. Pour over the pods and seal when cold. Leave for 2–3 weeks before using as a substitute for capers.

Note: If you have also picked buds, put them aside as you work on the pods. Pinch stems from buds and rinse buds lightly in a sieve. Drain well and spread onto paper towels to dry. Leave for 3–4 hours until they wilt a little. Add to pods in jar and pour on spiced vinegar.

Pickled Beetroot

2 kg medium-sized beetroots
cooking salt
1/2 teaspoon black peppercorns
1 fresh red chilli, halved
1 star anise
1/2 teaspoon whole cloves
3 cups white wine vinegar
1 1/2 cups sugar

1 Wash beetroot well and trim tops, leaving about 2 cm of stems in place. Place in a large boiler with water to cover and about 2 teaspoons cooking salt. Cover, bring to the boil, and boil gently for 40–50 minutes or until just tender. Test with a fine skewer. Cool, then drain and remove skins and top, trim bases.
2 Quarter, slice or dice beetroot and pack into cold, sterilised jars.
3 Put remaining ingredients in an enamelled or stainless steel saucepan and add 1 tablespoon salt. Stir over heat until sugar is dissolved. Cover and simmer gently for 20 minutes.
4 Strain hot vinegar over beetroot in jars to cover completely. Seal when cold with plastic lids. Store in a cool, dark place and leave for 3–4 days before using.

AUSTRALIAN VINEGARS

With such a thriving wine industry, it is surprising that wine vinegars are not produced in abundance. The vinegar-using public probably has something to do with it, as the biggest seller is white vinegar, followed by cider and malt (brown) vinegar. Of these, mild-tasting cider vinegar is excellent for culinary uses, and a good malt vinegar is often overlooked for dressing salads — it is really very good. White is best reserved for pickles that require a light-coloured vinegar.
However, some wine makers have turned their hand to wine vinegar production. Both red and white wine vinegar is produced. Cornwell's markets a white wine vinegar in 750-ml bottles, which is far better than white vinegar for general use. They also make a Gourmet range of white

and red wine vinegars, reasonably priced and as good as some of the imports. A couple of South Australian wine producers, Coriole of McLaren Vale, and Yalumba of Angaston, make red wine vinegar by the French Orleans method, placing these vinegars on a par with French imports. Yalumba also makes a sherry vinegar using their fino sherry, and production of a balsamic-style vinegar, based on a rich tawny port, proved satisfying enough to merit further development of this rich, mellow-flavoured vinegar presently imported from Italy. To be able to make balsamic in the traditional way requires casks of particular woods, and many years of maturation. In the not-too-distant future, we could have our own balsamic vinegar.

Mustard Pickles
Makes about 12 cups

500 g cauliflower, chopped
½ green and ½ red pepper, diced
2 Lebanese cucumbers, unpeeled and diced
250 g green beans, chopped
2 large onions, chopped
¼ cup cooking salt
4 cups good white vinegar
2 tablespoons powdered mustard
3 teaspoons curry powder
1 teaspoon ground turmeric
1¼ cups firmly packed brown sugar
¾ cup white vinegar, extra
¼ cup plain flour

1 Place the prepared vegetables in a large glass or china bowl, add cooking salt and toss well. Cover bowl and leave overnight.
2 Next day tip vegetables into a colander and rinse under cold water. Drain well.
3 Put vinegar, mustard, curry powder, turmeric and brown sugar in a stainless steel or enamelled pan. Heat, stirring until sugar dissolves, then add drained vegetables. Boil gently, uncovered, for 12–15 minutes until vegetables are just tender.
4 Pour extra vinegar into a screw-top jar, add flour, seal and shake well to mix (this prevents flour lumping). Pour into simmering pickle, stirring constantly, and simmer, stirring constantly, for 5–8 minutes until lightly thickened. Pickle will thicken further on cooling. Ladle into hot, sterilised jars and seal when cold. Store in a cool place.

Curing Olives

In autumn fresh olives appear in the markets. Usually they are a mixture of green and black, with shades in between. Pick out the green olives and put aside. Remaining olives of various hues are prepared separately. With curing, the coloured olives turn darker, so these will be referred to as black olives in the following instructions.

1 Cut three slits on the sides of the olives, using a Stanley knife with a new blade. Place green and black olives in separate, clean buckets and cover with cold water. Keep olives submerged with a plastic bag filled with water and tied. Change water each day for 7–10 days until bitterness is only just evident. Black olives could be ready 2–3 days before the green ones.

2 Measure last lot of water from each bucket, totalling amounts. This gives an indication of amount of brine required.

3 Leave olives aside to drain in separate colanders.

4 Put required amount of water in a large boiler and add 1/3 cup pickling salt (from the butcher) to each litre of water. Bring to the boil, stirring to dissolve salt. Cool the brine. Check salt level of brine — a fresh egg should float just under the surface. Add more salt or boiled water to increase or decrease brine density.

5 Pack olives into jars, again keeping green olives separate. Cover with brine solution. Float some vegetable oil on top of each jar, seal and leave for 6–8 weeks for black, 2–3 months for green. They are ready when there is no trace of bitterness.

6 Sometimes a skin forms over the olives. Remove this carefully and remove any olives in contact with the skin that have discoloured. Float more oil on top and leave until required.

7 As you need olives for the table, remove and drain well. They can be served as they are, or pack into clean jars, cover with brown vinegar and add 2 cut cloves garlic, 2–3 sprigs thyme and float some olive oil on top. Leave for 2–3 days then use as required.

Mexican Chilli Sauce

It is not possible to make a genuine chilli sauce in Australia as we do not grow the vast range of peppers and chillies available to Mexicans and Americans of the southern states. However, you can make a good substitute using the available peppers and chillies.

Makes about 2 1/2 cups

1 large green pepper
1 large onion, chopped
2 tablespoons maize or sunola oil
3 cloves garlic, chopped
4 small red chillies, seeded and chopped
500 g ripe tomatoes
2 teaspoons chopped fresh oregano
salt to taste

Parisian Essence

This is a very old Australian cooking additive which has taken a back seat to soy sauce. Actually its principal ingredients are food colouring, salt and preservative, and it was popular for adding a rich, brown colour to stews and casseroles. It is still used to add colour to Christmas puddings and rich fruit cakes. These days, soy sauce is often added to non-Asian type recipes for its colour more than its flavour; in future, add a little Parisian essence instead.

1 Wash pepper, remove stem, seeds and white membrane. Chop roughly.
2 Heat oil in a pan, add onion and peppers and cook gently for 10 minutes, until onion is soft.
3 Halve and seed chillies, taking care not to touch eyes or lips with hands. Chop chillies finely. Add to onion mixture with garlic and fry gently for a few seconds.
4 Peel tomatoes, halve and flick out seeds. Chop roughly. Add to pan with remaining ingredients, cover and simmer for 30 minutes.
5 Process in blender or food processor to a smooth sauce. Store in sterilised jars in refrigerator, reheating if necessary when serving.

Mango and Peach Chutney

Mango chutney has to be one of our favourite preserves. While Australian-made mango chutney is available, most of such chutneys are imported. The following recipe includes peaches for a real taste of summer, but you can use an additional 3 mangoes in place of the peaches if you prefer.

Makes about 8 cups

6 firm mangoes
6 free-stone peaches
1 large onion, finely chopped
2 cloves garlic, crushed
1 cup chopped raisins
½ cup currants
3 teaspoons grated fresh ginger
1 teaspoon chopped fresh red chilli
2 teaspoons mixed spice
3 teaspoons salt
1½ cups sugar
2 cups malt vinegar

1 Mangoes need only be partly ripe. Peel, slice and cut into cubes. To peel peaches, place in a large bowl, cover with boiling water, stand 2 minutes then drain and peel. Cut into cubes.
2 Place fruits and onion in a large enamelled cast-iron or stainless steel pan. Stir in remaining ingredients. Place over medium heat and bring to the boil, stirring well to dissolve sugar.

Minced Ginger or Garlic

These convenient items are often imported, although local manufacturers also prepare them. It is easy to do this yourself. Peel and shred fresh ginger root; put peeled garlic cloves into food processor and process to a coarse paste. Place each in a sterilised, dry jar. Add dry sherry to just cover, seal and refrigerate.

Using Australian Pickles, Sauces and Condiments • 179

3 Adjust heat so that chutney boils gently, and cook, uncovered, for 1 hour or until thick. Stir towards end of cooking to prevent chutney sticking to pan. Pour into hot, sterilised jars, seal and label when cold. Store in a cool, dark place.

Chutney variations

Once you have mastered this chutney, the same basic recipe may be used for other chutneys.

Apricot and Apple Chutney

Replace mangoes and peaches with 1 kg fresh apricots, pitted and chopped, and 2 Granny Smith apples, peeled, cored and chopped. Use the same quantity of brown sugar in place of the white sugar, and use cider vinegar instead of brown vinegar. Makes about 6 cups.

Tomato Chutney

Replace mangoes and peaches with 1.5 kg tomatoes, peeled and chopped, and 2 Granny Smith apples, peeled and chopped. Add an extra chopped onion. Use 1 cup sultanas in place of the raisins and currants and brown sugar in place of white sugar. Makes about 8 cups.

Peanut Sauce

Peanut Sauce is easy to make and stores well in the refrigerator. It goes well with beef, chicken, lamb and pork, particularly on satays. It may be used as a marinade for these meats, a basting sauce or merely served with grilled or barbecued meats.

Makes about 2 cups

1 tablespoon peanut oil
3 tablespoons grated onion
2 cloves garlic, crushed
1–2 teaspoons chopped fresh red chillies
1 teaspoon ground coriander
1 teaspoon ground cumin
½ cup water
½ cup canned coconut milk
1 cup crunchy peanut butter
2 tablespoons lemon juice
1 tablespoon soy sauce
1 tablespoon brown sugar

1 In a saucepan, place oil, onion, garlic and chilli to taste. Cook gently for 3–4 minutes. Add spices and cook for a further minute.

2 Stir in water and coconut milk, then add remaining ingredients. Stir until combined and bring to a simmer. If very thick, add a little more coconut milk or water.
3 Cool and store in a sealed jar in refrigerator. Use as it is as a sauce, bring it to room temperature, or heat and make more liquid with water and coconut milk if a thinner sauce is required for a marinade or basting sauce.

Note: If using as a marinade, and remaining marinade is required to serve as a sauce, bring it to the boil and boil gently for 2–3 minutes before serving.

Cherry Sauce for an Australian Christmas

In attempts to australianise Christmas, many recommend that we change our fare to feature seafoods and serve cold turkey and ham. Admittedly such changes suit our climate, but is it what we want?

It is obvious, from sales figures of festive foods and cookery editorials, that the average Aussie much prefers traditional fare, influenced by English and American traditions. This is where we can make subtle changes. The following recipe is one of them; using in-season cherries, it substitutes for the imported Cranberry Sauce and the English Cumberland Sauce, usually made with imported redcurrant jelly.

Serves 10–12

2 cups halved, pitted cherries
2 teaspoons grated orange rind
1 teaspoon grated lemon rind
1 cup sugar
½ cup lemon juice
½ cup port

1 Place pitted cherries in a saucepan with remaining ingredients. Stir occasionally over medium heat until sugar is dissolved.
2 Bring to the boil and boil gently for 10 minutes. Remove cherries to a bowl with a draining spoon.
3 Boil syrup for 10 minutes to reduce by a third. Cool syrup and pour over cherries. When cold, transfer to a sterilised jar, seal and store in refrigerator until needed.
4 To serve, bring to room temperature and serve in a bowl or sauce jug. It goes well with hot or cold turkey or ham.

Note: The sauce keeps for months in the refrigerator, but you can make it early in December when cherries are usually less expensive.

Jams, Syrups and Honey

*I*mports of sugars and derivatives are minor, but with jams, syrups and honey, imports account for some $20 million (confectionery is covered in a separate chapter).

Fruit jams and jellies account for half of the imports; add to this the fruit brought in to process into jam here and the amount almost doubles. Jam manufacturers source their fruits locally, but have to make up any shortfall in a particular fruit with imports.

When I have argued the toss with friends on local versus imported, so often their answer is that the imported product is better. We have jams, jellies and marmalades to suit all tastes and pockets. The larger manufacturers fill the average requirements; the growing band of 'boutique' jam and preserve makers produce an exciting range of superb quality, attractively packaged. Some also make uniquely Australian jams such as quandong and rosella.

It is difficult to put a dollar value on imports of certain types of jams and jellies as they are not itemised individually, except for marmalades.

Buyer's Guide
CHOOSING AUSTRALIAN JAMS, SYRUPS AND HONEY

Product	Australian-produced	Imported	What we can do
JAMS AND JELLIES			
Apricot jam and conserve	Yes, imported fruit sometimes used	Yes	Buy local product; make your own when apricots are in season.
Blackberry jam and jelly	Yes, sometimes using imported fruit	Yes	Buy local product; make your own if blackberries are still growing in your area.
Blackcurrant jam and jelly	Yes, mostly from imported fruit	Yes	Buy locally made product.
Cherry jam	Yes; from local and imported fruit	Yes	Buy local product; make your own when cherries are in season.
Fig jam	Yes	Yes	Buy local product; make your own if you have a fig tree.
Marmalade — orange, lemon, lime, grapefruit, mixed citrus, etc.	Yes, most types	Yes, over $1 million worth	Buy local product; for special marmalades, check types made by local 'boutique' jam makers.
Melon — with lemon, ginger or pineapple	Yes, a truly Australian jam	No	Buy it because you can be sure it is a wholly Australian jam. Easy to make too.
Peach jam and conserve	Yes, from local and imported fruit	Yes	Buy local product or make your own if you can get cheap fruit.
Plum jam	Yes	Yes	Buy local product or make your own when plums are in season.
Quince jam and jelly	Yes, jelly mostly	Yes, some jam	Not readily available; look for it in autumn/winter when fruit is in season or make your own.
Raspberry jam	Yes, from local and imported fruit	Yes	Buy locally made product.
Redcurrant jam and jelly	Yes, from local and imported fruit	Yes	Buy locally made product, even if fruit is imported.
Strawberry jam and conserve	Yes, from local and imported fruit	Yes	Buy local product or make your own when strawberries are in season.

Product	Australian-produced	Imported	What we can do
SYRUPS			
Corn syrup — clear, light and dark	No	Yes	Glucose can substitute for clear corn syrup, golden syrup for light and dark corn syrup.
Maple syrup	No, but a maple-flavoured syrup is made	Yes	Use maple-flavoured syrup in place of imported product.
HONEY			
Honey — clear, candied and in comb	Yes, sufficient for local demand and for export	Yes, small quantity	Buy local product; exciting, truly Australian honeys are now readily available.

Recipes
USING AUSTRALIAN JAMS, SYRUPS AND HONEY

Make a Marmalade

Marmalades are very easy to make as citrus fruits have good pectin and acid content, two essentials for jam to set. If you have never made jam before, start with a marmalade — it will give you confidence to try other jams. Testing for setting point and sterilising jars is given on pages 188-9.

Basic Marmalade
Makes about 8 cups

1 kg citrus fruits, see end of method
6 cups water
about 7 cups sugar
juice of 1 lemon

1 Wash fruit, halve lengthwise and slice finely. Remove pips as you slice, putting them in a bowl. If fruit slices are large, cut them in half. Put sliced fruit in a large bowl, add all but 1 cup water and leave overnight. Put remaining cup water with the pips.
2 Next day, pour fruit and water into a large boiler and strain liquid from pips into fruit. Bring to the boil, cover and boil gently until fruit rind is very soft; the time depends on each fruit or fruit combination listed.
3 Measure fruit and liquid, return to boiler and add 1 cup sugar to each cup fruit. Add lemon juice and heat, stirring occasionally, until sugar is dissolved, without allowing it to boil.
4 Bring to the boil and boil rapidly until mixture reaches setting point. Remove marmalade from heat while testing. When marmalade is ready, stand off the heat for 5 minutes, then pour into hot, sterilised jars and leave until cool. Seal when cold and store in a cool, dark place.

Orange Marmalade

Use 1 kg Valencia or Seville oranges — Seville make a more bitter marmalade. For speed of preparation, halve fruit crosswise and remove pips to a bowl. Trim off stem ends and chop oranges in rough pieces. Put through a mincer. Boil for 45 minutes or until peel is tender. Measure and finish as above. It takes about 25 minutes to reach setting point; begin testing after 20 minutes.

Kumquat and Brandy Marmalade

This is worth making if you have kumquats growing. The oval kumquats are easier to prepare as they are seedless. Halve, remove pips and slice or mince, but make sure all pips are removed if you mince the fruit. Soak pips and fruit separately. Boil gently, covered, for about 30 minutes and finish as above. It takes about 30–35 minutes to reach setting point; begin testing after 25 minutes. When ready, stir in 3 tablespoons brandy, stand 5 minutes, then bottle. The longer this marmalade is kept, the more it darkens and matures, giving it a rich flavour.

Three-Fruit Marmalade

Prepare 1 grapefruit, 1 orange and 1 lemon; the fruit should total 1 kg in weight. Add another orange if necessary. Prepare, slice or mince and soak pips and fruit separately. Boil gently for 30 minutes until peels are soft. Omit lemon juice after adding the sugar and finish as above.

Melon and Passionfruit Jam

Melon Jam is one of those old Australian favourites which should be upheld in our culinary traditions. Look for jam melons in autumn or order one from your greengrocer. It takes time to peel and dice the melon, but it is well worth the trouble. If you end up with more than the 1.5 kg of prepared melon required in the recipe, divide the remainder into 1.5 kg lots into containers, sprinkle each with ½ cup sugar, cover and store in the refrigerator for making up into another version in 2–3 days time if necessary.

Makes about 5 cups

1.5-kg diced jam melon
4½ cups sugar
pulp of 6 passionfruit
3 tablespoons lemon juice

Sealing Jams with Paraffin Wax

If you make a lot of jam and want to keep it for some time, the best way to seal it is with paraffin wax. Buy this from the chemist in blocks. Heat gently in a small pan until it melts but do not let it get hot. Pour a thin layer on top of jam or marmalade, and when set pour in another layer and immerse a piece of string into wax, letting short ends of string protrude. When set, seal jars with lids, tucking string under lid. When jam is to be used, remove the paraffin with the aid of the string.

PUTTING THE LID ON JAM

Traditional jam-making is usually done in a preserving pan — a wide pan with slightly sloping sides, but no lid, because it was never deemed necessary. Experienced jam-makers simply boiled the fruit and let the evaporation take care of the final water content. Recipes given call for lid to be placed on pan (use a large boiler). This serves two purposes: Firstly, you can save energy because it takes a lower heat to keep food boiling gently if pan is covered; secondly, because evaporation is kept at a minimum, the jam-making novice does not have to guess if sufficient evaporation has occurred before adding sugar to the softened fruit. Water quantities in recipes have taken the reduced evaporation into account. Once sugar is added and dissolved, jam or jelly is boiled without a lid.

1 Put diced melon in a bowl and sprinkle on 1/2 cup of the sugar. Leave to stand overnight to allow moisture to be drawn from the melon. No water should be added.

2 Turn bowl contents into a preserving pan, add passionfruit and bring to the boil. Cover and simmer on gentle heat for 30–35 minutes until melon is soft.

3 Remove lid and add remaining sugar. Stir over heat until sugar is dissolved but do not allow jam to boil. Wipe down any sugar crystals from side of pan with a wet brush. Add lemon juice.

4 Bring jam to the boil and boil rapidly, uncovered, for 45–55 minutes until setting point is reached. Stir gently with a wooden spoon towards end of cooking to ensure jam is not sticking to base of pan.

5 When jam has reached setting point, pour into hot, sterilised jars, leave until cool, then seal and label. Store in a dark, cool place.

Variations

Melon and Lemon Jam

At the start of cooking the melon, add 2 tablespoons grated lemon rind. When melon is soft, add sugar as in Step 3 above and add 1/2 cup lemon juice. Complete as above.

Melon and Ginger Jam

Wash and bruise a 3-cm piece of fresh ginger (place ginger on a board and flatten with a cleaver or mallet). Tie in a piece of muslin and add to melon with 1/2 cup sugar. Proceed with Step 2, adding 1/2 cup finely chopped crystallised ginger. When melon is soft, remove bruised ginger and add sugar as in Step 3. Add 3 tablespoons lemon juice and complete as above.

Melon and Pineapple Jam

At the start of cooking the melon, add 2 cups finely chopped fresh pineapple. When melon is soft, add 3 tablespoons lemon juice with the remaining sugar plus an extra cup of sugar. Complete as above. Makes about 6 cups.

Stone Fruit Jams

The enjoyment of apricots, cherries, plums and peaches can be extended past their season by making the fruit into jam. Stone fruits are not as rich in pectin and acid and do not set as well as most other fruits.

Apricot and Cinnamon Jam
Makes about 5 cups

1.5 kg fresh, slightly under-ripe apricots
1½ cups water
8-cm piece cinnamon stick
about 5 cups sugar
3 tablespoons lemon juice

1 Wash apricots, halve and remove stones. Cut halves in 2–3 pieces. Place in a preserving pan with water and cinnamon stick.
2 Bring to the boil and boil gently until apricots are very soft — about 25 minutes. Remove cinnamon stick and discard, or leave in with fruit. Measure pulp and return to pan.
3 For each cup pulp, add 1 cup sugar. Stir over heat without allowing jam to boil until sugar is dissolved. Add lemon juice, bring to the boil and boil rapidly for 18–20 minutes until jam reaches setting point. Gently stir the jam with a wooden spoon during latter stage of cooking to prevent it sticking to the base of the pan.
4 Stand jam off the heat for 5 minutes, then ladle into hot, sterilised jars. If you have left cinnamon stick in jam, break apart and add a piece to each jar. Seal when cold.

Variations

Plum and Port Jam
Use 1.5 kg plums in place of the apricots and omit cinnamon. Use 1 cup water and ½ cup port. Cook as for Apricot and Cinnamon Jam.

Peach Jam
Use 1.5 kg peaches in place of the apricots; peel and stone peaches and chop roughly. Omit cinnamon and proceed as for Apricot and Cinnamon Jam.

SETTING POINT

In jam and jelly making, setting point is the stage the preserve has reached whereby it will set or jell when cooled. If such preserves are cooked beyond this stage, the natural jelling properties of the fruit are destroyed and the resultant preserve becomes syrupy. Chill a small plate in the freezer and drop a teaspoonful of jam or jelly onto cold plate. Return to freezer just to cool sample to room temperature — preserve should be removed from the heat while testing. Push sample with fingertip — if surface wrinkles, setting point has been reached, otherwise return preserve to heat and test again in a few minutes.

Sterilising Jars and Bottles

Jams, jellies, chutneys and pickles must be stored in sterilised glass jars or bottles, otherwise the contents could become contaminated and spoil. Wash containers in hot, soapy water, rinse and drain. Place upright on a baking tray covered with a folded sheet of newspaper and place in a cold oven. Turn oven onto 100°C (200°F) and leave jars in oven for 20–30 minutes. Fill jars while hot or when cooled, as indicated in recipe. Boil lids in water for 15 minutes, drain while hot and dry with clean paper towels before sealing jars.

Cherry Jam

Use 1.5 kg cherries in place of apricots. Remove stalks and pit cherries with a cherry stoner. Place in preserving pan with only 1 cup water and add $^1/_2$ cup lemon juice, omitting cinnamon. Bring to the boil, cover and simmer for 10 minutes until soft. Measure pulp and add 1 cup sugar for each cup pulp. Return to pan, add 50-g packet of Jamsetta, stir to dissolve and finish as for Apricot and Cinnamon Jam. There is no need to add the 2 tablespoons lemon juice with the sugar, as lemon juice is added in the initial cooking. Store jam in refrigerator.

Pineapple Honey

When you have a particularly sweet and fragrant pineapple, use the skin to make this delicious honey. I have not given amounts because pineapples vary in size, and you might want to do more than one pineapple.

pineapple skins
water
sugar
strained juice of 1 lemon

1 Rinse the pineapple before removing skin. Cut skin roughly and place in a boiler.
2 Cover with water and bring to the boil. Boil gently, covered for 1 hour until skin is very soft. Strain through a fine sieve and leave for a while for liquid to drain off skins.
3 Measure liquid into a clean pan and add 1 cup sugar to each cup liquid. Stir over heat to dissolve, add strained lemon juice and bring to the boil.
4 Boil on medium heat for 10 minutes; test a little on a cold saucer and chill in freezer for 1–2 minutes. Syrup should be the consistency of honey when cooled. Skim off any froth and pour into hot, sterilised jars. Seal when cold. Store in a cool, dark place. Refrigerate when in use. Serve like honey.

Fruit Jellies

Tangy fruit jellies are very satisfying to make, particularly if you use fruits rarely found in commercially made jellies. While redcurrant jelly is made locally, imported fruit is often used to make up the shortfall in local supplies. This jelly is frequently used in savoury and sweet dishes. Other jellies can be used in its place.

Fruit Jelly
Makes 5–7 cups, depending on fruit

2 kg fruit, see end of recipe
8 cups water
about 6 cups sugar
¼ cup strained lemon juice

1 Fruit should be as fresh as possible and slightly under-ripe for highest pectin content. Wash large fruit well, particularly quinces (to remove the fuzz). Leave unpeeled and uncored and chop roughly.
2 Place in a large boiler with the water and bring to the boil. Cover and leave to boil gently for times indicated for each fruit or fruit combination, until fruit is very soft.
3 Place a colander over a large bowl and line with a damp, fine cloth — butter muslin is good. Pour fruit and liquid into colander, gather up the ends of the cloth and tie with strong string.
4 Tie other end of string onto a cupboard handle or tap and suspend over the bowl. Remove the colander. Leave to drip overnight. Do not squeeze or finished jelly will be cloudy.
5 Next day, measure juice into a clean pan and bring to the boil. Add 1 cup sugar for each cup juice and the lemon juice and stir over heat, without boiling, until sugar is dissolved.
6 Bring to the boil and boil rapidly for 15–25 minutes, depending on fruit used. When testing for setting point, remove jelly from heat. When ready, skim and pour into sterilised jars, leave until cool then seal and label. Store in a cool, dark place. If jelly is properly set, refrigeration is not necessary, but refrigerate after opening.

Quince Jelly

Boil quinces in Step 2 for 1½ hours until very soft with the fruit nicely pink. Setting point is usually reached in 25–30 minutes; begin testing after 20 minutes.

Apple Jelly

Use new season's apples and have a combination of red and green apples. If you happen to have some crab-apples growing, use on their own or add to other apples. Boil for 1 hour. Setting point is usually reached in 15–20 minutes; begin testing after 15 minutes.

Apple and Blackberry Jelly

Use 1 kg green apples and 1 kg blackberries. Chop apples, leave blackberries whole, and leave on stems if present. Boil for 1 hour. Setting point is usually reached in 12–15 minutes; begin testing for setting point after 10 minutes. Mulberries or raspberries may be used in place of the blackberries.

Redcurrant Jelly

If you grow redcurrants or can obtain them cheaply, then certainly make this jelly. Leave in bunches, rinse and cook as they are, stems and all. Reduce water to 6 cups and boil gently for 30 minutes or until fruit is very soft. Reduce lemon juice to 1 tablespoon. Setting point is usually reached in 12–15 minutes; begin testing after 10 minutes.

Confectionery and Snack Foods

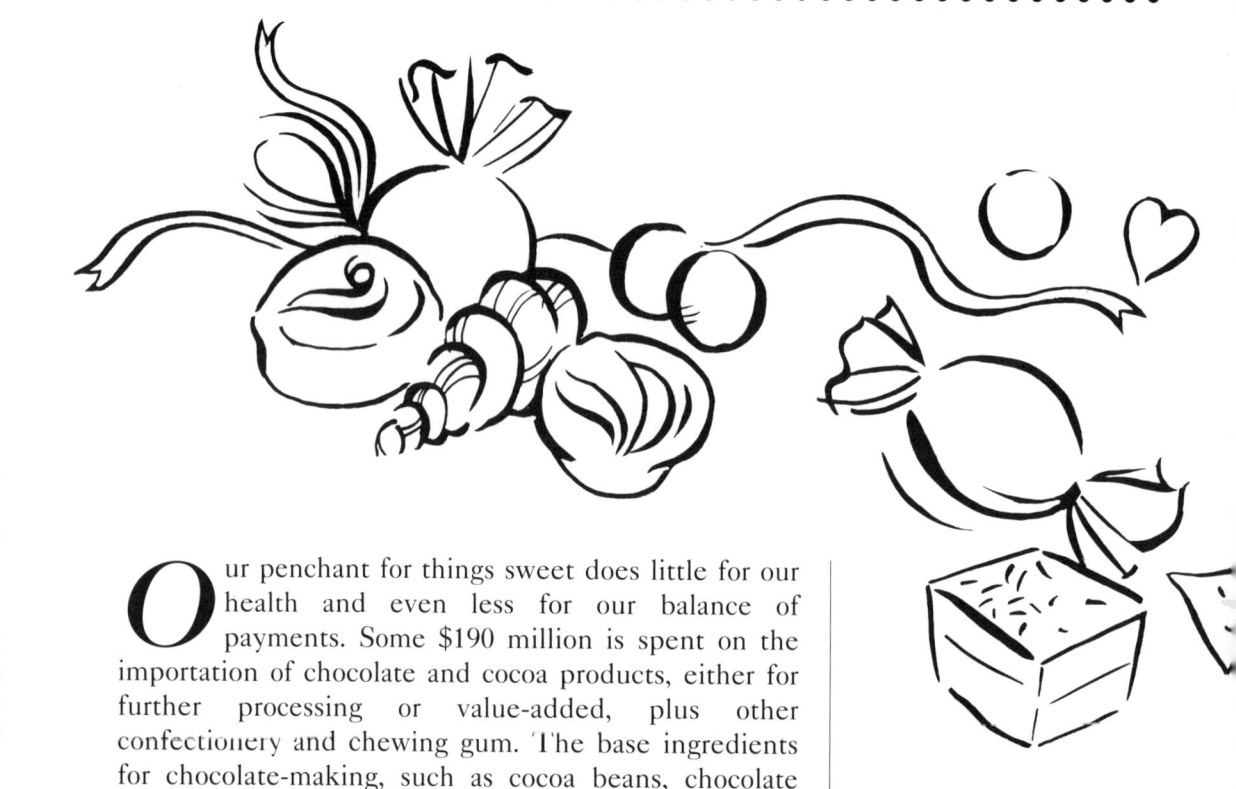

Our penchant for things sweet does little for our health and even less for our balance of payments. Some $190 million is spent on the importation of chocolate and cocoa products, either for further processing or value-added, plus other confectionery and chewing gum. The base ingredients for chocolate-making, such as cocoa beans, chocolate and cocoa butter, account for almost half of this amount.

Chocolate, Confectionery and Chewing Gum

While we do not cultivate the cacao tree in Australia (although we could do in the future), there are ways of changing our buying habits to reduce the cost of chocolate imports. We have a number of efficient large chocolate and confectionery manufacturers, and many independent chocolate makers who produce excellent chocolates. We should give greater preference to their products rather than imported, value-added chocolates. For example, the big-selling chocolate shells that have all been imported until recently are now being made by Darrell Lea, as well as the cocoa-coated Belgian truffles, and both items are competitively priced. These are two changes we can make, and there are many more.

Many local ingredients are used in the manufacture of all value-added chocolates — sugar, milk powder, fruit and nuts — not to mention the labour and resources involved. These are good enough reasons to support the local manufacturers.

Other confectionery contains local products, with a small quantity of imported products for certain lines. The base for chewing gum, chicle, is imported (it is the latex from the sapodilla tree of Central America), but the other ingredients are mostly sourced locally.

Snack Foods

These exclude dried fruit and nuts, which are covered in other chapters. It is difficult to put a figure on snack foods such as potato crisps (especially the imported, formed crisps), rice snacks, and so on, as these are not itemised separately in statistics.

Buyer's Guide
CHOOSING AUSTRALIAN CONFECTIONERY AND SNACK FOODS

Product	Australian-produced	Imported	What we can do
CHOCOLATE CONFECTIONERY			
Chocolate bars — filled, nougat, honeycomb, etc.	Yes, using imported and local ingredients	Yes, some $60 million worth of value-added chocolate, chocolate bars and boxed chocolates	Most popular items are locally made. Use fewer imported bars, such as the triangular bar with nougat; these are aggressively advertised.
Chocolate blocks — plain, filled, fruit and nut, almond, cashew, coconut, white, etc.	Yes, using imported and local ingredients	Yes, some lines	Buy locally made chocolate blocks rather than imported blocks. Fruit and nut content of local chocolate could be imported.
Chocolates — dipped, shells, Belgian truffles, etc.	Yes, using imported and local ingredients	Yes	Buy locally made chocolates and support new lines produced locally, such as chocolate shells, Belgian truffles.
Chocolate — cooking, chocolate compound, bits and sprinkles	Yes, using local and imported ingredients	Yes, small amount	Easy to buy local products.
CONFECTIONERY AND CHEWING GUM			
Barley sugar, boiled sweets, butterscotch, etc.	Yes, with local ingredients	Yes, over $50 million worth, all confectionery	Buy locally made products — check labels on unfamiliar brands. Avoid buying any of these unpackaged as they may be imports.
Caramels, including flavoured	Yes, mostly using local ingredients	Yes	Buy packaged products which give country of origin and check for local product. Avoid buying unpackaged as they may be imports.
Chewing gum, bubble gum	Yes, with local and imported ingredients	Yes, almost $10 million worth of finished gum, half of this is for bubble gum	Buy well-known, locally made gum; all novelty bubble gum is imported.
Coconut ice	Yes, using local and imported ingredients	No, but coconut is imported	Buy it if you want to be sure confectionery is locally made.
Fudge — caramel, vanilla, chocolate, etc.	Yes, using local and imported ingredients	Yes	Buy from fudge specialists if possible; favour caramel and vanilla over chocolate.

Product	Australian-produced	Imported	What we can do
Health bars — apricot, almond, carob, fruit and nut, sesame, etc.	Yes, all varieties with local and imported ingredients	Some, particularly sesame seed confections	Use sparingly; while containing some healthy ingredients, they are high in fats and sugars.
Licorice, licorice allsorts	Yes, with local and imported ingredients	Yes, licorice extract, finished licorice	Buy locally made licorice and allsorts such as Darrell Lea's.

SNACK FOODS

Product	Australian-produced	Imported	What we can do
Cheese snacks	Yes, from local and some imported ingredients	Not as finished product; some ingredients imported	Use sparingly because of high fat content.
Corn chips (see Cereals and Grains)			
Nuts — various types (see Pulses, Nuts and Seeds)			
Popcorn	Yes; microwave popcorn especially popular	No; imports not permitted	A healthy snack food if salt and fat are kept to a minimum.
Potato crisps, formed crisps, plain and flavoured	Yes, with local potatoes; frying fat has imported components	Yes, the formed crisps in various flavours	Buy local products. Avoid the formed crisps in cylindrical packs that are aggressively advertised.
Pretzels	Yes, in a range of flavours	Yes, plain and salted	Buy local products only.
Pulse snack foods — roasted chick peas, spiced blue peas, etc.	Yes, and range increasing gradually	Yes	Check labels for these healthier snack foods made from dried beans and peas.
Rice snacks (small, multi-coloured)	No	Yes	Avoid buying them; use other local snack foods instead.

Choosing Australian Confectionery and Snack Foods • 195

Recipes
USING AUSTRALIAN CONFECTIONERY AND SNACK FOODS

Nut Chocolates
Yield depends on the size of the moulds

½ cup coarsely chopped nuts
250 g block dark chocolate

1 For the nuts, use untoasted macadamias, toasted blanched almonds or roasted peanuts with skins rubbed off. Chop selected nuts coarsely.
2 Break up chocolate and place in a bowl. Select a saucepan on which bowl can sit, with base of bowl not touching water. Put water in the pan and heat with bowl in place. Stir chocolate occasionally until melted and barely warm, but do not allow it to overheat or finished chocolates will be dull.
3 Remove bowl and stir in nuts. Spoon into chocolate moulds or small foil cases and leave to set at room temperature. If weather is hot, set in refrigerator. Unmould or leave in foil cases.

Variations

Nut Clusters
As above, adding 1 cup selected nuts; chop in largish pieces; leave peanuts whole. Drop in heaped teaspoonfuls onto foil and set at room temperature or in refrigerator.

Fruit and Nut Clusters
As for nut clusters, using ½ cup sultanas and ½ cup selected nuts.

Ginger and Sultana Clusters
Rinse ¾ cup preserved ginger to remove syrup, and dry with paper towels. Chop into smallish chunks. Add to melted chocolate with ½ cup sultanas. Finish as for Nut Clusters.

AUSTRALIAN CASHEW NUTS

Per capita, Australians are the largest consumers of cashew nuts in the world; we imported over $20 million worth in the twelve months to June, 1993. Since the tree thrives in tropical regions, there was every reason to hope that it would thrive in Australia's north. Research, trial and error have finally seen our first commercial cashew crop come onto the market in 1994. Experimentation with varieties still continues, to find those most suited to particular regions. So far, commercial quantities are harvested at plantations in the Wildman River region of the Northern Territory, and Dimbulah on the Atherton Tableland of

> ## Buderim Ginger
>
> Preserved ginger produced in Buderim, Queensland, is regarded by connoisseurs as being the best in the world. Young, tender rhizomes are peeled and steeped in brine for some months before being processed in sugar syrup. The best eating ginger is packed in sugar syrup; glacé and candied ginger are also excellent for eating as they are, or use in baking or savoury foods.

north Queensland, these sold under the Tableland brand. Mechanical harvesting is used, but the shell containing the nut also contains a liquid with irritant properties. Here and overseeas, many attempts have been made to develop a shelling machine, but none have been successful. Hand-shelling is still required, and our cashews are sent to India and China for shelling, then re-imported. In the Atherton Tableland, yields are 6 tonnes per hectare at present, compared with 0.5–1 tonne per hectare in traditional cashew-producing countries, which augurs well for our own industry.

Mars Bar Slice
Makes about 40 pieces

3 x 65-g Mars Bars
90 g butter
3 cups rice bubbles
½ cup chopped, mixed nuts

Chocolate Topping:
200 g dark chocolate
30 g butter

1 Chop Mars Bars and place in a large, heavy-based saucepan with butter. Stir until smooth and creamy without allowing mixture to boil.
2 Stir in rice bubbles and nuts and turn into a greased 18- x 28-cm lamington pan. Press into pan, levelling top.
3 Break up chocolate and place in a bowl with the butter. Set bowl over a pan of simmering water, but do not allow base to touch water. Stir until smooth without overheating chocolate.
4 Pour over pan contents and spread thinly with a palette knife. Chill until set. Cut into squares. Store in a sealed container in refrigerator.

Nuts and Bolts
Oven temperature: 150°C (300°F)

Makes about 1 kg

275-g packet long pretzels
500-g packet Nutrigrain cereal
250 g salted peanuts
125 g butter
3 tablespoons canola oil
2 teaspoons Worcestershire sauce
1 teaspoon garlic salt
1 teaspoon paprika
½ teaspoon cayenne pepper

1 Break pretzels into 2-cm lengths. Place in baking dish with Nutrigrain and peanuts. Toss gently to mix.
2 In a saucepan, heat butter and oil over low heat until butter is melted, mix in Worcestershire sauce, garlic salt, paprika and cayenne. Pour evenly over cereal mixture and mix in gently.
3 Cook in preheated oven for 45 minutes, turning mixture occasionally with a wide spatula so that it toasts evenly. Cool and store in an airtight container.

Using Australian Confectionery and Snack Foods

Beverages

Slaking our thirst is an expensive business. We spend almost $650 million a year on tea, coffee, cocoa and drinking chocolate, fruit juices, mineral water, beer, wine, spirits and liqueurs. Expenditure on non-alcoholic beverages or beverage bases (tea, coffee, etc.) accounts for some $360 million. (Herb teas are covered in the chapter on Herbs and Spices.)

Tea, coffee and cocoa account for over $320 million, and considering we grow very little tea or coffee and produce no cocoa, we must somehow reduce our expenditure in other ways. While our coffee industry is in its infancy, it is good to see one coffee company, Vittorio's, marketing a breakfast blend of Australian-grown coffee beans. It is also an Australian-owned company! We should support local coffee processors who value-add locally, rather than buying value-added coffee from a European country that does not produce the coffee bean. The same applies to tea — support local processors.

Growers supplying the orange juice industry have been battling for survival and have recently gained government support. Now it is easy to recognise Australian-produced juice by a distinctive bright green label proclaiming '100% Australian Orange Juice'. However, local sales of Australian orange juice are less than 50 per cent of total sales. Total orange and other juice imports account for over $35 million of our total beverage expenditure, which might not seem a lot, but it is enough to affect our growers.

Importing aerated mineral and still waters is another area where we need to make changes. We have plenty of both, from the bottle or the tap, yet imports cost us some $11 million.

Beer, wine and spirit imports of almost $280 million could be reduced considerably if we used more of the Australian products. We have a reputation for excellence with regard to beers and wines, and there are a few spirits that we do reasonably well. With a concerted effort, we should be able to reduce this figure; if you have a preference for a particular imported beer or wine, ask your wine merchant to suggest a comparable Australian product.

Buyer's Guide
CHOOSING AUSTRALIAN BEVERAGES

Product	Australian-produced	Imported	What we can do
COFFEE			
Coffee beans, ground coffee — various blends	Yes, grown in a small way, with potential to increase. Beans value-added locally	Yes, over $180 million worth in total, all coffee products and substitutes	Buy coffee roasted and/or ground locally; do not buy if value-added outside Australia. Local organically grown coffee available at health food stores.
Coffee bags, single-serve filter coffee	Yes, coffee bags using imported coffee processed locally	Yes, single-serve filter coffee	Buy coffee bags; avoid single-serve filter coffee. Use fine-mesh tea ball filled with ground coffee for single serve; effective and much cheaper than either product.
Coffee, instant, freeze dried and decaffeinated	Yes, processed locally from imported coffee	Yes	Buy local or locally packed products. Avoid imports.
Coffee essence, coffee and chicory	Yes, processed locally from imported products	Yes	Buy locally processed product. Avoid imported processed product.
Coffee mixes — instant with dried milk products and flavours	Yes, using imported and local ingredients	The coffee is imported but processed locally	A good convenience item — flavours include Vienna, Brazil, French, Cappuccino and Bavarian.
COCOA			
Cocoa, drinking chocolate, Milo, ovaltine, instant flavoured chocolate	Yes, packaged and/or processed locally from local and imported products	Yes, some $8 million, value-added or for further processing	Buy locally packed/processed products. Avoid imported value-added cocoa and drinking chocolate.
TEA			
Tea — blended and packaged in boxes or tins	Yes, grown locally, some organically grown; most teas imported and blended locally	Yes, over $60 million worth, all teas and tea extracts	Buy teas blended and packaged locally. Try locally grown teas. Avoid imported packaged teas.
Tea — bags	Yes, blended and packaged locally, including locally grown tea	Yes	Buy local products only. Try tea bags with locally grown tea. To save money, use a tea ball instead of tea bags.
Tea, iced — instant powder, canned and bottled	Yes, instant powder	Yes, canned and bottled	Use locally made product or make your own, see recipe page 205.
Tea — fruit or flower flavoured, various types	Yes, blended locally with local and imported ingredients	Yes	Look for them at health food stores and tea specialists.

Product	Australian-produced	Imported	What we can do
JUICES			
Apple juice — pure and apple drink	Yes, both types using local and imported juices	Yes, some $19 million worth	Check labels for local product — see Orange entry.
Fruit drinks — tetra and bulk packs of single and mixed juices, water, sugar, etc.	Yes, using local and some imported ingredients	Yes, various citrus juices, apple, grape, mixed juices, pineapple	Labels mostly indicate 'Product of Australia' — see Orange entry. High in sugar content — use less.
Orange juice — pure and fruit drink	Yes, both types using local and imported juices	Yes, over $7.5 million worth	Buy juice with green symbol indicating 100% Australian. Chances are other products of these brands contain local juice.
Pineapple juice — pure and fruit drink	Yes, both types using local and some imported juices	Yes, almost $1 million worth	Buy well-known brands; check labels on house brands.
BOTTLED WATERS			
Mineral waters — aerated and still	Yes, both types in abundance	Yes, over $11 million worth, mineral aerated, flavoured and still	Buy local products only. Ask for local waters in hotels, etc. Check labels.
Mineral waters — aerated, sweetened and flavoured, other non-alcoholic beverages	Yes, in abundance	Yes, see Mineral Waters	Buy local products only. Check labels on unfamiliar brands.
Spring and pure waters	Yes, in abundance	Yes, see Mineral waters	Buy local bottled waters, install spring water dispenser or fit a filter to tap if local tap water is not to your liking.
ALCOHOLIC BEVERAGES			
Beers — all types	Yes, most types, including boutique beers	Yes, some $19 million worth	Buy only local beers. Boutique beers should satisfy those with discerning tastes.
Liqueurs — various types, such as Benedictine, Cointreau, Grand Marnier, Curaçao	Yes, fruit liqueurs, advocaat, crème de menthe — Seagrams, Vok, Baitz	Yes, over $55 million worth	Use special imported liqueurs sparingly. Try local products, especially for cooking and cocktails.
Spirits — brandy, cognac, calvados, gin, rum, saki, vodka, whisky (various types)	Yes, some of very good quality — brandy, gin, rum, vodka; saki produced in small way — rice growers are working on saki production	Yes, over $150 million worth, the majority in whisky	Use local spirits as much as possible. Whisky is not made locally but a Tasmanian is working on making malt whisky with local barley and pure, mountain water.

Choosing Australian Beverages

Product	Australian-produced	Imported	What we can do
Wines, table — red, rosé and white	Yes, excellent range to choose from, including French and Italian types	Yes, some $19 million worth	Buy only Australian wines; many are world-class.
Wines, fortified — port, sherry, madeira, muscat	Yes, all types named, excellent in quality	Yes, just under $1 million worth	Buy only local fortified wines.
Wines, sparkling — champagne, sparkling rosé, spumante, etc.	Yes, very good champagne-style whites, rosés. Spumante also produced	Yes, over $27 million worth	Buy local sparkling wines — many of good to excellent quality.

Recipes
USING AUSTRALIAN BEVERAGES

AUSTRALIAN BRANDY

Brandy is a spirit distilled from wine made from fresh grapes, and strictly regulated to ensure that only sound grapes are used. This results in a spirit of utmost purity. Even the less expensive Australian brandies are better than the cheapest imports. Yalumba, Hardy's and Mildara make brandies that compare more than favourably with French three-star and VSOP (very superior old pale). High quality, well-aged Australian brandies can substitute very well for imported cognacs. Cognac cannot be made here as it requires very old brandy (aged 60–100 years), blended with younger stock. Besides, if we could make it, it couldn't be called cognac, as this superior spirit comes from the region surrounding the town of Cognac in France.

Brandied Kumquats

If you want to make this for the kumquats, then the oval-shaped variety are much nicer to eat; the round ones tend to be bitter because of the larger number of seeds they usually contain. However, the resultant kumquat brandy makes a delicious tipple, or may be used in cooking to replace the imported orange-flavoured liqueurs.

500 g kumquats
1½ cups sugar
1 cup brandy

1 Wash kumquats, drain and spread out to dry on paper towels. Prick each kumquat in three or four places with a darning needle and pack into a large sterilised jar.
2 Add sugar to kumquats and pour on brandy. Seal and store in a dark, cool cupboard.
3 Each day, for about a week, tilt jar back and forth to agitate liquid and dissolve sugar gradually. When no sugar granules are visible, leave undisturbed for 2 months before using. Drained kumquats may be served with after-dinner coffee or to decorate sweet or savoury dishes. Use the brandied syrup as a liqueur to drink or in cooking.

Fresh Fruit Drinks

Remember the fruit drinks in those Greek cafés? That was in the days before the cartonned and bottled juices we drink in such quantities these days, so much so that we have to import juices to keep up with demand. When juice processors dare to put orange zest (grated rind) into their pure fruit juices, there is a general hue and cry. The orange and lemon squashes of the old Greek cafés always contained zest to give the drink zing. Here are two of those recipes, much reduced in quantity.

Using Australian Beverages • 203

Fresh Orange Drink

Makes about 2 litres

1 cup sugar
grated rind of 4 oranges and 2 lemons
1 cup sugar
1 cup hot water
1½ teaspoons citric acid
extra 6 oranges for juice
5–6 cups cold water
orange food colouring (optional)

1 Place sugar in a bowl and grate orange and lemon rinds onto sugar. Mix rind thoroughly into sugar with hand or wooden spoon to release as much of the flavoursome oils as possible.
2 Add hot water and citric acid and stir to dissolve. Strain syrup into a large container through a fine sieve or cheesecloth, press or squeeze well to extract moisture.
3 Juice all the fruit, including those with grated skins, and add to syrup with cold water, adding amount of water to taste. Add a few drops of orange food colouring if liked. Pour into clean plastic bottles and refrigerate. Will keep for several days.

Variation

Fruit Cocktail

Follow Steps 1 and 2 in Fresh Orange Drink. Juice the oranges and lemons with the grated skins and add to the cooled syrup. Juice 1 small pineapple (peel, core and chop and process in food processor) and add with the pulp of 4 passionfruit. Add to syrup with the cold water. A few drops of yellow food colouring may be added if desired. Bottle and store in refrigerator.

AUSTRALIAN COFFEE

Growing coffee is no easy task, as our small band of dedicated coffee growers will attest. These dedicated Australians are the backbone of what could be a thriving industry in the future. In north Queensland and the north coast of New South Wales, excellent coffee is being produced. The Queensland operations rely on mechanical irrigation and harvesting to make their ventures viable, and many have had to put in coffee roasters to value-add and sell locally, in order to get a reasonable return. If you travel up as far north as Port Douglas, or west to the Atherton Tableland region, you can buy locally grown and roasted coffee,

sold under brands such as Domigo, Tableland and Skybury.
At the Wombah plantation, near Grafton, New South Wales, coffee is hand-picked, processed and roasted, and sold through their coffee shop. Other local growers are also contracted to supply coffee for the Wombah enterprise.
Thanks to Vittoria Coffee, an Australian-owned coffee processor, we can sample some of the Australian coffee in their Breakfast Blend, which contains over 50 per cent Australian coffee beans from north Queensland. But if you are travelling up north, make it a coffee tour. You won't be disappointed.

Iced Tea

This beverage has not attained the same popularity it enjoys in the United States, more's the pity, as it is most refreshing on a hot, summer's day. You can buy an Australian-processed instant tea for convenience, or brew your own. Tea bags are all right if the tea is to be served soon after brewing, but if the brew is refrigerated it becomes cloudy. Cloudiness in brewed tea can even be a problem with loose leaf tea, and can be reduced if filtered or pure water is used — hard water is one cause of cloudiness.

Brew tea in a china, glass or stainless steel pot, letting it infuse for 10 minutes. Strong tea is required, as the ice dilutes it. Strain into a jug and stir in sugar or honey to taste. When cool, pour over ice cubes in tall glasses and add a lightly crushed sprig of mint and lemon slices if desired.

Another method is an American one, and it works well. The tea doesn't cloud and the flavour is good. Put tea into a clean bottle and add cold water — $1^{1}/_{2}$ teaspoons tea to each cup of water. Seal and store in refrigerator overnight. In fact it will keep well for several days. When required, strain into glasses, add sugar or honey, mint and lemon, according to taste.

WEIGHTS AND MEASURES

*C*up and spoon measures are used in recipes as much as possible as it is a much more efficient way to cook. It is important to have the Australian standard cup measure of 250-ml capacity with graduated markings of 1/4, 1/3, 1/2, 2/3, 3/4 and 1 cup, as well as 50-ml graduations up to 250 ml. A set of graduated cup measures from 1/4 to 1 cup capacity is also desirable for measuring dry ingredients — fill and level with a palette knife when measuring.

Standard spoon measures are also essential. A set includes 1 tablespoon (20-ml capacity), 1 teaspoon (5-ml capacity), 1/2 and 1/4 teaspoon. Level when measuring dry ingredients.

Mass (weight) of ingredients is given in kilograms (kg) and grams (g) for ingredients purchased by weight, or which require weighing for convenience, such as butter. Metrics have been around long enough for us not to want to convert to pounds and ounces — it only adds to confusion. However, if you still think in such terms, or have tried and true recipes in imperial measures, the following is a guide to approximate equivalents as used in Australia. Note that a recipe using metric measures gives a yield 10 per cent greater than the same recipe using imperial measures, as we adopted a logical system based on the kilogram rather than converting ounces and pounds to exact equivalents in grams and kilograms

MASS (Weight)

Metric	Imperial (Approx. equivalents)
15 g	1/2 oz
30 g	1 oz
45 g	1 1/2 oz
60 g	2 oz
90 g	3 oz
125 g	4 oz
155 g	5 oz
185 g	6 oz
250 g	8 oz
375 g	12 oz
500 g	1 lb
1 kg	2 lb

LIQUID MEASURES

Metric	Imperial (Approx. equivalents)	Standard Cup or Spoon Measures
5 ml	1/6 fl oz	1 teaspoon
20 ml	2/3 fl oz	1 tablespoon
30 ml	1 fl oz	
60 ml	2 fl oz	1/4 cup
90 ml	3 fl oz	
125 ml	4 fl oz	1/2 cup
185 ml	6 fl oz	
250 ml	8 fl oz	1 cup
300 ml	10 fl oz (1/2 pint)	
500 ml	16 fl oz	2 cups
1 litre	1 3/4 pints	4 cups

LINEAR MEASURES

Metric	Imperial
5 mm	1/4 inch
1 cm	1/2 inch
2 cm	3/4 inch
2.5 cm	1 inch
3 cm	1 1/4 inches
5 cm	2 inches
8 cm	3 inches
10 cm	4 inches
12 cm	5 inches
15 cm	6 inches
18 cm	7 inches
20 cm	8 inches
23 cm	9 inches
25 cm	10 inches
28 cm	11 inches
30 cm	12 inches (1 foot)

OVEN TEMPERATURES

Description	Celsius (°C)	Fahrenheit (°F)
Cool	100	200
Very slow	120	250
Slow	150–160	300–325
Moderately slow	160–170	325–350
Moderate	180–190	350–375
Moderately hot	190–200	375–400
Hot	210–230	425–450
Very hot	230–250	450–500

Note: Where two temperatures are given, use lower temperature for gas ovens, higher temperature for convenional electric ovens. These are a guide only. As fan-forced ovens vary from brand to brand in temperature settings according to heat descriptions, consult your oven manual for the correct temperature setting. As a general rule, decrease temperature by 10°C for the lower Celsius setting given; Fahrenheit doesn't apply.

Weights and Measures • 207

GLOSSARY

Certain terms which appear frequently, particularly in the Buyer's Guides, require definition.

Boutique: Actually means a small shop selling exclusive clothing, etc.; in recent years, it is a term applied to small manufacturers of specialty food products, as against large manufacturers and companies.

Cholesterol: A sterol (type of fat) found in all animal tissues; plant tissues contain a different sterol. Plant foods labelled with 'cholesterol free' statements cause much confusion to the consumer. Medical opinion has varied over the years about the intake of foods high in cholesterol content and its link to elevated blood cholesterol levels. To eliminate many of these foods from the diet can cause deficiencies in other essential nutrients. However, high intakes of saturated fats have been linked to elevated blood cholesterol levels; reduce such fats and increase consumption of fibre-rich foods in the diet, and blood cholesterol levels can be reduced in most instances.

Formed: Food which is processed to a state whereby it can be formed into shapes of uniform size and weight, such as formed potato crisps made by forming pulverised potatoes, usually with additional flavourings, into uniformly shaped crisps.

Further processed: A basic food item which is milled or processed to another form without the addition of other ingredients, such as the grinding of whole spices, the roasting and blending of coffee beans.

Health food stores: Stores which primarily cater to the needs of vegetarians and vegans, and to those who feel they require supplements to their diet. Many organically grown foods are also sold through these outlets, such as coffee, tea, herb teas, cereals, flours and breads from such flours. Check labels as some of these products could be imported. Some cereals, grains and flours, locally grown, are also available in supermarkets.

House brand: Certain supermarket chains have products packaged under their own particular house brand. These are packed by large food companies under special agreements, and are usually cheaper than known brands of similar products. Check that the product is Australian, as some are imported.

Local product/locally produced: Grown or manufactured in Australia.

Logo: A trademark or symbol used to identify a company, or, as it relates to food labelling, to convey a special message to the consumer.

Value-added: A basic food item further processed with additional ingredients to add value to the original item.

FURTHER READING

The following books were used as references or are recommended if you want to find out more about Australian foods, for whatever reason.

Alexander, Stephanie, *Stephanie's Australia*, Allen & Unwin/Haynes, Sydney, 1991

Australian Farmhouse and Specialty Cheese Book, Publicity Press, Melbourne, 1992

Bacon, Vo, *The Fresh Vegetable Cookbook*, Regency, Melbourne, not dated

Bacon, Vo, *The Fresh Fruit Cookbook*, Regency, Melbourne, not dated

Burke, Don, *Burke's Backyard Information Guide*, Vols 1–5, Random Century/Margaret Gee, Sydney, 1989–1993

Cherikoff, Vic, and Isaacs, Jennifer, *Bush Food Handbook*, Ti Tree Press, Sydney, not dated

Edmanson, Jane, *Jane Edmanson's Working Manual for Gardeners*, Lothian Books, Melbourne, 1992

Glowinski, Louis, *The Complete Book of Fruit Growing in Australia*, Lothian, Melbourne, 1991

Goodman, Cheryl, and Bacon, Vo, *The Fresh Seafood Cookbook*, Regency, Melbourne, not dated

Hemphill, John and Rosemary, *Herbs: Cultivation and Usage*, Lansdowne, Sydney, 1983 (now published by Weldon, Sydney)

Isaacs, Jennifer, *Bush Food*, Weldon, Sydney, 1987

Mallos, Tess, *The Greek Cookbook*, Paul Hamlyn, Sydney, 1976 (now published by Weldon, Sydney)

Mallos, Tess, *The Complete Middle Eastern Cookbook*, Ure Smith/Paul Hamlyn, Sydney, 1979 (now published by Weldon, Sydney)

Mallos, Tess, *The Fillo Pastry Cookbook*, A.H. & A.W. Reed, Sydney, 1983

Mallos, Tess, *The Bean Cookbook*, Summit Books, Sydney, 1980 (title changed to *Wholefood Cookery*, Lansdowne, Sydney, 1985)

Passmore, Jackie, *The Encyclopedia of Asian Food and Cooking*, Doubleday/Weldon Russell, Sydney, 1991

Rogers, Jo, *What Food Is That?*, Weldon Publishing, Sydney, 1990

Smith, P., and Reid, C., *Efficiency of Australian Seafood Marketing*, Australian Bureau of Agricultural Resource Economics (ABARE), Canberra, 1993

Stackhouse, Shirley, *Five Minute Vegetable Gardener*, Lothian Books, Melbourne, 1993

Thomas, Gail, *A Gourmet Harvest*, Five Mile Press, Melbourne, 1986

Thomas, Gail, *Australia's Gourmet Resources*, Hyland House, Melbourne, 1989

ACKNOWLEDGEMENTS

The author and publisher wish to thank the following people and organisations for their invaluable assistance in the research and photography for this book.

Research

Apples: Sue Dodds of The Sydney Market Authority.

Brandy and liqueurs: Mike Lawrence of the Cognac Information Centre.
Cameron Levick of Seagram Australia Pty Ltd, Sydney, for information on Australian-made liqueurs.

Cereals and Grains: Doreen Badger of the Bread Research Institute of Australia, for information on flours.
Diane Miskelly of Goodman Fielder Wattie, Sydney, whose knowledge of noodles is second to none.
Trevor Wiles of Sunrice Australia, for information on Australian rice.

Cheeses: Jim Conas of the Hellenic Cheese Farm, Melbourne, for information on goat's and sheep's milk cheeses.
Sandy and Julie Cameron of Meredith Dairy for information on sheep's milk cheeses.

Confectionery and chocolate: Peter Mallach and George Paul of Darrell Lea, Sydney, for information on chocolate and confectionery production in Australia.
Timothy Piper of the Confectionery Manufacturers of Australasia, for answering queries regarding the effects of imports on local production.

Dairy foods and cheeses: Australian Dairy Corporation, especially Campbell Jeffery, for information regarding the dairy industry and cheese statistics.

Dried fruits: Geoff Sheppard of Australian Dried Fruit Sales, for matters relating to dried vine fruits.

Food labellings: National Food Authority, Canberra, for information regarding food labelling, especially Rose Too.

The Federal Bureau of Consumer Affairs, Canberra, regarding food labelling legislation, especially Anne Rawson.
Advance Australia Foundation, Melbourne, for information regarding labelling logos.
Australian Owned Companies Association's President, Harry Wallace, for his interest and support. If you would like to know more about this organisation and their AusBuy Guide, write to Australian Owned Companies Association, PO Box 440, Rydalmere, NSW 2116, or fax (02) 638 5670.

Grocery statistics: Gary Esdaile, Food industry marketing consultant, for patiently answering many queries on vegetable imports, tariffs and statistics.
Peter Arentz of the Grocery Manufacturers of Australia.

Herbs and spices: Ian Hemphill of Master Foods of Australia, for information on herbs and spices.

Nuts: Gary Barron of Barron Process Company, Kingaroy, Qld, for information on the state of the peanut industry.
Robin and Tom Ellis for information regarding chestnut growing.
Ian Wallace for information on Australian chestnut growing.
The Chestnut Growers of Australia Ltd, Melbourne, for information on the state of the industry.
Loxton Horticultural Centre for information on walnut and pistachio growing in Australia.
Graham Gates of the Almond Co-operative, Berri, SA, for information on almonds.
Jane Dean for information on the growing of hazelnuts in Australia.
David Noel, The Tree Crops Centre, Subiaco, WA, for information on cashew nut growing in Australia.
Chris Joyce of Kyalite Pistachios, for information on the pistachio nut industry.
Peter and Jenny Shearer of Dimbulah, Qld, for information on the cashew nut industry.

Dr Elias Chacko, of CSIRO Tropical Horticultural Research, Darwin, on the cashew nut and coffee industries.

Oils: Rachel MacSmith of Australian Country Canola, Borenore, NSW, for information on their cold-pressed canola oil and for supplying samples of the splendid product.
Greg Husband and Andrew McIver of Meadow Lea Foods Ltd, Sydney, for information on vegetable oil, canola and sunola oils in particular.
Mark and Anne Lloyd of Coriole Vineyards, McLaren Vale, SA, for supplying samples of their extra virgin olive oil, fermented red wine vinegar and their delicious cured Australian Kalamata olives.
Simon Johnson of McDonald and Johnson, for information on Joseph extra virgin olive oil and for supplying samples of this excellent oil from the Primo Estate, SA.

Pepper: Levi and Louis Campagnola of Silkwood, Qld, for information on their pepper plantation. Contact Queensland Wholesale Industries, Brisbane, for supplies.

Pork: John Creagh of the Australian Pork Corporation, for information on pork and the impact of imports on the industry.

Pulses: Michael Goldring of All Gold Foods, Leeton, NSW, for information regarding pulse production in Australia.
Brian Greenup of McKean & Son, Sydney, for information regarding pulse imports.

Seafoods: Terry Kennedy of the Fish Marketing Authority, NSW, for answering queries re the state of the fishing industry.
Perry Smith of ABARE (Australian Bureau of Agricultural and Resource Economics) for information on seafood consumption.

Statistics: The Australian Bureau of Statistics, Sydney, especially John Arena.

Vinegar: Mauri Foods, Sydney, for information on Cornwell's and vinegars in general.
Yalumba Wines, Angaston, SA, for information on wine vinegars.

Wines: Cameron Hills, of The Winemakers' Federation of Australia, Adelaide, for wine import statistics and information on wines.

General assistance: Maggie Venerys, Perth, WA, for tracking down contacts in certain WA food industries.
John Mallos, my ever-patient husband, for the hours he spent checking labels, shopping for my food-testing ingredients and cleaning up the kitchen.

Photography credits

Australian-made ceramics, pottery, glassware etc. were used in many of the photographs. Our thanks to those who supplied these excellent examples of Australian crafts.

Cover photograph (Salads): Glass bowl by Keith Rowe, ceramic bowl by Krypton, Melbourne; from Punch Gallery, Balmain, NSW. Australian horn salad servers from Linen & Lace, Balmain, NSW.

Pesto and Pasta, facing page 57: Ceramic ware by Kathrin McMiles of Pandora Productions, Wahroonga, NSW.

Seafoods, facing page 120: Lemon bowl by Genevieve Loxley, from Studio Showcase, Rozelle, NSW. Blue plates by Barbara McIvor, Eumundi Markets, Queensland.

Turkey and Ham with Cherry Sauce, facing page 152: Cydonia green glass dinner plate from Artizana, Paddington, NSW and Punch Gallery, Balmain, NSW.

Macadamia Shortbread and Fruit and Nut Ring, facing page 88: Red and green plate with nuts by Jolanta Janavicius, from Studio Showcase, Rozelle, NSW.

Australian Cheese Platter: Australian granite from Natural Stone, Alexandria, NSW. Thank you also to The Bay Tree Kitchen Shop, Woollahra, NSW, for providing china, ceramic ware, glassware, linen and cutlery, and to Linen & Lace, Balmain, NSW, for tablecloths and napkins.

Index • Recipes

Almond fruit tarts 152
Almond pesto 53
Anzac biscuits 36–7
appetisers
    avocado dip 148
    felafel 45–6
    fillo pastry triangles 66–7
    fillo rolls 67
    fried calamari 98
    hommos with peanut butter 47
    mango seafood salad 98–9
    sausage rolls 117
    smoked salmon appetiser 90–1
    taramosalata 92–3
    refried beans 49
Apple and blackberry jelly 191
Apple jelly 191
Apples (poached) 149
Apricot and apple chutney 180
    and cinnamon jam 188
    chicken in fillo 123
    purée 150
Apricots (poached) 149
Asparagus, stir-fried 132
Atlantic salmon mousse 88–9
Australian nut-flavoured dressing 82
Australian trifle 73
Avocado dip or sauce 148

Bacon and egg pie 118
Bagel crisps 25
Baked custard 72
Barbecued honey prawn skewers 96
Basic butter cake 31
Bean and tuna salad 47–8
Bean soup, Italian 48
Beans, Mexican-style 48–9
Beans, refried 49
Beef and feta patties 113
    and onion skewers 108
    and pepperoni pizza 26
    casserole, quick 108–9
    dinner, corned 111
    Frypan moussaka 114
    in red wine 110
    Lasagne 112–3
    pie 109
    Roast stuffed topside 106
    Sharp steak 110
    Steak Diane 107–8
    stroganoff 109
Beetroot, pickled 176
Berry fruit purées 151
biscuits and cookies
    almond Anzac 37
    Anzac 36
    basic refrigerator 34–5
    oat and apricot 38
    oat and raisin 37–8
    passionfruit 35
    peanut Anzac 37
    pecan 35–6
    sugar and nut-topped 35
Black-eyed bean stew 52
Blue-eyed cod steaks with orange butter 95
Boiled carrot fruit cake 156–7
Brandied custard cream 71
Brandied kumquats 203
Bread and butter custard 72–3
Broccoli soup, cream of 131
    stir-fried 133
    with cheese sauce 135
Brown rice, see rice
Burghul salad, chick pea and 46

cakes
    almond fruit tarts 152
    apple 32
    apricot and walnut loaf 33
    banana loaf 33
    basic butter 31
    boiled carrot fruit 156–7
    cheesecake, lemon 74
    chocolate 32
    fruit and nut ring 155–6
    fruit loaf 33
    lamingtons 32
    loaf 32
    Mars bar slice 197
    patty 32
    orange 31
Calamari, fried 98
Canape bases 25
Capsicums, preparing dry, sun-dried 139
Carrot and beetroot salad 142
    fruit cake, boiled 156–7
    soup, cream of 131
Cauliflower with cheese sauce 135
Cheese and bacon flan 64–5
Cheese filling (for fillo pastries) 66
Cherry jam 189
    sauce for an Australian Christmas 181
Chestnut and chocolate dessert cake 57
chestnuts, preparation of 55–6
Chicken, avocado and cheese, focaccia with 28–9
    cacciatore 119
    drumsticks, chilli 121–2
    herb and lemon 119
    in fillo, apricot 123
    in fillo, Swiss 122–3
    in red wine 110
    parcels 122
    mango and ginger 118–9
    roast, with fruit stuffing 120
    thighs in fillo 123
    wings, chilli 121
    wings, glazed honey and ginger 122
Chick pea and burghul salad 46
Chilli chicken wings 121
Chilli chicken drumsticks 121–2
Chocolates, nut 196
Chokoes with cheese sauce 135
Christmas pudding, last-minute 157–8
Citrus rack of veal 115
Corned beef dinner 111
Cream of broccoli soup 131
Cream of carrot soup 131
Cream of pumpkin soup 130
Croutons 25
Curried prawns 96–7
Custard, baked 72
    baked pumpkin 72
    bread and butter 72–3
    cream 71
    cream, brandied 71
    stirred 70–1
Damper 18–19
Damper loaves, herbed 19
desserts
    Almond fruit tarts 152–3
    Baked custard 72
    Baked pumpkin custard 72
    Bread and butter custard 72–3
    Butternut crunch icecream 75
    Chestnut and chocolate dessert cake 58
    Christmas pudding, last-minute 157–8
    Fruit crumble 153–4
    Fruit fools 151–2

Lemon meringue pie 159
Macadamia pie 54–5
Mango icecream 75
Pantry-shelf icecream 75
Passionfruit meringue pie 159
Passionfruit sauce pudding 154–5
Peach Melba 150
Peach trifle 74
Pecan or walnut pie 55
Poached fruit 149–50
Raspberry ripple icecream 75
Refreshing fruit desserts 151
Sticky toffee pudding 160
Trifle 73–4

Easy white sauce 67–8
Eggplant and kumara pizza 27
    marinated 143
    parmigiana 136

Felafel 45–6
    with broad beans 46
fillo pastry
    basic handling 17
    parcels 18
    rolls 17, 67
    sheets for large pies 17
    triangles 17, 66–7
    working with 16
fish
    Atlantic salmon mousse 88–9
    Bean and tuna salad 47
    Blue-eyed cod steaks with orange butter 95
    cakes 91
    fillets with avocado sauce, microwave 94
    florentine 92
    poaching 88
    Sardines with tomato sauce 94–5
    Simply salmon 89–90
    Smoked salmon appetiser 90–1
    with fresh mango relish, grilled 93
Flans, savoury 64–5
Focaccia 27
    with caramelised onions and red peppers 28
    with chicken, avocado and cheese 28–9
    with prosciutto and mozzarella 28
French dressing 81
Fried calamari 98
Fried potato wedges 134–5
Fried brown rice 23
Fried rice 22–3
Fried rice, vegetarian 23
Fruit and nut clusters 196
    and nut pilaf 24
    and nut ring 155–6
    cocktail 204
    crumble 153–4
    drinks, fresh 203–4
    fools 151–2
    jellies 190–1
    poached 149–50
    purées 150–1
    stuffing 120–1

Garlic and herb bagel and pita crisps 26
Garlic mayonnaise 83
Ginger and sultana clusters 196
Glacé icing 33
    chocolate 34
    orange 34
    passionfruit 34
    vanilla 33
Glazed carrots 131
    Honey and ginger chicken wings 122
    kumara 131
    pumpkin 132

Gooseberry purée 151
Green salad with macadamia dressing 140–1
Green sauce 167
Grilled fish with fresh mango relish 93

Ham and pineapple pizza 26
Hamburgers, tender 113
Herb and lemon chicken 119
Herb teas, fresh 169
Hommos with peanut butter 47
Honey-glazed lamb racks 103

Icecream, pantry-shelf 75
Iced tea 205
Icing, glacé 33
Italian bean soup 48
    dressing 81
    meat sauce 112
Kumquat and brandy marmalade 186
Kumquats, brandied 203

lamb
    and spinach pie 105
    curry crumbed cutlets 104
    dinner, roast 102–3
    Middle-eastern kebabs 106
    racks, honey-glazed 103
    with orange and mint jelly 104
Lamingtons 32
Lasagne 112–13
Lemon cheesecake 74
Lemon meringue pie 159

Macadamia pesto 53
    pie 54–5
    shortbread 54
Mango and ginger chicken 118–19
    and peach chutney 179–80
    icecream 75
    relish, grilled fish with fresh 93
    Seafood salad 98–9
Marinade, herbed wine 169
    rosemary red wine 169
Marmalade, basic 185
    orange 186
    kumquat and brandy 186
    three-fruit 186
Mars bar slice 197
Mayonnaise 82–3
Mediterranean-style vegetables 133
Melon and ginger jam 187
    and lemon jam 187
    and passionfruit jam 186–7
    and pineapple jam 187
Mexican chilli sauce 178–9
Mexican-style beans 48–9
Microwave fish fillets with avocado sauce 94
Mint sauce 167
Muffins, banana and raisin 30
    basic mix 29–30
    berry 30
    orange and pecan 30
    savoury herb and cheese 30–1
Mustard pickles 177

Nasturtium pods, pickled 175–6
Nut chocolates 196
Nut clusters 196
Nuts and bolts 197

Oat and raisin cookies 37–8
Oatmeal porridge 13
Olives, curing 177–8
Orange
    and pecan muffins 30
    cake 31
    drink, fresh 204
    marmalade 186

Pancakes and pikelets 30
Passionfruit biscuits 36

meringue pie 159
sauce pudding 154–5
Pasta and tomato salad 140
Pastry, shortcrust 15
    sweet shortcrust 15
    wholemeal shortcrust 15
Pea and ham soup 50
Pea soup, vegetarian 50
Peaches in champagne 151
Peaches (poached) 149
Peach jam 188
    Melba 150
    trifle 74
Peanut Anzac biscuits 37
Peanut sauce 180–1
Pears (poached) 149
Pecan biscuits 35–6
Pecan or walnut pie 55
Peppers, pickled 174
Pesto, almond 53
    macadamia 53
Pickled beetroot 176
    nasturtium pods 175–6
    peppers 174
Pickles, mustard 177
Pies, open (pie cases), using pastry for 16
Pikelets, pancakes and 30
Pilaf, basic 23
    fruit and nut 24
    vegetable 24
Pineapple honey 189
Pita crisps 25
Pizzas, true blue 26–7
    beef and pepperoni 26
    eggplant and kumara 27
    ham and pineapple 26
Plum and port jam 188
poaching fish 88
Pork and apricot skewers 116
Pork with prunes and apples, roast 115–16
Porridge, oatmeal 13
    microwave 14
    additions for 14
    quick-cooking oats 13
    instant oat 13
Potato salad with pesto dressing 142
    salad with sun-dried tomato dressing 141
    wedges, fried 134–5
Prawn skewers, barbecued honey 96
Prawns, curried 96–7
Prosciutto and mozzarella, focaccia with 28
Pumpkin flan 65
Pumpkin soup, cream of 130–1

Queen of puddings 73
Quince jelly 191
Quinces (poached) 150

Raspberry ripple icecream 75
Redcurrant jelly 191
Refreshing fruit desserts 151
Refried beans 49
Refrigerator biscuits, basic 35
Rhubarb purée 151
rice
    boiled 20
    boiled, absorption method 21
    boiled brown 21
    freezing 20
    fried 22
    fried brown 23
    quick-cooking brown 21
    parboiled long grain (Sungold) 22
    microwave cooking 22
    vegetarian fried 23
Roast chicken with fruit stuffing 120
    lamb dinner 102

pork with prunes and apples 115–16
stuffed topside 106
turkey 123–4

salad dressings 81
    Italian 81
    French 81
    Australian nut-flavoured 82
    macadamia dressing 140
    mayonnaise 82–3
    sun-dried tomato 141
    pesto 142
Salad oil 80
salads
    bean and tuna 47
    carrot and beetroot 142
    chick pea and burghul 46
    green, with macadamia dressing 140
    mango seafood 98–9
    pasta and tomato 140
    potato with sun-dried tomato dressing 141
    potato, with pesto dressing 142
    tabouli 168
    tomato and basil 139–40
    tomato and basil with mozzarella 140
    tossed tomato and basil 140
Salmon appetiser, smoked 90–1
    filling (for fillo pastries) 66
    mousse, Atlantic 88–9
    Simply 89–90
Sardines with tomato sauce 94–5
sauces
    avocado 148
    cherry 181
    green 167
    Italian meat 112
    Mexican chilli 178–9
    mint 167
    mornay 68
    parsley 68
    peanut 180
    tartare 83
    tomato pasta 136–7
    white, easy 67–8
Savoury herb and cheese muffins 30–1
Schnitzels, popular 114
Scones, quick 33
Sharp steak 110
Simply salmon 89–90
Soup, chilled potato and leek 130
    cream of broccoli 131
    cream of carrot 131
    cream of pumpkin 130–1
    Italian bean 48
    pea and ham 50
    vegetarian pea 50
Spiced vinegar 174
Spinach filling (for fillo pastries) 66–7
Spinach flan 65
Split pea patties 51
Squid, preparing fresh 97
Steak Diane 107–8
Sticky toffee pudding 160
Stir-fried vegetables 132–3
Stirred custard 70–1
Stone fruit jams 188–9
Stuffing, bacon and herb 125
    chestnut 124
    fruit 120–1
'Sun-dried' tomatoes 138–9
    preparing dry 139

Tabouli 168
Taramasalata 92–3
Tartare sauce 83
Tomato and basil salad 139–40
    chutney 180

Index • 213

pasta sauce 136–7
paste 137–8
Tuna salad, bean and 47

Veal, citrus rack of 115
Vegetable pilaf 25
Vegetables, Mediterranean-style 133
  stir-fried 132–3
vegetarian dishes
  Mexican-style beans 48–9
  Almond pesto 53
  Black-eyed bean stew 52
  Chick pea and burghul salad 46
  Felafel 45–6
  Hommos with peanut butter 47
  Refried beans 49
  Split pea patties 51
  Vegetarian pea soup 50

Vegetarian fried rice 23

White sauce, easy 67–8

Yoghurt and cucumber dip or sauce 70
  making 68–9
  serving suggestions 69

Zucchini flan 65

Index • General

abalone, canned 87
adzuki beans 41
alfalfa, see seeds for sprouting 43
almond paste, see nut pastes 43
almonds 42
  blanching 52
  confectionery 42
  ground 42
  salted 42
  to toast 56
anchovies 85, 86
anchovies, Bela del Tindari 85
anchovy sauce, see fish sauces 172
apple juice 201
apple sauce 172
apples 146
  Australian 153
apricot jam and conserve 183
apricots 146
  dried 144, 146, 149
Auschovies 85
artichokes, globe 128
asparagus 128
  freezing 132
Attiki 60
Australian apples 153
  brandy 203
  canned fish 85
  cashew nuts 196
  coffee 204–5
  fillo 17
  flours 16
  pepper 170
  pistachio nuts 50
  rice 22
  sesame seeds 47
  smoked salmon 90
  vinegars 176–7
Australia-New Zealand Closer
  Economic Relations Trade Agreement
  (ANZCERTA) 144
Australian Food Standards Code 2
Australian-owned Companies
  Association 5
avocados 146
  to ripen 148

bacon, see pork 101
bagel crisps, see toasted breads 12

bake blind, to 16
baked beans, see haricot beans 41
bakery products 10
baker's cheese, see fresh cheese types 62
bananas 146
  dried 144, 146
  storing 160
barley sugar 194
basmati rice 11
Bass River red, see cheddar cheese types 62
bean curd/tofu, see soy beans 42
beans, green 128
beef 101
  corned 101
beer, wine and spirit imports 199
beers 201
bengal gram, see chick peas 41
biscuits, savoury 12
  sweet 12
black bean sauce, see sauces 173
black beans, salted Chinese 41
blackberry jam and jelly 183
blackcurrant jam and jelly 183
black-eyed beans 41
blanching almonds 52
blueberries 146
blue brie cheese 59
blue castello, see mould-ripened types 62
blue peas, dried 41
blue-vein cheese, see mould-ripened types 62
bocconcini, see fresh cheese types 62
boiled sweets 194
borlotti beans 41
bouquet garni 167
brans 11
brawns 101
brazil nut paste, see nut pastes 43
brazil nuts 42
breadcrumbs, making 25
bread, choosing 27
  storing 26
breads, toasted 12
breadsticks 12
brie cheese, see mould-ripened types 62
broad beans, dried 41
broccoli and cauliflower, storing 141
bubble gum 194
Buderim ginger 197
bunch of flavouring herbs 167
burghul/bulgar 11
butter 78
  blends 78
butterscotch 194

cake cooked? is the 34
cake mixes 10
cakes 12
calcium in the diet 68
calrose rice 11
camembert cheese, see mould-ripened types 62
camembert cheese, sheep's milk 60
canape bases 12
candied citrus peel, see oranges 147
canned fruit imports 145
cannellini beans 41, 43
canola oil 77, 80
canola oil, cold-pressed 77
capers 172
caramels 194
cashew nut paste, see nut pastes 43
cashew nuts 42
cashew nuts, Australian 197
caviar 87
champignons, canned 128
champagne, see wines, sparkling 202

cheddar cheese 62
cheese (cow's milk) 59, 60, 62
  grating hard 65
  snacks 194
  storing 70
cheeses, Australian and imported 62, 63
  goat's and sheep's milk 60, 63
  some special Australian 59, 60
cherries 146
cherry jam 183
cheshire cheese (Maffra farmhouse) 60
cheshire, see cheddar cheese types 62
chestnuts 42
  Australian 55
  boiling 56
  freezing 56
  microwave preparation 56
  peeling 56
  purée 56
  roasting 56
  shelling 56
  water 42
chèvres 60, 63
chewing gum 192, 194
chicken, thawing frozen 122–3
  with care (handling) 118
chick peas/garbanzos 41
chilli, dried 164
  minced, jar-packed 172
  sauce 172
chocolate 192
  bars, filled 194
  blocks 194
  cooking 194
  dipped 194
  drinking 200
  imports 192
  shells 192, 193
chutneys 172
clams, canned 87
club cheese, Mersey Valley vintage 59
  reduced fat 60
  Tilba blue club 60
  Tilba club vintage 60
cockles, see storing scallops etc. 98
cocoa 200
  imports 198
coconut 42
  cream 42
  ice 194
  milk 42
  oil 77
coffee 198, 200
  Australian 204–5
  imports 198
  mixes 200
colby, see cheddar cheese types 62
cooking oils and fats, disposal of 82–3
cooking pasta 24
cooking times, pulses 44–5
copha butter, see coconut oil 77
corn chips 12
corn cobs, baby 129
cornflour 11
cornflours, maize and wheaten 20
corn syrup 184
cost comparison (fresh and canned salmon) 85
cottage cheese, see fresh cheese types 62
cotton seed oil 77
crab 87
cranberry sauce and jelly 172
cream 63
cream cheese, double and triple, see fresh cheese types 62
cream cheese, see fresh cheese types 62
crispbread, flat 12

214

crispbread, Falwasser   29
croutons, see breads, toasted   12
cucumbers, pickled   172
currants, red, white, black   146
currants, see vine fruits   147
curry powder   164
curry pastes   172
custard, see dairy desserts   63
custards and sauces, cooling   71

dairy desserts   63
dairy foods, use-by dates   66
dates   146
disposal of cooking oils and fats   82–3
dried fruit imports   144
dried apricots   149
drinking chocolate   200

edam cheese, see round-eye types   62
egg storage   67
emmental, see round-eye types   62
   St Claire   62
   Swissfield   62

Falwasser crispbread   28
fenugreek, see seeds for sprouting   43
feta cheese   60, 63
fig jam   183
figs, dried and fresh   146
fish, fresh   86
   frozen and frozen products   86
   canned   85, 86
   roes   86
   salted   86
   sauces   172
   smoked   86
   storage   95
flans, using shortcrust pastry for   16
flour paste for thickening   21
flours, rye   10
   wheaten   10
fontina cheese, see round-eye types   62
food and beverage imports, cost of   vii
fromage frais, see dairy desserts   63
frozen, cooked rice   11
frozen desserts, see dairy desserts   63
fruit, canned imports   145
   dried imports   144
   drinks   201
   fresh imports   144
   frozen imports   145
   juice imports   198, 199
frying oil   81
fudge   194

garam masala   164
garbanzos, see chick peas   41
garlic   128
   minced   128, 179
ghee   78
gherkins, pickled   172
ginger, Buderim   197
   ground   164
   minced   172, 179
gloucester, see cheddar cheese types   62
glutinous rice   11
gorgonzola cheese   58
gorgonzola cheese, see mould-ripened types   62
gouda cheese, see round-eye types   62
grapeseed oil   77
grating hard cheese   65
graviera cheese   61
great northern beans, see cannellini beans   41, 43
'green' oranges   156
grissini, see breads, toasted   12
gruyère cheese (Maffra farmhouse)   60
gruyère cheese, see round-eye types   62

haloumy cheese, see stretched curd

types   62
halva, see sesame seeds   43
ham, see pork   101
handy hints
   coating foods with flour   106
   chopping canned tomatoes   133
   cooking fruit cakes   157
   springform tin   74
   storing Christmas pudding   158
havarti cheese, see round-eye types   62
hazelnut oil   77
hazelnuts   42
   to skin   53
haricot/navy/pea beans   41
health bars   195
Heidi emmental cheese, see round-eye types   62
Hellenic cheese farm   60, 61
herbal teas   162, 168–9
herbs   162–3
   bunch of flavouring   167
   drying   166
   storing fresh   166-7
hoisin sauce, see sauces   173
honey   184
horseradish   162

icecream and ice confections   63
infant foods   12
instant rice   11
iron for good health   104–5

jam, putting the lid on   187
jams, sealing with paraffin wax   186
jarlsburg cheese, see round-eye types   62
jasmine/thai rice   11
Jindabyne cheesemakers   60
jumbuck gourmet feta cheese   60
jumbunna cheese   59, 62
jumbunna cheese, see mould-ripened types   62

kashkaval cheese   63
kasseri cheese   61, 63
keep meat and poultry cool   103
keeping weevils and moths at bay   14
kefalotiri cheese   61
Kervella goat's milk cheese   61
King Island (Butterfield's)   59
kiwi fruit   146

Lactos cheesemakers   59
lamb and mutton   101
lard, see animal fats   78
leicester, see cheddar cheese types   62
lemons   146
lentils, brown and red   41
licorice   195
lighthouse blue cheese, see blue brie   59
lima beans   41
limes, giant   154
liqueurs   201
lobster   87
lumpfish roe   87

Macadamia nut paste, see nut paste   43
macadamia nuts   42
   chopping   57
   oil   77
   to toast   56
madeira, see wines, fortified   202
Maffra farmhouse, see cheddar cheese types   62
maize and wheaten cornflours   20
maize/corn oil   77
making breadcrumbs   25
mandarins   146
mangoes   146
maple syrup   184
margarine   79
marmalade   183

marzipan, see almonds   42
mascarpone, see fresh cheese types   62
matzo, matzo meal   12
meat with care, preparing   108
medicinal herbs   162
melon jam   183
Mendolia seafoods   85
Meredith dairy   60
Meredith dairy blue cheese, see mould-ripened types   62
merino gold cheese   61
Milawa blue cheese, see mould-ripened types   62
Milawa cheese company   60
milks   63
   fat-modified, no cholesterol   72
mineral waters   199, 201
   flavoured   201
mint   163
mousse, see dairy desserts   63
mozzarella cheese, see stretched curd types   62
mungabareena cheese   59
mung beans   41
muscat, see wines, fortified   202
muscatels, see vine fruits   147
mushrooms   126–7, 128
   champignons   128
   dried   127, 128
   enoki   127
   morels   127
   oyster   127
   shiitake   127
mussels   87
   storing   97
mustard   164
mustards, prepared   172

National Food Authority   2
National Food Standards Council   3
neufchatel, see fresh cheese types   62
no added salt (food labels)   142
noodles   12
nut imports, cost of   40
nutmeg   164
nut pastes/butters   43
nuts   39, 42
nuts, shell your own   54

oats and oat products   10
octopus   87
olive oils   77, 80
olives   172
omega-3 fatty acids   80, 89
onions   128
   dried   128
   peeling small   137
   pickled   173
   spring   136
   without tears   137
orange juice   201
oranges   147, 156
oyster sauce, see fish sauces   172
oysters   87
   storing fresh   97

palm oil   77
panettone, see cakes   12
panforte, see cakes   12
parboiled rice (sungold)   11
parisian essence   178
parmesan cheese, see hard grating types   62
pasta, cooking   24
pasta, noodles   12
pastorello cheese   59
pastries   10
pastry mixes   10
pâtés   101
peach jam and conserve   183
peaches   147
peanut butter, see nut pastes   43

Index • *215*

peanuts 43
peas, green 128
    snow 128
pecan nuts 43
pecorino cheese, see hard grating types 62
pecorino romano cheese 59–60, 63
peeling small onions 137
pepato cheese, see hard grating types 62
pepitas, see pumpkin seeds 43
pepper 164, 170
peppers, pickled 173
pineapple 147
    dried 145, 147
    juice 201
pine nuts 43
    pinto beans 41
pipis, see storing scallops etc. 98
pistachio nuts 43, 50–1
    nut paste, see nut paste 43
pita crisps 12
pizza bases 12
plum jam 183
plum sauce, see sauces 173
polenta, see corn meal 10
polished rice 11
popcorn 195
pork 101
port, see wines, fortified 202
port of Sale cheese 59
port salut cheese 59
potato crisps 195
potatoes 128
poultry 101
poultry livers, preserved 101
poppy seeds 43
prawn cutlets, crumbed 86
prawns 86
preparing meat with care 108
pretzels 195
provolone cheese, see stretched curd types 62
prunes 147
pulse nutrition 49
pulses, basic cooking 44
    cooked, to store 44
    cooking times 44–5
    imports 39
    nutrition 49
    snack foods 195
    soaking 44
    some tips on 48
pulses, nuts and seeds, storing 46
pumpkin seeds/pepitas 43
putting the lid on jam 187

quark, see fresh cheese types 62
quince jam and jelly 183

raclette cheese, see round-eye types 62
raisins, see vine fruits 147
raspberries 147
raspberry jam 183
red clover seeds, see seeds for sprouting 43
redcurrant jam and jelly 183
red kidney beans 42
red wines, see tables wines 202
refried beans, see pinto 41
ricotta, see fresh cheese types 62
rice 11
    cakes 12
    crackers 12
    flour 11
    mixes 12
    snacks 195
Riverslei red cheese 60
rosé, see table wines 202

rosé, sparkling, see sparkling wines 202
roes, fish 87, 92
romano cheese, see hard grating types 62
roquefort cheese 58
roquefort cheese, see mould-ripened types 62
roquefort-style, see sheep's milk cheeses 60
royal Victorian blue 60
rusks, see breads, toasted and infant foods 12

safflower oil 78
saffron 165
salmon, canned 85, 86
    canned Australian 85
    cost comparison 85
    smoked 86
    smoked Australian 90
    roe 87
salt, no added (food labels) 142
samsoe cheese, see round-eye types 62
sardines 85, 86
satay sauce, see sauces 173
sauces 172–3
scallops 87
    storing 98
scarmorza cheese, see stretched curd types 62
seafood imports 84
seafood sticks 87
seafood storage 94–5
sealing jams with paraffin wax 186
seeds 40, 43
    imports 40
    for sprouting 43
sesame seeds 40, 43
    Australian 47
    confections 43
    oil 78
setting point 188
shellfish 87
shortening, solid 79
shrimp sauce, see fish sauces 172
silverbeet isn't spinach 134
smallgoods 101
smoked fish 86
soups and broths, imported 131
soy beans 42
    drink 42
    drink substitute 63, 72
    import costs 39
    flour 42
    oil 78
    sauce 173
spices 163–5
spinach, leaf/English 128
spirits 201
split peas 42
spring and pure waters 201
spring onions 136
spumante, see sparkling wines 202
springform tin, handy hint 74
squid 87
sterilising jars and bottles 189
stews and casseroles, storing 109
stilton cheese 58
stilton cheese, see mould-ripened types 62
storing bread 26
    bananas 160
    broccoli and cauliflower 141
    crisphead lettuce 140
    crustaceans 96
    fresh herbs 166–7
    mussels and oysters 97
    pulses, nuts and seeds 46

scallops etc. 98
smallgoods 111
smoked fish 99
stews and casseroles 109
stracchino, see fresh cheese types 62
strawberries 147
strawberry jam and conserve 183
suet 79
sultana bran money saver 159
sultanas, see vine fruits 147
sunflower seeds 43
sunflower oil 78
sungold rice 11
sunola oil 78, 80
sweet corn 129
sweet yeast breads 12
Swiss cheese, see round-eye types 62
Swissfield 59

tabasco sauce, see chilli sauce 172
tacos 12
tahini, see sesame seeds 43
tarama 87, 92
Tarrago River blue orchid cheese, see mould-ripened types 62
Tarrago River cheese company 60
tea 200
    flavoured 200
    iced 200
terrines 101
textured vegetable protein, see soy beans 42
tic/ful/ful medamis beans 42
tilsit cheese, see round-eye types 62
tofu, see soy beans 42
tomato, Italian pasta sauce 173
    ketchup 173
    paste, money saver 133
    sauce 173
tomatoes 129
    dried 129
    home-grown 138–9
    paste 129
    purée 129
Top Paddock cheeses 59
tortillas 12
tortillas, wheat 18
Trade Practices Amendment (Origin Labelling) Bill 3
Trade Practices Act 3
true blue cheese, Lactos, see blue brie 59
true blue cheese, see mould-ripened types 62
tuna, canned 85, 86

United Dairies 59
use-by dates (dairy foods) 66

vanilla 165
veal 101
vegans 7
vegetable oil blends 78
vegetables, mixed 129
vegetarians, ovo-lacto 7
vine fruits, dried 147
vinegars 173
    Australian 176–7
Vittoria coffee 198, 205

walnut oil 78
walnuts 43
warming pita breads 29
wheat tortillas 18
which bread? 27
white wines, see table wines 202
wild rice 11
working with fillo pastry 16

yoghurt 63

zwieback, see breads, toasted 12